MAXIMUM

DELIVERY

Project Management Toolkit

KENNETH ASH

2025 by Kenneth Ash
Published by Asha One, Inc.

Asha One Inc. Publishing

ASHA ONE

ASHA ONE

INFORMATION SYSTEMS TECHNOLOGY

www.ashaone.com
www.maximum-delivery.com
www.maximum.delivery.com
www.project-toolkit.com

Printed in the United States of America
Publisher's Cataloging-in-Publication data

Kenneth Ash
Maximum Delivery : Project Management Toolkit / Kenneth Ash
p. cm.

Paperback ISBN: 979-8-9994529-0-0
Hardback ISBN: 979-8-9994529-2-4
eBook ISBN: 979-8-9994529-1-7

Library of Congress applied
BUS101000 BUSINESS & ECONOMICS / Project Management
COM051430 COMPUTERS / Software Development & Engineering / Project Management

First Edition

Copyright

Registration Number / Date
TXU002503327 / 2025-07-02

CONTENTS

INTRODUCTION

Why: The Silent Miner: A CIO's Nightmare

THE ALERT CAME in at 3:14 AM, an automated usage anomaly notification. At first glance, it seemed like an error. Our cloud infrastructure was suddenly consuming compute resources at an exponential rate, far beyond our usual workloads. Our reserved instances had been maxed out, and the system had automatically spun up new bare metal GPU shapes, driving costs into the stratosphere. Someone was burning through our cloud credits, but it wasn't us.

By the time my team and I dug into the logs, it was clear what had happened. A misconfigured IAM policy had left an administrative API endpoint exposed, allowing an unknown intruder to create and manage new resources without detection. Our Cloud Guard and Security Zones features designed to detect and prevent such activity, had been disabled for "testing" weeks ago, and no one had reinstated them. Worse, our audit logs were incomplete, thanks to a lack of Logging and Monitoring rules. The attacker had quietly deployed a fleet of high-performance BM.GPU4.8 instances, the most powerful NVIDIA-based shapes in our cloud solution, ideal for heavy compute tasks like machine learning, or in this case, mining Bitcoin.

For days, the intruder had been running an illicit cryptomining operation, siphoning off our cloud resources unnoticed. Had we properly implemented budget alerts, anomaly detection, and Cloud Infrastructure Security Advisor, we would have caught this within hours. Instead, the damage was already in the tens of thousands of dollars. The only reason we caught it now? Our monthly billing threshold had been breached.

The fallout was immediate. The Threat Intelligence Service confirmed that our exposed IAM credentials had been harvested from a public repository, an accidental commit to GitHub by a careless developer. Basic IT governance controls, such as automated scanning for leaked credentials and enforced Zero Trust IAM policies had been overlooked. In a matter of days, our negligence had turned the high-performance cloud infrastructure into a criminal's goldmine.

As the CIO, I had no choice but to own this failure. Our security team was already isolating the compromised instances, revoking API keys, and reporting the incident to law enforcement. But the damage was done, not just in cost, but in reputation. We had learned a costly lesson: in cloud security projects, it's never just about technology, it's about discipline, governance, and vigilance.

THE EXTENT OF PROJECT FAILURES

Unfortunately, this is not a unique situation, the numbers speak for themselves: McKinsey & Company estimates that large IT projects typically run 45% over budget and deliver 56% less value than expected.[1] These statistics are not mere outliers; they reflect a systemic challenge across industries, where ambitious undertakings frequently devolve into costly disappointments. Studies like the Chaos Report by the Standish Group reveal that success isn't a matter of luck; it's about applying the right strategies.[2] While these reports highlight that only a fraction of projects currently achieve their goals, the remaining disappointments represent incredible untapped potential, opportunities to redefine your processes and outcomes with expert guidance.

Take for example, the high-profile failure that unfolded in recent years with the U.S. Department of Defense's (DoD) Defense Enterprise Human Resources Information System (DEHRIS) project.[3,4] Initiated to modernize the Pentagon's HR systems, DEHRIS aimed to consolidate disparate legacy systems into a unified platform to manage personnel data for millions of military and civilian employees. The project, launched in the late 2010s, was heralded as a critical step toward improving efficiency and data accuracy within one of the world's largest employers. However, by March 2025, the DoD abruptly terminated DEHRIS after it ballooned to a staggering 780% over its original budget and suffered years of delays, marking it as one of the most dramatic public-sector IT failures in recent U.S. history.[5,6]

Originally budgeted at approximately $100 million, DEHRIS was intended to streamline payroll, benefits, and workforce management processes. Yet, costs spiraled to nearly $880 million, driven by a combination of scope creep, technical missteps, and mismanagement. Reports indicate that the project's timeline, initially set for completion within three years, stretched to over seven, with no functional system delivered by the time of cancellation. The DoD cited "unacceptable performance" and "insufficient progress" as reasons for pulling the plug, but the underlying issues mirror the broader trends identified by McKinsey.[7,8]

First, overoptimism plagued DEHRIS from the outset. The initial budget and timeline underestimated the complexity of integrating dozens of legacy systems, each with unique data structures and operational requirements. This optimism was compounded by a failure to conduct a thorough diagnostic of existing systems; a step McKinsey recommends to identify potential pitfalls before committing resources. Second, stakeholder misalignment played a significant role. With multiple branches of the military and civilian agencies involved, conflicting priorities led to frequent changes in requirements, inflating the project's scope beyond its original intent.

Technological challenges further derailed DEHRIS. The system relied on a commercial off-the-shelf (COTS) solution that proved ill-suited to the DoD's bespoke needs, requiring extensive customization that drove up costs and timelines. This echoes McKinsey's finding that mastering technology is a critical yet often neglected dimension of project success. Finally, poor project management exacerbated these issues. The absence of strong stage gates, checkpoints to assess progress and adjust course, allowed problems to accumulate unchecked. By the time the DoD intervened, the sunk costs were too high to salvage the effort, leading to its termination in early 2025. [9, 10]

LESSONS LEARNED AND PATHS FORWARD

The DEHRIS failure underscores the need for a paradigm shift in how large projects are approached. Maximum Delivery: Project Management Toolkit offers a roadmap: centering on DNA, "Date Name Action" accountability, alignment with stakeholder needs, securing top-tier technical talent, fostering cohesive teams with intrinsic incentives, and the enforcement of disciplined project management practices. For DEHRIS, this could have meant a more realistic initial assessment, clearer communication among stakeholders, a better-fit technology solution, and regular progress reviews to catch issues early.

Broader lessons emerge as well. Organizations must resist the temptation to rush into projects without adequate planning, as haste often breeds waste. Investing in pre-project diagnostics, as seen in successful cases like a public-sector organization that replaced 50 legacy systems within budget, can preempt costly missteps. Additionally, adopting flexible methodologies, breaking projects into smaller, iterative phases, can enhance flexibility and reduce risk, a tactic that turned around a claims-system modernization effort cited by McKinsey after an initial $200 million failure.[11]

THERE IS A SOLUTION

What if the high failure rates of IT projects could become a thing of the past? The benefits of mastering project management extend far beyond mere cost savings; they directly impact project success rates, and stakeholder satisfaction through behavioral change. According to PMI's research, organizations that implement robust project management frameworks are 20% more likely to achieve their objectives, maintain stakeholder confidence, and consistently deliver high-quality outcomes.[12] Readers will find solutions to pervasive challenges like scope creep, ineffective communication, and resource mismanagement through step-by-step guidance on methodologies, emotionally intelligent leadership, and conflict resolution.

Dive in and discover a transformative guide that tackles the daunting reality of project failures head-on, offering a lifeline to leaders navigating the complex world of project management. From gripping challenges, where the silent threat of project derailments is exposed, to the actionable frameworks in later chapters, this book unveils why projects fail and how to turn the tide. Expect a deep dive into the anatomy of successful projects, exploring critical elements like governance, Agile methodologies, and decision making, all while distinguishing between management and leadership. With real-world use cases, such as cloud-based IT projects and innovative scheduling solutions, readers will uncover practical tools like Information Gathering and Work Breakdown Structure examples,

Risk Assessment Processes, and the magic thread that empowers them to steer projects toward success with confidence and clarity.

To help you harness these advantages, the following sections provide exclusive resources, and practical tools designed to elevate your project management approach and drive measurable success.

- **Reference Dictionary:** A comprehensive Project Manager Professional encyclopedia tailored for decision-makers to boost profitability, streamline project execution, and quickly find innovative solutions to complex problems.
- **Use Case Examples:** Real life examples on how to apply the reference material to challenges and experiences for every project.
- **Comprehensive Toolkits**: From project templates and mind maps to useful dashboards that streamline every phase of your project.
- **Expert Cheat Sheets:** Quick-reference guides and short cuts to accelerate decision-making and problem-solving that hurry but not rush the project.

WWW.MAXIMUM-DELIVERY.COM

CHAPTER I

What: Tiny Seeds, Big Dreams

I CUPPED A HANDFUL of seeds in my palm, letting them slide between my fingers like grains of sand. Each one was small, unremarkable on its own, yet holding something unseen within, a **PROMISE**. The soil, dark and waiting, had seen generations before me cast their hopes into its depths. With a careful hand, I pressed the seeds into the earth, covering them gently, knowing that nothing would change overnight. But in time, with warmth, rain, and patience, something new would rise.

Days turned to weeks, and where there had been only dirt, tiny shoots emerged, stretching toward the sun. The green was timid at first, delicate against the wind, but as roots deepened, so did its strength. Leaves unfurled, and buds formed, carrying the quiet determination of life pushing forward. It was easy to forget that everything, every towering tree, every golden field, every full harvest had once been like this. Just a seed, small and waiting.

By season's end, the land was full, golden and swaying under a sky as wide as time itself. The harvest came, and with it, new seeds, each one a beginning, carrying within it the memory of seasons past and the hope of those yet to come. And so, I gathered them in my hands once more, knowing that in something so small, everything begins again.

I stood at the edge of the field, watching the cycle come full circle, and it struck me, this was no different from the projects I had managed. Every endeavor begins with a seed; an idea planted with intention and care. The early stages demand patience, discipline, and faith, even when progress is invisible. Like tending a crop, a project requires structure, nurturing, and resilience against unforeseen storms. And when the harvest comes, the completed work, the lessons learned, it provides not just an outcome, but a catalog of knowledge, a guide for the next season.

THE PROMISES

Like a seed, every project begins with a promise, one of transformation, innovation, or success that ignites ambition and sets the stage for what's to come. This promise is the foundation of every endeavor, a vision that inspires teams to turn ideas into reality. Yet, promises alone don't guarantee success; they require careful nurturing, strategic planning, and unwavering leadership to flourish. This chapter starts at the beginning then builds through each section in detail because the fundamentals never change; the discipline to follow them is what turns seeds into legacies.

The problem isn't what managers don't know, but what they mistakenly think they know about projects. So, what is a project?

Project: *A temporary endeavor undertaken to create a unique product, service, or result.*

This means that every project has a defined beginning and end, and the outcome it aims to deliver is not part of the organization's day-to-day operations. Whether it's launching a new application, building a facility, or implementing a process improvement, the distinctiveness and impermanence of projects require a tailored management approach.

PROJECT CHARACTERISTICS

Projects are defined by two primary characteristics: they are inherently unique and uncertain.

A project's **uniqueness** means that it involves delivering something that has not been done before in exactly the same way. This could be a new software system, a business process reengineering effort, a product launch, or the construction of infrastructure. Even if similar projects have been completed in the past, the specific context, such as the stakeholders involved, the timing, the scope, or the resources, will always be different. This uniqueness eliminates the possibility of relying solely on standardized procedures or historical data; instead, it requires customized strategies, careful scoping, and adaptive decision-making.

At the same time, projects are marked by **uncertainty**. Unlike operational work, which typically follows established workflows with predictable outcomes, projects must deal with unknowns in technology, requirements, timelines, costs, and risks. As a result, assumptions may change, issues may arise without precedent, and course corrections often become necessary. Managing this uncertainty requires proactive risk management, flexible planning, and continuous stakeholder engagement.

Together, uniqueness and uncertainty mean that projects cannot be treated like ongoing business operations. They demand a dedicated management framework that emphasizes clarity of objectives, structured planning, milestone-based progress tracking, and responsive leadership capable of adapting to change. We incorporate these characteristics into a statement of work, SOW, for management to monitor and control the project.

STATEMENT OF WORK (SOW)

A Statement of Work, SOW, is a legally binding contract, between the signor and the signee, where both are bound by the four corners of the agreement. A well written contract leaves enough room for ambiguity filled with assumptions that the obligor more than likely is responsible for at least likely to understand the vision of the future or the meaning. These assumptions are critical to the success of the project and must be aligned with management before moving forward. The problem is the contract has a very structured document, offer plus agreement equals acceptance, and once accepted they are bound by the covenants within. The key to success in building a statement of work must be to provide visibility into the ambiguity the acceptance of change and write that in as part of the preamble to the statement of work. Too often clients close on a deal and think that it is fixed and unchangeable, change must be included in the document using buckets of time and costs as window buffers understood up front that things are going to change a change order is coming and we're going to adapt and pivot to the needs of the company.

In practice, the SOW acts as both a planning tool and a legal safeguard, minimizing misunderstandings by setting mutually agreed-upon expectations. In complex projects (such as ERP implementations, software development, or major construction efforts), a well-written SOW ensures that multiple parties stay aligned and accountable, reduces scope creep, and forms the baseline for managing change requests or disputes. A strong SOW is specific but flexible enough to adapt to unexpected changes, and it reflects a balance between clear instructions and pragmatic allowances for real-world challenges.

Statement of Work: *A formal, detailed document that defines the scope, objectives, deliverables, timelines, resources, and responsibilities associated with a project or contract. It serves as a foundational agreement between a service provider (or vendor) and the client, outlining what work is to be performed, how it will be executed, and under what conditions.*

An SOW typically includes key elements such as:

- **Project Purpose and Goals:** the "why" behind the project
- **Detailed Scope of Work**: what is included (and sometimes what is explicitly excluded)
- **Deliverables and Milestones:** clear outcomes, deadlines, and acceptance criteria
- **Project Schedule:** key dates, phases, or sprint timelines
- **Roles and Responsibilities**: who is accountable for what, including points of contact
- **Performance Standards:** expectations for quality, compliance, and methods of measurement
- **Payment Terms and Conditions**: how and when vendors or contractors will be paid
- **Assumptions and Constraints:** known limitations, dependencies, and risks

PROJECT MANAGEMENT KNOWLEDGE AREAS EXPLAINED

Now that we understand what a Statement of Work entails, it's time to put this foundation into action by leveraging the project management knowledge areas. These core areas, such as scope, time, cost, quality, and risk management form the backbone of any successful project, guiding us through planning and execution.

Project Management Knowledge Areas*: Each of these knowledge areas is essential to successfully managing projects, project integration management, scope, schedule, cost, quality, human resources, communications, risk, procurement, and stakeholder management.*

Here's a summary breakdown of what each one does; a detailed analysis in the succeeding chapters provide a seamless transition into mastering these essential disciplines, offering practical insights to ensure project success.

I. **Project Scoping**
   Defines the work that needs to be done.
   - Establishes **project objectives, deliverables, and boundaries**.
   - Identifies **in-scope vs. out-of-scope** work.
   - Prevents **scope creep** (uncontrolled changes that derail projects).
   - Uses tools like the **Work Breakdown Structure (WBS)** to break down tasks.

2. **Project Scheduling**

   Ensures tasks are completed on time.

   - Develops a **timeline** with task dependencies and milestones.
   - Uses **Gantt charts, Critical Path Method (CPM), and Agile sprints** for planning.
   - Manages **delays and adjustments** to keep the project on track.

3. **Project Cost Management**

   Controls project budgeting and financial resources.

   - Estimates costs for labor, materials, and resources.
   - Sets and tracks **budgets vs. actual spending**.
   - Uses techniques like **Earned Value Management (EVM)** to measure financial performance.

4. **Project Communications Management**

   Ensures clear and effective communication.

   - Defines **who, what, when, and how** information is shared.
   - Creates communication plans, status reports, and stakeholder updates.
   - Uses tools like **email, dashboards, meetings, and collaboration platforms** (e.g., Slack, Teams).

5. **Project Risk Management**

   Identifies and mitigates risks that could derail the project.

   - Identifies **potential risks** early on.
   - Assesses risks using **qualitative and quantitative risk analysis**.
   - Develops **mitigation strategies** and contingency plans.

6. **Resource Management**

   Manages people, materials, and tools needed for the project.

   - Allocates the right **people, equipment, and materials** at the right time.
   - Prevents **bottlenecks and over/underutilization** of resources.
   - Includes **capacity planning and workload balancing.**

7. **Quality Management**

   Ensures deliverables meet required standards.

   - Sets **quality standards and benchmarks.**
   - Uses **Quality Assurance (QA) and Quality Control (QC)** processes.
   - Prevents defects and ensures **customer satisfaction.**

8. **Procurement Management**

   Handles buying goods and services for the project.

   - Selects **vendors, contracts, and suppliers.**
   - Manages **negotiations, compliance, and contract execution.**
   - Ensures timely delivery of materials/services without cost overruns.

9. **Stakeholder Management**

   Manages expectations and engagement of people affected by the project.

   - Identifies key **stakeholders (clients, executives, team members, customers, etc.).**
   - Engages stakeholders to **gain buy-in and address concerns.**
   - Uses tools like **stakeholder analysis and communication strategies** to manage expectations.

MANAGEMENT VERSUS LEADERSHIP

The key to success lies in recognizing when a manager must step into a leadership role, balancing mechanical precision with dynamic, moment-to-moment leadership to drive the project forward. Project management focuses on applying knowledge, skills, tools, and techniques to meet project requirements, emphasizing the day-to-day mechanics of task delegation, goal achievement, and issue resolution. Managers often adopt a transactional approach, maintaining order and efficiency while addressing risks and challenges with a structured, confident style. However, project leadership goes beyond these mechanics, requiring deep engagement with the team and the project's purpose to inspire and guide. For a project to truly thrive, a manager must embrace moments of leadership, blending disciplined execution with the ability to motivate and connect, fostering a collaborative and dynamic path to success.

Project Manager: *The person responsible for working with the project sponsor, the project team, and other stakeholders involved to meet project goals.*

Leadership is communicating to another their worth and potential so clearly, they are inspired to see it in themselves.[13] Leadership is the ability to guide, direct, and influence the behavior and actions of others. It involves the use of communication, motivation, and decision-making skills to achieve a common goal or objective. Leadership can be exercised in a variety of settings, including in the workplace, in community organizations, and in government. It can also be exhibited by individuals at all levels of an organization, from entry-level employees to top executives. The specific characteristics and behaviors that define effective leadership can vary depending on the situation and context. These individuals are considered great leaders because they were able to inspire and mobilize large groups of people towards a common goal, they demonstrated courage and integrity in the face of adversity, and they left a lasting positive impact on their countries and the world.

Definitions from Oxford, Webster, and Google left me lacking in my information-seeking pursuit. Turning to my office library, Sinek, Covey, Greene, Follett, Gladwell, Knight, Thich Nhat Hahn, the Bible, and more, it was clear that the quest for knowledge of leadership was unbounded. Yet, expressing the relationship between the part and the whole of the term leadership was formless and elusive. Was it the symbolism of Ralph's conch, Henry's moment in time, or Joesph's faith that defined them as leaders? My personal experience has observed two hallmarks analogous to leadership, timing and opportunity. First, the situation must demand action and energy management; second, when placed in a group, one person rises to that calling. Leadership has a proactive vision of what needs to be done and a mastery of human interaction interdependence. Using these characteristics, an effective leader unleashes the potential of others in pursuit of a common goal.

Leader: *Generally, a leader is a person who focuses on long-term goals and big-picture objectives while inspiring people to reach those goals. What I've found is many different definitions, next section is my perspective.*

LEADERSHIP STYLES

Dick Dash is the president and CEO of the OwnIT information technology corporation. He is beloved and respected by all that come into contact with him because he makes you feel important. A natural trait leader born in India, his father positioned him inside the factory as part of the team, commanding him to enter the building from the employee entrance and work beside the kilns during the hot summer months of Hyderabad. Charismatic and transformational, his vision and empathic understanding gravitate one toward his power of influence. Through his ability to form interpersonal relationships, he sows a spirit of certainty that you are valuable and full of limitless capabilities. He is my definition of leadership.

Leadership style is a function of strategic choice rather than personality. Which style to utilize depends on any particular situation. Leadership styles include charismatic, coercive, authoritative, affiliative, democratic, pacesetting, servant leader, transactional, transformational and coaching. Leaders learn to focus their own attention, being focused is about filtering out distractions, drawing on different neuropathways some of which work in concert while others stand to oppose. Grouping these attentions into three buckets focusing on yourself, focusing on others, and focusing on the wider world is the new light of practice for essential leadership skills. Focusing inward constructively helps leaders cultivate the primary elements of emotional intelligence. Every leader must focus on cultivating the triad of awareness, cognitive empathy, emotional empathy and empathetic concern.[14]

The type of leadership that is needed to be successful depends on the project and people. I've found that a mix of the leader-member exchange (LMX) approach, and a transformational approach has yielded the best results overall. A unique, trust-based relationship leader develops over time with employees and the key to leadership effectiveness. The emphasis on selecting what's important varies from serving others and adopting an emotionally intelligent-oriented view in leadership. Another recent focus is on the importance of being true to oneself as a leader, embracing authenticity as a cornerstone of effective leadership. True leadership is not about mere authority but about integrity, self-awareness, and the courage to lead with conviction. When a leader stays genuine, aligning actions with values and fostering trust, they inspire those around them to do the same. In a world of constant change, authenticity remains the anchor that grounds teams, fuels innovation, and transforms vision into reality. While each leadership approach focuses on a different element of leadership, effective leaders will need to change their style based on the demands of the situation as well as using their own values and moral compass.

Charismatic Leadership: *A leadership style in which people inspire others based on their enthusiasm and confidence. More than just a commanding presence, charismatic leaders ignite passion and purpose in those they lead. Their energy is contagious, their vision compelling, and their ability to connect with others deeply transformative. Through empathy, storytelling, and unwavering self-belief, they create an environment where people feel valued, motivated, and empowered to achieve greatness. Charismatic leadership is not just about influence; it is about fostering a shared sense of purpose that drives teams toward extraordinary outcomes.*

Interactional Leadership: *A leadership style in which people use a combination of transactional, transformational, and charismatic approaches. This dynamic style recognizes* *that effective leadership is not one-size-fits-all but rather a blend of structure, inspiration, and personal connection.*

Servant Leader: *Servant leaders put employees first to achieve their goals; employee happiness is tantamount not corporate goals. Effort to help others. A leadership style in which people focus on relationships and community first and leadership is secondary. Subscribe to empathy, social awareness, and using social skills to produce effective results. However, reject this style of leadership when it enables weak entitled team members that focus more on their vacation time during project planning than delivery.*

Transactional: *Ensure behaviors through benefits and incentives. A leadership style using a management by exception approach that focuses on achieving goals or compliance by offering team members appropriate rewards and punishments. This type of leadership should be used sparingly and cannot be the sole basis for motivation for delivery. A team member's responsibility comes from being mission driven. Barriers must be removed from that handicap and rob the hourly worker of the right to be proud of his or her work.*

Transformational: *Align leadership goals with employee goals. Charismatic and inspire, motivate with a vision, intellectual stimulation allowing creativity and breaking norms. Show personal care with their followers. Trust, integrity, fairness, and predictability. A leadership style in which people work with others to identify needed changes to empower others and guide changes through inspiration. Ability to recruit others into wanting to be part of something bigger than themselves. Very effective leadership style.*

Authentic Leadership*: An authentic leader must be genuine and derive their strength from past experiences, embracing both triumphs and trials as guiding lessons. True leadership is not about imitation but about embracing one's unique journey, values, and perspectives. By being themselves, authentic leaders foster trust, inspire loyalty, and cultivate an environment where others feel empowered to do the same. Their credibility is not built on perfection but on honesty, vulnerability, and the courage to lead with integrity. In a world that often demands conformity, the most powerful leaders are those who remain unapologetically true to who they are.*

The primary goal of leadership is to reduce ambiguity and make the correct decisions. This pursuit requires not only strategic clarity but also a consistency of character that permeates every action. The adage "how you do anything is how you do everything" underscores the idea that a leader's true nature is revealed in their everyday behaviors, from the smallest gestures to the most critical choices. Observing a leader in action, how they handle challenges, interact with others, and uphold their principles, offers a clearer measure of their integrity and capability than any spoken promises. Words, while persuasive, carry little weight compared to the tangible impact of deeds, as actions consistently reflect a leader's values and shape the trust and direction of those they lead.

Ethics: *A set of principles that guides decision making based on personal values of what is considered right and wrong.*

One is immediately drawn to the conclusion that there are no right or wrong decisions, only consequences. The question in my mind isn't if there are right and wrong decisions; the question is are my decisions right or wrong. During the course of human events, great leaders, politicians, and everyday people find themselves in situations requiring difficult choices. The older I get, the more I question what is right or wrong and for whom, and under which lens do I perceive, understand and interpret the moral and ethically right thing to do. Born in the image of God as an imperfect person, the differences between right and wrong seem inherent in nature when faced with easily distinguished counter positions. Do unto others, thou shalt not kill, thou shalt not steal seem clear moral and ethical positions intrinsic to the soul. The cases we are asked to evaluate in business are not as simple. Life imposes many complex decision-making opportunities that cast judgment on the differentiation between right and wrong. A leader's moral compass not only shapes their own conduct but also sets the tone for the values and culture of their team. Leading practices can act as a framework or guide, when faced with these difficult decisions, offering structured approaches and proven strategies to navigate organizational demands.

LEADING PRACTICE: MELDING OPERATIONS WITH DEVELOPMENT

Leaders adopt leading practices to drive organizational success. Modern DevOps methodologies are leading practices designed to bridge the gaps between software development "Dev" and IT operations "Ops" to optimize software development, reduce delivery time.[15] DevOps patterns can be derived from the Three Ways.[16] The Three Ways provide value to customers by creating a culture where collaboration between employees and departments work together, understanding the interdependencies of the system. The First Way helps create fast flow of work as it moves from Development into IT Operations, because that's what's between the business and the customer. One example is to create a Kanban board to help visualize work and pull work through the system. Index cards on a Kanban board puts work in process on display so everyone can see. The Second Way fixes quality to avoid rework by shortening and amplifying feedback loops. This action attempts to eradicate unplanned work from happening with faster detection. The result prevents resource interruptions, shielding resource bottlenecks by making wait times visible. In addition, improving daily work will dilute the technical debt created from patchwork resulting from emergencies. Furthermore, the Third Way shows us how to create a culture that simultaneously fosters experimentation, learning from failure, and understanding that repetition and practice are the prerequisites to mastery.[7] Learning from failures and creating separate work packages can properly plan resources and be decoupled from firefighting requests. Decoupling from other projects makes changes easier and do not put other projects at risk.

DevOps: *DevOps is a set of practices and tools that integrate software development and IT operation, a culture of collaboration between software development and operations teams to build, test, and release reliable software more quickly.*

Leading Practice: *An optimal way recognized by industry to achieve a stated goal or objective.*

Upon entering the office, we received the memo: the term "best practice" is no longer permitted due to potential liability concerns for the organization. Instead, we are to use "leading practice," as it allows for flexibility and adaptability in our approach. This shift in terminology enhances marketability and persuasiveness, aligning with industry trends. Many consultants and advisors employ this strategic language to elevate their influence when engaging with clients. Companies that use language effectively guide and inspire action, leveraging resources with deep knowledge of the organization's people, products, and processes to achieve meaningful outcomes.

TOOLS & TECHNIQUES

Having explored the promise of a project, its key characteristics, the essential knowledge areas, and the critical distinction between management and leadership, we now shift our focus to empowering project managers to elevate their leadership capabilities. While understanding project frameworks and management principles is vital, true leadership in project management requires practical tools and techniques to inspire teams, drive value, and navigate complex organizational dynamics. In the following section, we introduce a suite of tools, ranging from prioritizing value over constraints, enterprise software, leveraging project management organizations and other resources that project managers can adopt to foster collaboration, enhance decision-making, and lead with greater impact in today's dynamic project environments.

In the vast landscape of project management, Enterprise Project Management (EPM) software stands as a powerful yet imperfect tool. It excels at structuring the grand architecture of a project, defining tasks, allocating resources, setting deadlines, and mapping deliverables with precision. The work breakdown structure it provides is a backbone of organization, ensuring that every major phase is accounted for and properly linked to the overall goal. However, where these tools often fall short is in the day-to-day navigation of project execution. They lack the agility to track the real, nuanced flow of progress, the conversations, quick adjustments, and problem-solving moments that truly drive a project forward.

Success does not come from simply adhering to a high-level plan but from breaking down milestones into manageable, actionable steps. While EPM software is adept at painting the big picture, producing large unusable Gantt Charts, it often struggles to provide the flexibility needed for teams to handle daily tasks, unexpected obstacles, and incremental progress. The key to project success lies not just in defining the major phases but in ensuring that every small, essential action, every meeting, review, and task completion contributes meaningfully to reaching those milestones. Without this level of adaptability, even the most well-structured plans risk becoming rigid roadmaps that fail to reflect the true nature of project execution.

Enterprise Project Management Software: *Asana, Microsoft Projects, Procore, Smartsheet are all software solutions that integrate information from multiple projects to show the status of active, approved, and future projects across an entire organization; also called Portfolio Project Management Software.*

Gantt Chart: *A standard format for displaying project schedule information by listing project activities and their corresponding start and finish dates in a calendar format; sometimes referred to as bar charts.*

Ethan sat at his desk, staring at the massive Gantt chart sprawled across his Enterprise Project Management (EPM) software. At first glance, it was a masterpiece of organization, every task carefully linked, resources allocated, and dependencies mapped with precision. It gave the illusion of control, a roadmap promising clarity. But as he scrolled endlessly from left to right, trying to make sense of a project that stretched well beyond the visible screen, frustration set in. For a short-term initiative, a Gantt chart might have worked, but for a project spanning a year or more, it was a logistical nightmare. Even printed versions were absurd, pages upon pages of bars and lines that meant nothing when detached from their digital context. No matter how detailed the plan was, the inconvenience of constantly sliding back and forth between screens to track progress made it nearly impossible to see the bigger picture.

Ethan had learned the hard way that a better approach was to manage the project with high-level timelines marked by key milestones, providing a clear, strategic view of progress without getting lost in the weeds. Rather than obsessing over an endless string of tasks, he focused on monthly date calendars to track short-term execution, ensuring that each milestone was met without the burden of unnecessary complexity. This allowed his team to remain agile, adjusting priorities without being trapped in the rigidity of a bar chart that failed to reflect the fluid nature of real work. Gantt charts, while impressive in theory, had become more of a burden than a benefit, proof that in long-term project management, clarity and adaptability far outweigh the illusion of structure.

The exemplum illustrates a timeless truth: our choices in allocating time and energy shape our outcomes. Whether it's the farmer who sows seeds haphazardly or the merchant who prioritizes profit over purpose, the story reveals that without intentional focus, we risk squandering our most precious resource, time. In the chapters ahead, we'll explore practical strategies for scheduling and managing projects that align with this wisdom. From tools to streamline workflows to methods for identifying high-impact tasks, these solutions will help you reclaim control over your time. Ultimately, prioritizing value, whether it's the time you invest or the purpose driving your actions, stands as the cornerstone of a meaningful and productive project.

PRIORITIZING VALUE

To attain significant levels of improvement in an organization we have to address how performance is measured. Conventional project management measures performance using scope, schedule and cost. In these cases, scope was the primary driver because of false assumptions made that the scope was known early in the project and the cost and the schedules varied. The Triple Constraint, also known as the Traditional Triangle, represents the three key factors that influence project success: scope, schedule, and cost. These constraints are interconnected, any change to one impacts the others, requiring careful balancing to maintain project viability. Traditionally, project management focused on optimizing these constraints, but modern approaches prioritize delivering value over strict adherence to scope, time, or budget.

Triple Constraint: *Balancing scope, time(schedule), and cost goals, serves as a practical model for understanding the impact of decision-making during a project.*

The traditional triple constraints of scope, schedule, and cost, while still important, are no longer the primary focus, value is. Value deals with business or organizational outcomes, which is related to financial gains. Delivering in a timely manner is important, however even more important may be delivering a high-quality product that is easily adaptable to future needs. The Value Triangle shifts the emphasis toward delivering meaningful outcomes to the customer by balancing value, quality, and constraints.[18] At the top of the triangle, the ultimate goal is to build a releasable product that meets customer needs. Quality ensures that this product is not only reliable but also adaptable for future growth. Constraints, rather than having rigid limitations, serve as flexible boundaries that support the achievement of value and quality goals within acceptable limits. As the project progresses, these constraints may be adjusted to maximize customer value, reinforcing the idea that true success is not just about staying within budget and timeline but about delivering sustainable, high-impact results.

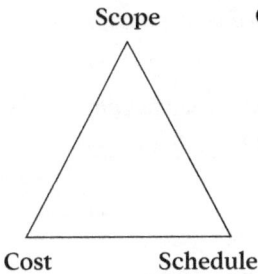

Traditional Triangle	Iron Triangle	Value Triangle [19]
Scope	Cost Scope	Value
△	▽	△
Cost Schedule	Schedule	Quality Constraints

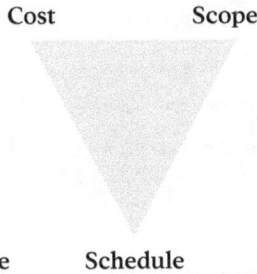

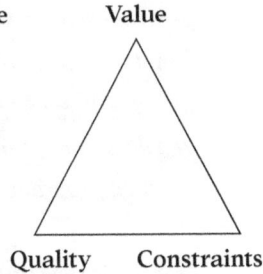

Predictive, illusion of control ⟶ Adaptive, rewarded for delivering value

ORGANIZATIONAL PROJECT MANAGEMENT

In today's fast-paced and competitive business environment, organizations strive to deliver value through strategic initiatives, and a

Project Management Office (PMO) plays a pivotal role in achieving this goal. By serving as a centralized hub for coordinating project management functions, the PMO ensures alignment with organizational objectives, driving efficiency, consistency, and success across projects, programs, and portfolios. A PMO oversees individual projects while also managing programs, groups of related projects coordinated to deliver amplified benefits, and portfolios, which encompass multiple projects and programs aligned to strategic goals. Guided by standards from the Project Management Institute (PMI),[20] a global authority in advancing the project management profession, the PMO fosters excellence through frameworks like the Project Management Professional (PMP) certification, which equips professionals to lead with expertise and uphold ethical standards.[21]

Program: *A group of related projects, subprograms, and program activities managed in a coordinated way to obtain benefits and control not available from managing them individually. The Program Manager provides leadership and direction for the project managers heading the projects within a program.*

Portfolio: *Many or multiple projects, programs, subsidiary portfolios, and operations managed as a group to achieve strategic objectives.*

Project Management Office [PMO]: *An organizational group responsible for coordinating project management functions throughout an organization.*

A Project Management Office (PMO) provides structure and governance for managing projects within an organization. While it can significantly improve efficiency and standardization across projects, programs, and portfolios, it also has some drawbacks such as potential bureaucratic overhead that may slow decision-making processes and the risk of becoming disconnected from on-the-ground project realities if not properly integrated with operational teams. Here are the pros and cons of a PMO structure:

Pros of a PMO

- **Standardization & Best Practices** – A PMO establishes methodologies, templates, and frameworks that create consistency across projects, reducing inefficiencies.
- **Improved Governance & Oversight** – It ensures compliance with policies, manages risks, and aligns projects with strategic goals.
- **Better Resource Management** – The PMO provides a clear view of resource allocation, reducing bottlenecks and improving efficiency.
- **Enhanced Reporting & Transparency** – By centralizing project tracking and reporting, a PMO gives stakeholders better visibility into project status, risks, and progress.
- **Increased Success Rates** – Organizations with strong PMOs often see better project outcomes due to structured planning and risk management.

Cons of a PMO

- **Bureaucracy & Rigidity** – Standardized processes can slow down projects, making it harder to adapt to fast-changing environments.

- **Resistance to Change** – Teams may push back against PMO oversight, seeing it as unnecessary control rather than support.
- **High Costs** – Establishing and maintaining a PMO requires investment in personnel, tools, and training, which can be costly.
- **One-Size-Fits-All Approach** – A rigid PMO might not be suitable for all project types, especially in agile or highly innovative environments where flexibility is key.
- **Slower Decision-Making** – Additional layers of governance can create bottlenecks, delaying critical project decisions.

Everything needed to become a Project Management Professional (PMP) or prepare for the certification exam can be learned through the structured guidance and resources provided by Maximum Delivery: Project Management Toolkit. Beyond theoretical knowledge, practical application is emphasized, equipping candidates with real-world skills through hands-on scenarios, case studies, and mentorship, enabling readers to effectively manage people, processes, and business priorities in dynamic project environments. The Project Management Institute (PMI) includes comprehensive study materials, training courses, and practice exams that cover the PMBOK Guide and PMI's standards.[22]

Project Management Institute [PMI]: *The international professional society is a nonprofit organization that promotes the project management profession. https://www. pmi.org*

Project Management Professional [PMP]: *The Project Management Professional® certification acknowledges candidates who are skilled at managing the people, processes, and business priorities of professional projects. Certification provided by PMI requires documenting project experience and education, agreeing to follow the PMI code of ethics, and passing a comprehensive exam.*

CHAPTER 2

How: This isn't just a diet, folks, it's a SYSTEM!

THIS ISN'T JUST a diet, folks, it's a **SYSTEM**! There he was a guy in a tight polo, standing in front of a whiteboard covered in arrows, circles, and words like "metabolic synergy" and "thermogenic optimization." He spoke fast, with the confidence of a man who had just discovered the secret to human existence. "Using my proprietary systems approach, I break down weight loss into its components: nutrition, exercise, mindset, and hydration. We identify limitations, what's holding you back? Junk food? Lazy mornings? Your in-laws bringing over cake? We fix that! Follow our thermogenic system, so you don't just lose weight, you become weight-loss itself! All thanks to my scientifically proven, AI-enhanced, bio-optimized, SYSTEM!"

At this point, I almost admired the audacity. As a CIO, I had spent years advocating for real systems thinking, the kind pioneered by W. Edwards Deming and Peter Senge, not the kind that came with a free shaker bottle if you ordered in the next 10 minutes. Yet, beneath the sales pitch, he wasn't entirely wrong. Everything is a system. Our IT infrastructure, our project roadmaps, even the way my team prioritizes tasks, it all follows patterns, dependencies, and feedback loops. Systems management ensures our cloud deployments don't turn into a budgetary nightmare. Systems philosophy helps us antic-ipate problems before they happen. Even weight loss, at its core, is about managing inputs, outputs, and constraints.

So maybe this guy in the polo was onto something. I wasn't about to buy his "thermogenic synergy meal plan," but I had to respect his appreciation for a good system.

Systems Approach: *A holistic and analytical approach to solving complex problems that includes using a systems philosophy, systems analysis, and systems management.*

PROJECTS AS PART OF A SYSTEM

Projects do not exist in isolation; they operate as dynamic compo-nents of larger organizational systems. Viewing projects as inter-dependent systems allows managers to consider the overall impact of decisions on organizational goals. Systems thinking provides a framework for managing these interdependencies focuses on busi-ness, technical, and organizational issues. By embracing a systems reasoning, project managers can anticipate challenges, balance competing demands, and adapt to change.

Systems Thinking: *A broad, interconnected perspective that helps organizations understand and manage complex situations by recognizing how different parts influence one another within a larger system.*

Systems Analysis: *A structured problem-solving method that involves defining the boundaries of a system, breaking*

it down into individual components, and evaluating its
challenges, opportunities, limitations, and requirements.

Systems Management: *The practice of overseeing the*
business, technological, and operational aspects of a system
to ensure its efficient creation, maintenance, and adaptation
to evolving needs.

The greater the interdependence between components, the greater will be the need for communication and cooperation between them. Appreciation on systems work involve understanding how different components of a system interact with each other to produce outcomes. In order to appreciate a system, managers need to understand the connections between different components of the system, and how changes in one component can impact the entire system.

APPRECIATION OF A SYSTEM

Edwards Deming's principle of appreciation for a system emphasizes that organizational success depends on understanding and optimizing the interconnected processes and people within a system, rather than blaming individuals for systemic flaws.[23] Consider the scenario of an open role to lead a Project Management Office (PMO) overseeing multiple programs, where departments have competing interests. The project management system was designed to prioritize delivery and customer needs, but systemic issues, such as a poorly configured timesheet system lacking proper capitalization and CapEx distinctions created inefficiencies. Management's focus on cash flow forecasting, which relied on weekly timesheet entries but was reported monthly, was misaligned with the project delivery focus. This disconnect was greater than a timing difference, it was compounded by a "widget mentality," treating human resources like machines in a manufacturing process, ignoring the reality that project management is a service industry where adaptability and human factors are critical. Replacing the PMO leader without addressing these systemic flaws would have been futile, as Deming's philosophy suggests that true improvement requires management's commitment to a total system transformation, aligning processes to support delivery and customer satisfaction.

The systemic issues extended to financial forecasting and billing, further illustrating the need for a holistic approach. Management's obsession with meeting covenants and growth targets led to unrealistic expectations that forecasts should mirror actuals, ignoring the dynamic nature of multi-million-dollar projects with dozens of resources. The forecasting system, semi-connected to timesheet entries, lacked flexibility to accommodate project evolution, creating friction during management reviews. Worse, the interconnected billing system failed to capture critical details, individual roles, rates, and work performed, resulting in invoices with single-line entries lacking supporting documentation. Clients, unsurprisingly, rejected these invoices, demanding breakdowns by person, role, rate, and work performed, which should have been captured in the timesheet system at the outset. This misalignment forced project managers to divert focus from delivery to administrative tasks, such as chasing billing details, highlighting a lack of appreciation for the system's interdependencies. Deming would argue that management's failure to recognize these interconnections and their impact on both project managers and clients perpetuated inefficiencies, as they targeted individuals rather than the flawed system.

Ultimately, the PMO's challenges stemmed from a lack of systemic thinking, as Deming's principles advocate. Project managers, caught between delivery demands and administrative burdens, were not accountants or billing specialists, yet the system required them to fill these roles due to inadequate processes. The absence of detailed timesheet coding for capitalization, operating expenses, and billing purposes created downstream issues, from forecasting inaccuracies to client dissatisfaction. Management's focus on financial metrics over service delivery ignored the human element of project management, where adaptability and customer collaboration are paramount. Deming's insight that systems drive outcomes, not individuals, underscores that no new PMO leader could succeed without a fundamental transformation. By redesigning the system, integrating timesheet, forecasting, and billing processes to capture necessary details upfront and aligning incentives with delivery, management could create a cohesive system that supports project managers, satisfies clients, and meets financial goals, embodying true appreciation for the system.

THE EXPERIMENT

The red bead experiment is designed to show how the performance of workers is largely determined by the system in which they work, rather than by their individual effort or skill. The game had participants pretend to be workers in a factory that produces white beads and red beads. The white beads represented good quality products, and the red beads represented defects or errors. Participants were given a paddle that has small cups on the bottom, which were used to scoop beads out of a container. The container contained a mixture of white and red beads, and the task of the participants was to scoop out as many white beads as possible, while avoiding the red beads. Participants were later scored based on the number of white beads they scooped out, and the number of red beads they scooped out were subtracted from their score.[24] The result of the red bead experiment was that the performance of workers is largely determined by the system in which they work, rather than by their individual effort or skill. No matter what the workers did they were restricted by the tools they were given because the system itself is flawed, making it difficult or impossible to achieve good results. Deming used this example to illustrate the idea that managers should focus on improving the system in which workers operate, rather than blaming or punishing individual workers for poor performance.[25]

PROJECT GOVERNANCE

Understanding governance is crucial for ensuring projects are executed efficiently and align with organizational goals. The **Three Pillars of Governance, Structure, People, and Information** provide a solid foundation for decision-making, accountability, and transparency.

Structure: Structure refers to the organizational framework that defines roles, responsibilities, and processes. It ensures clear chains of command, decision-making protocols, and resource allocation, helping teams work efficiently within a well-defined system.

People: Governance is only as strong as the individuals who enforce and uphold it. This pillar focuses on leadership, stakeholder engagement, and team dynamics. Effective governance requires empowered, skilled, and accountable individuals who can navigate challenges and drive strategic objectives.

Information: Accurate, timely, and transparent information is critical for governance. This pillar ensures that data flows effectively, enabling informed decision-making, risk management, and performance tracking. Well-structured reporting mechanisms and knowledge-sharing frameworks are essential for maintaining project alignment and mitigating risks.

By balancing these three pillars, organizations can establish strong governance that supports project success, risk management, and continuous improvement. Subsequent chapters will cover each of these line items in detail.

Structure	People	Information
· Project Methodology, Approach & Purpose	· Center of Excellence	· Mission Statement
		· Scope Definition
· Financial Management	· Standard Communications Plan - to whom, what format and frequency	· Project Execution Plan
· Risk Tracking and Resolution		· Critical Success Factors
· Issue Tracking and Resolution	· Change Management	· Change Control
	· Process for On-Boarding Resources	· Work Plan Control
· Quality Standards, Project Standards, including Naming Conventions and Standard Look and Feel, Quality Reporting		· Project Documentation Archiving Policy and Process
	· Procurement Process, if required	· Work Product Deliverables
	· Execution of Planned Quality Checkpoints and Validations	· Status Reporting
· Configuration Control and Release Management	· Responsibility assignment Matrix	· Requirements Capture

Project Governance: *Governance refers to the framework of authority and control that oversees key activities within an organization, including the management of project infra-*

structure, the strategic use of resources, and the execution of project-related projects.

ORGANIZATIONAL FRAMEWORKS AND CULTURE

As the saying goes, *culture eats process for breakfast*, underscoring that even the most meticulously designed governance and structural systems will falter without a supportive culture to drive collaboration, adaptability, and alignment across the organization. While structures like functional, project-based, or matrix organizations define how resources and authority are allocated, it is organizational culture, the shared assumptions, values, and behaviors, that truly shapes their effectiveness.

Organizational Culture: *A set of shared assumptions, values, and behaviors that characterize the functioning of an organization.*

Organizational Structures: *such as **functional, project-based,** and **matrix** structures, determine how resources and authority are allocated. While functional structures focus on departmental expertise, project-based structures prioritize cross-functional collaboration. Matrix organizations blend these approaches, allowing for flexibility but requiring careful management to balance dual reporting lines.*

The effectiveness of project management planning and integration is influenced significantly by organizational structure and culture.

Boleman's **Four Frames of an Organization,**[26] enhances those outlined by scholars like Robbins & Judge, and offer insights into these dynamics:

Structural Frame: *This frame focuses on roles, responsibilities, and hierarchies. Projects thrive in well-defined structures where accountabilities are clear.*

Operations in companies show the action of people and products moving and interacting. A formal org chart of boxes showing the names and managers is an important starting point but does not reflect actual processes. RACI charts have never been very useful as they create another document no one reads or understands, never to be seen again after its creation. Organigraph modeling is a more revealing way to depict people in operations. It's not a chart; it's a map that overviews the company's functions in a way that people organize themselves at work; most importantly, they can help managers unearth competitive opportunities.[27]

A functional organizational structure is a hierarchical framework in which employees are grouped based on their specific expertise or job functions, such as Information Technology (IT), manufacturing, engineering, and human resources. This structure is designed to enhance efficiency by allowing specialists in each field to collaborate closely within their respective departments, nurturing deep expertise and streamlined processes. For example, in a large automobile manufacturing company, the engineering team would focus solely on vehicle design and innovation, while the manufacturing team would be responsible for assembling the cars. Meanwhile, the IT department would ensure that all digital systems, from production software to employee communication tools, operate smoothly. This clear division of labor allows for better resource allocation, improved coordination within specialized teams, and a structured chain of command. However, while this approach promotes efficiency within departments, it can sometimes create communication silos, making cross-functional collaboration more challenging.

A matrix organizational structure is a hybrid framework that assigns employees to both a functional manager, who oversees their department-specific responsibilities, and a project manager, who directs their work on specific initiatives. This dual-reporting system enables organizations to leverage expertise across departments while maintaining flexibility in project execution. For example, in a technology company developing a new mobile app, a software engineer might report to the head of engineering for technical development while also working under a project manager responsible for delivering the app on time and within budget. This setup allows the engineer to receive technical guidance while ensuring their work aligns with project goals.

Organigraph tools are designed to visualize organizational structures and can be particularly useful in mapping matrix structures by clearly illustrating the overlapping relationships between employees, functional departments, and projects. By doing so, companies can identify bottlenecks, optimize workflows, and ensure transparency in responsibilities, ultimately improving efficiency and collaboration across teams.

Human Resources Frame: *The Human Resource (HR) frame, as described in organizational theory, emphasizes the people-centric aspects of a company, focusing on employee needs, relationships, motivation, and overall well-being.*

This perspective views organizations as communities where individuals seek meaning, belonging, and personal development. Within this frame, concepts like otherness become particularly important, as they highlight the ways in which certain employees may feel excluded or marginalized due to differences in background, identity, or work style. For example, an international company expanding into new markets might struggle with integrating employees from diverse cultural backgrounds, leading to unconscious biases or barriers in communication. A strong HR approach ensures that these differences are recognized, respected, and embraced through inclusive policies, mentorship programs, and open dialogue. By addressing otherness proactively, organizations foster a more inclusive workplace where all employees feel valued, ultimately leading to higher engagement, innovation, and productivity.

Emphasizing harmony among team members ensures effective collaboration and morale. Otherness relates to the social desirability bias that reinforces characteristics and behaviors deemed generally socially desirable by the group and deny those who are not. Otherness in this concept relates to the open mindedness for the acceptance of those who are different from oneself. Increasing the number of positive experiences produces effective outcomes, however, it is a gradual process. Unproductive emotions established in each of our paradigms will not instantly revert to pleasant experiences. One must have an openness and willingness to talk with one another knowing that differences exist to gain an understanding of one another and form new perceptions.

Political Frame: *Understanding power dynamics and interpersonal relationships can mitigate conflicts and align stakeholder interests.*

Stakeholders range from team members and executives to external clients and end-users, each with varying degrees of interest and power. We refer to this as the "NOC" list, a metaphor for sensitive complex human capital. A frame that addresses organizational and personal politics.

Symbolic Frame: *Cultural symbols, shared meanings, and organizational values inspire team commitment and alignment.*

Paul O'Neill, during his tenure as CEO of Alcoa, used the symbolism of "safety first" to initiate transformative change within the company.[28] When he took over in 1987, O'Neill made worker safety his primary focus, stating that no one should ever be injured on the job. This was a radical departure from traditional corporate priorities, like profitability or shareholder returns, but it served as a powerful symbol for organizational culture. By focusing on safety, O'Neill introduced a simple, clear, and unifying goal that resonated with every level of the company, from factory workers to executives.[29]

NAVIGATING PHASE GATES: A PROJECT MANAGER'S PERSPECTIVE

Cultural change must ensure that governance practices, such as phase reviews, decision checkpoints, and quality gates, are not seen as bureaucratic hurdles, but as essential components of delivering value and mitigating risk. Embedding this perspective into the culture helps project teams embrace governance as a strategic enabler, not an obstacle, paving the way for more consistent execution and better outcomes. Navigating phase gates, throughout the Software

Development Lifecycle, SDLC,) requires more than technical compliance; it demands a shift in mindset where teams value discipline, accountability, and transparency.

Systems Development Life Cycle (SDLC): *(SDLC) is a structured framework that outlines the phases involved in the creation, implementation, and maintenance of information systems, ensuring they meet business and technical requirements effectively. Project and product lifecycles are similar but different collections of processes and phases specific to deliver those strategic goals.*

As an IT Project Manager leading the development of a new customer-facing mobile application, I knew that phase gate reviews would be critical in ensuring the project stayed on track while minimizing risks. From initial planning to final deployment, we had several structured checkpoints, each serving as an opportunity to evaluate progress, assess deliverables, and make key decisions about the project's future. To illustrate how cultural change can support effective governance, consider the following use case that demonstrates a practical approach to embedding accountability and ownership during phase gate reviews. This example highlights how structured interventions can align team behavior with governance expectations.

Checkpoint 1: Planning Phase Gate Review

Phase Gate Review: *Management reviews that keep projects on track and determine if they should be continued, redirected, or terminated; also called phase exits or kill points.*

After weeks of stakeholder meetings, requirements gathering, and feasibility studies, we reached our first phase gate review. In this session, executives, key stakeholders, and product owners assessed whether we had a clear project scope, realistic budget, and defined technical architecture. With all deliverables in place and risks identified, we got the green light to move into the development phase.

Checkpoint 2: Development Phase Exit

Phase Exit: *A management review that should occur after each project phase to determine if projects should be continued, redirected, or terminated; also called a kill point.*

Midway through the project, we hit our development phase exit, where we evaluated our prototype, sprint progress, and integration testing results. Although we had made good progress, the stakeholders flagged performance issues that could impact user experience. After a heated discussion, we redirected resources toward optimizing the backend before continuing to full-scale testing. This phase exit helped us identify and fix issues early, preventing costly rework later.

Checkpoint 3: The Kill Point Decision

Termination Point: *A management review that should occur after each project phase to determine if projects should be continued, redirected, or terminated; also called a phase exit*

By the time we reached the final review before user acceptance testing (UAT), new risks had emerged. A competitor had launched a similar app, and market research suggested a declining demand for our product. Meanwhile, testing uncovered security vulnerabilities that would require additional time and budget to fix. This was our kill point, a moment of hard decision-making.

The leadership team analyzed the situation:

a. Could we pivot the project to salvage value?
b. Was the additional investment justified given the declining market interest?
c. Would continuing introduce more risk than potential return?

After extensive discussion with the executive steering committee, we made the difficult decision to terminate the project before full deployment, preventing further financial loss. While disappointing, this kill point protected the organization from investing in a product with diminished viability. Resources were reallocated to a different initiative with higher strategic value, demonstrating the importance of structured reviews in project governance.

In the end, the phase gate review process ensured that each phase added value, and when it no longer made sense to continue, the kill point provided a controlled, rational way to stop before further losses accumulated. As a project manager, these checkpoints were not just bureaucratic steps but essential tools for strategic decision-making.

CHAPTER 3

PIM: The Tale of Code & Conquest: A Project Integration Journey

---

Project Integration Management (PIM): *Processes that coordinate all project management knowledge areas throughout a project's life, including developing the project charter, drafting the preliminary project scope statement, creating the project management plan, directing and managing the project, monitoring and controlling the project, providing integrated change control, and closing the project.*

Once upon a deadline dreary, in a land where projects ran weary,
Our company sought to build an app quite grand
To streamline logistics with AI's guiding hand.

Their journey through Project Integration Management was one
    of trials and might,
But with careful planning and leadership bright,
They conquered scope creep, change requests, and more,
And emerged victorious—strong to the core.

Before the first line of code was typed, the CEO declared,
"We shall create an AI-powered logistics app, for customers
    ill-prepared!
Our trucks arrive at odd times, inventory goes amiss,
With real-time tracking, we'll ensure nothing's amiss."

A project charter was drafted, a project manager was crowned,
Her name? Sarah Sprintwell, with leadership renowned.
She defined objectives, stakeholders, and scope,
And with sign-off secured, the team held hope.

With the charter in hand, Sarah declared with flair,
"A plan we need, one thorough and fair!"
She gathered her leads, devs, QA, and design,
And built a plan where all goals aligned.

From scope to schedule, from cost to risk,
Each detail was logged, no piece was missed.
A risk register held their fears at bay,
For scope creep lurked just one sprint away.

With a roadmap in place, the coding began,
Developers typed with keyboards in hand.
Features took shape, UI looked neat,
Until... a customer said, "We need voice control, that would
    be sweet!"

Sarah sighed but kept morale tight,
Approving changes (within scope) with insight.
She tracked progress, resolved blockers with grace,
Her agile sprints kept a steady pace.

"Wait!" cried a junior, fresh on the scene,
"Didn't we solve this? I swear—it's been seen!"
Alas, the documentation was thin and unclear,
So Sarah decreed, "A wiki shall appear!"

A knowledge repository—simple yet grand,
Held solutions, decisions, a guide close at hand.
No more guessing, no knowledge astray,
For future devs, lessons paved the way.

Sarah sat at her dashboard, charts full of hues,
Red meant trouble, green meant good news.
A bottleneck here, a delay over there,
But with monitoring tools, she handled with care.

"Dev velocity's low, the backlog's too wide!"
She adjusted resources—kept the ship in stride.
Stakeholders stayed happy, informed and content,
For Sarah ensured not a dollar was misspent.

A wild VP of Sales burst through the door,
"Add GPS alerts! We must do more!"
Sarah, composed, did not say "no,"
But assessed the impact before letting it go.

A Change Control Board weighed the request,
Cost, scope, timeline—what was best?
"Approved with caution," the team decreed,
A minor shift, not reckless greed.

And at last, the app was done,
AI-powered logistics? Second to none!

With sign-off secured, the final report,
ByteBridges had a product to support.

Sarah sighed, her job complete,
"Next project?" she asked, lifting her feet.
But before she left, she sent one last mail—
"Lessons learned are in the wiki, don't let them go stale!"

Epilogue: The Moral of the Tale
And so, dear reader, what have we learned?
A project's success is rightfully earned.
Integration management ties all threads tight,
With planning, control, and knowledge in sight.

Should you ever lead a project of scale,
Remember this story, this rhythmic tale.
For chaos lurks in unmanaged change,
But with integration, success is in range

THE PROJECT CHARTER

Having woven a poetic journey through the realm of Project Integration Management, highlighting how its processes thread together the fabric of a successful project from initiation to closure, it's only fitting to begin unpacking the introductory elements that give such integration its structure. At the heart of this coordination lies the Project Charter: a crucial document that sets the project in motion. Just as integration management ensures all parts move in harmony, the charter provides the formal authority, strategic direction, and stakeholder alignment that enable a project to take shape with purpose and clarity.

Project Charter: *A project charter is a formal document that authorizes the initiation of a project and provides direction on its objectives and management. It empowers the project manager to utilize organizational resources to achieve the project's goals. The charter is developed in collaboration with key stakeholders to ensure alignment with business needs and strategic priorities.*

PROJECT CHARTER TEMPLATE

I'm providing you with a Project Charter Template that you can use as a starting point for your project. This document outlines the foundational aspects of the project, defining its purpose, scope, stakeholders, key deliverables, and success criteria. It serves as a critical reference point for aligning the team, establishing expectations, and creating a framework for execution and accountability throughout the project lifecycle.

See Template below.

Project Information
- **Project Title:**
- **Date of Authorization:**
- **Project Manager:**

Project Objectives and Justification

The objective of this project is to <briefly describe the project's goals>. This initiative is necessary to <explain the business need, strategic alignment, or problem resolution>. By achieving these objectives, the organization aims to <explain the intended purpose>.

Project Scope
- **In-Scope:**
  - \<List key deliverables, functionalities, or features>
- **Out-of-Scope:**
  - \<Clarify areas beyond the project's focus>

Project Schedule and Milestones

Milestone	Planned Completion Date
Project Kickoff	/ /
Requirement Gathering	/ /
Design & Development	/ /
Testing & QA	/ /
Deployment	/ /
Project Closeout	/ /

Project Budget

A summary of the project's budget is provided below. Additional budgetary details can be found in the referenced financial documentation.

- **Estimated Budget:**
  - **Project Success Criteria**
    The success of this project will be determined by:
- **Project Approval Requirements:**
  Project Management Approach
  This project will be managed through structured methodologies, ensuring alignment with stakeholder needs and expectations. The approach will incorporate:
  - **Stakeholder Engagement:** Identifying and addressing stakeholder needs.

- **Key Assumptions & Constraints:** Documenting critical factors that may impact execution.
- **Risk Management:** Proactively identifying and mitigating project risks.
- **Communication Strategy:** Ensuring transparent and effective communication among all involved parties.

Roles and Responsibilities

A structured matrix defining the roles and responsibilities of key project stakeholders is provided below:

Role	Responsibility
Project Sponsor	
Project Manager	
Functional Leads	
Key Stakeholders	

Sign-Off Section

Name	Role	Signature	Date
	Project Sponsor		/ /
	Project Manager		/ /

Comments Section

Stakeholders may provide additional comments or considerations related to the project below:

PROJECT MANAGEMENT PLAN: A COMPREHENSIVE GUIDE

The development of a Project Management Plan relies on key inputs, including the Project Charter, outputs from other processes, enterprise environmental factors, and organizational process assets. It is created using tools and techniques such as expert judgment, data gathering, interpersonal and team skills, and meetings. The final output of this process is the Project Management Plan, which serves as the primary document guiding project execution and decision-making.

Project Management Plan: *A project Management Plan is a formal, structured document that integrates and coordinates all project planning artifacts and serves as a guiding framework for project execution, monitoring, and control. It outlines the methodologies, processes, tools, and techniques required to successfully complete a project within defined scope, time, cost, and quality constraints.*

KEY COMPONENTS OF A PROJECT MANAGEMENT PLAN

Mastering the Key Components of a Project Management Plan, also known as Knowledge Areas, is mission-critical to ensuring project success. These areas represent the core pillars of effective project management, providing a structured approach to tackling complex challenges. Without a clear scope, projects risk scope creep, leading to missed deadlines and budget overruns. Poor schedule management results in delays and costly inefficiencies, while inadequate risk management exposes projects to avoidable threats that could derail progress. Each knowledge area plays a strategic role, from aligning stakeholder expectations to optimizing resource allocation, enhancing communication, and ensuring compliance with quality standards.

Knowledge Areas:

1. **Project Scope Management Plan** – Defines the project's boundaries, objectives, deliverables, and acceptance criteria to ensure all stakeholders align on what is included (and excluded) from the project.

2. **Schedule Management Plan** – Provides a timeline with key milestones, task dependencies, and a structured approach for tracking and managing project timelines.

3. **Cost Management Plan** – Establishes the project budget, cost estimates, and financial tracking mechanisms to ensuring that the project stays within financial constraints.

4. **Quality Management Plan** – Specifies quality standards, processes, and metrics to ensure project deliverables meet required performance and compliance standards.

5. **Resource Management Plan** – Identifies the people, materials, and equipment needed for the project, along with allocation strategies to optimize efficiency.

6. **Risk Management Plan** – Documents potential project risks, their impact, likelihood, and mitigation strategies to proactively manage uncertainties.

7. **Stakeholder Engagement Plan** – Outlines strategies for communicating and engaging with project stakeholders to ensure alignment and support.

8. **Communication Management Plan** – Defines how project information will be shared optimally, including reporting frequency, communication channels, and key messages for stakeholders.

9. **Procurement Management Plan** – Details procurement processes, vendor management, and contract strategies to acquire necessary external resources.

10. **Change Management Plan** – Establishes processes for handling scope changes, approvals, and documentation to control project modifications effectively.

The project management plan is not a single document that addresses each knowledge area, but a collection of subsidiary organizational process assets that address key aspects of project management. It provides a roadmap for project execution, ensuring that all team members and stakeholders understand the project's direction, deliverables, and success criteria.

Organizational Process Assets (OPAs): *Organizational Process Assets (OPAs) encompass the plans, processes, policies, procedures, and knowledge repositories unique to an organization that influence project management and execution. These assets serve as a foundation for project governance and execution, incorporating best practices, historical data, and lessons learned from past projects.*

OPAs include essential project documentation such as completed schedules, risk assessments, earned value data, and performance reports, which help teams streamline project planning and decision-making. Because OPAs are internal to the organization, project teams can update and refine them as needed throughout the project lifecycle.

OPAs are typically categorized into two key areas:

a. Processes, Policies, and Procedures – Standard-ized guidelines and methodologies that ensure consistency across projects.
b. Organizational Knowledge Bases – Repositories of valuable project information, including histor-ical records, risk logs, and performance metrics, that aid in future project planning and execution.

Baseline: *A baseline is the approved project management plan, including all authorized changes. It serves as the reference point for measuring project performance and progress.*

THE NATURE OF KNOWLEDGE

You may be asking yourself now, *"Okay, I understand the bullet points and definitions of the knowledge areas, but how do I truly grasp them?"* It's one thing to know the textbook definitions of scope, schedule, cost, and risk management; it's another to apply them effectively in real-world situations. This is where the distinction between knowledge and information becomes critical. Information, such as charts, data points, or timelines is useful, but it only becomes powerful when it's interpreted, contextualized, and transformed into actionable knowledge. To take this a step further, we also need to understand the difference between explicit knowledge, which can be easily documented and shared, and tacit knowledge, which is gained through experience, intuition, and practice. Bridging this gap is key to becoming a competent and confident project manager. Let's explore how to move beyond definitions and data, and into the realm of applied, experiential understanding.

Explicit Knowledge: *Knowledge that can be easily explained using words, pictures, or numbers and is easy to communicate, store, and distribute, such as information in textbooks, project documents, and plans.*

Tacit Knowledge: *Sometimes called informal knowledge, this type of knowledge is difficult to express and is highly personal, such as beliefs, insight, and experience.*

Knowledge within organizations can be categorized into two forms: explicit and tacit. Explicit knowledge is visible, teachable, and easy to replicate. This includes standardized processes, templates, and technical skills that are straightforward to document and share. For example, a project's risk registers, or work breakdown structures (WBS) embodies explicit knowledge, clear steps that guide action and are easily communicated to team members. However, this type of knowledge is also easy for competitors to imitate, reducing its long-term competitive advantage.

Tacit knowledge, on the other hand, is intangible, deeply personal, and less observable. It is embedded in individual expertise, organizational culture, and the specific context in which it was created. For instance, a project manager's ability to navigate political dynamics within a team or an organization's unique approach to innovation represents tacit knowledge. This type of knowledge is far more complex and challenging to detach from its creator, making it a critical yet an underutilized asset in project management. People are the heart and pulse of the project.

To leverage tacit knowledge, organizations must prioritize knowledge sharing through mentorship, collaborative workshops, and creating an environment where experiential insights are valued. Tools such as retrospective reviews and lessons-learned sessions provide platforms for capturing and embedding tacit knowledge into future projects. Engaging with independent service providers can deliver leadership to navigate through the process. Improve the tacit knowledge of a project by encouraging self-organization within teams. By empowering team members to take ownership of their tasks, you unlock their creative potential to address challenges and seize opportunities. Self-organized teams, which emphasize adaptability and team autonomy, are particularly effective in harnessing this natural capacity for continuous improvement. When team members work closely and frequently together, they naturally develop a shared language, understand each other's strengths and habits, and pick up on non-verbal cues. This ongoing, often informal communication helps embed skills and insights in ways that formal documentation can't.

CHANGE MANAGEMENT: A COMPREHENSIVE GUIDE

Up to this point, we've been immersed in the structured, intellectual components of Project Integration Management, crafting project charters, defining comprehensive project management plans, and unpacking the nature of knowledge to bridge theory with application. But the moment we hand over these carefully prepared documents to the customer, the dynamic shifts. The challenge is no longer about planning; it's about behavioral change. A strong plan doesn't guarantee buy-in, engagement, or transformation. Bridging the gap between documentation and real-world adoption is where Change Management becomes essential. This next section focuses on how we move beyond formal planning into the human experience of change, navigating uncertainty, resistance, and the emotional side of project delivery.

Integrated Change Control: *Identifying, evaluating, and managing changes throughout the project life cycle.*

Change management is not about making people happy about change; it is about managing the risks associated with change and ensuring that they are addressed expediently. The ADKAR Change Management Model is a goal-oriented framework that helps organizations manage change effectively by focusing on individual transitions. Developed by Prosci, ADKAR stands for Awareness, Desire, Knowledge, Ability, and Reinforcement, representing the five key steps individuals must go through for successful change adoption.[30]

a. **Awareness** – Understanding why the change is necessary. Employees must recognize the need for change to begin the transition process.

b. **Desire** – Building motivation to support and participate in the change. Without personal commitment, resistance may hinder progress.

c. **Knowledge** – Providing the necessary information, training, and tools to implement the change effectively.

d. **Ability** – Developing the skills and competencies required to apply the change in daily operations.

e. **Reinforcement** – Ensuring long-term sustainability by reinforcing new behaviors through recognition, support, and continuous improvements.

By addressing both the people and process sides of change, the ADKAR model helps organizations drive successful transformations while minimizing resistance and ensuring lasting adoption.[31] But how do we know when there are warning signs that there is team resistance to change?

Warning Signs in Context to a Cloud Software Project

a. Lack of a clear project sponsor or having multiple conflicting sponsors.
b. History of past project failures within the organization.
c. Absence of official communication about upcoming changes.
d. No designated individual responsible for managing change.
e. Circulating rumors about the solution or concerns over job security.
f. Lack of a dedicated training center or training specialist.
g. A consensus-driven culture that slows decision-making.
h. Restricted or self-censored communication due to internal company politics.
i. No advocate or leader championing cloud adoption.
j. Misalignment between IT and business strategies, such as cloud vs. on-premises preferences.

When we acknowledge there's a problem and the warning signs are evident, the most effective way to address resistance is by beginning with a Change Readiness Assessment. This tool helps uncover where individuals, teams, or even the entire organization may be hesitant or unprepared for change, offering critical insights into underlying challenges. With this information, we can develop focused interventions and support strategies, transforming awareness into purposeful, informed action.

Change Readiness Assessment: *A structured process and tool designed to evaluate an organization's ability to support upcoming changes, mitigate associated risks, and recommend actions to enable a successful transition. This assessment serves as the foundation for the Change Management Roadmap, ensuring that the organization is prepared to implement and sustain the necessary changes.*

Here's an illustration of the process, step by step:

Information Gathering Process

To complete the Change Readiness Assessment, the Change Management Team gathers information through multiple channels, including leadership interviews, stakeholder analysis, a change readiness survey, reviews existing documentation, current processes, future process changes, and lessons learned from previous project initiatives.

Leadership Interviews

Leadership interviews are conducted to assess the organization's readiness for change and identify potential risks that could impact the success of the solution. The Change Management Team interviews executives and managers across all functional areas using a stakeholder register and power/interest grid to organize the dialogues. The interview questions are developed based on leading management practices, focusing on leadership alignment, past experiences with change, reactions to change, work environment, and training needs. Insights from these interviews provided a deeper understanding of the challenges and opportunities associated with the change.

Stakeholder Register: *A stakeholder register is a living document that contains essential information about identified stakeholders, including their names, roles, influence levels, expectations, communication preferences, and potential impact on the project. This register helps project managers tailor their engagement strategies, ensuring that each stakeholder is involved appropriately based on their level of interest and authority. Keeping this document updated throughout the project lifecycle enhances stakeholder management effectiveness.*

Power/Interest Grid: *This stakeholder management tool categorizes stakeholders based on their level of authority (power) and degree of concern (interest) regarding project outcomes. Stakeholders with high power and high interest require close engagement, while those with low power and low interest need* *minimal attention. This grid helps project managers prioritize communication and involvement strategies, ensuring effective stakeholder engagement throughout the project.*

Stakeholder Analysis

In addition to leadership interviews, the Change Management Team collaborates with functional teams to expand on the stakeholders register on how they would be impacted. This Stakeholder Analysis is crucial in determining the level of influence, disposition (positive or negative), and potential risks associated with each stakeholder group.

a. For each stakeholder, the following attributes are assessed:
b. Function, size, and location
c. Level of involvement in (High, Medium, Low)
d. Influence within the organization (High, Medium, Low)
e. Level of impact the project would have on their role (High, Medium, Low)
f. Potential resistance to change (High, Medium, Low)
g. Assessment tools needed to gauge their readiness

Stakeholder Analysis: *This technique involves gathering and analyzing stakeholder-related information to identify key individuals, their interests, influence levels, and potential impact on the project. By understanding stakeholders' needs and expectations, project managers can develop strategies to enhance support, mitigate resistance, and maintain positive relationships. Effective stakeholder analysis leads to smoother project execution and greater buy-in from critical participants.*

To gain further insights, the Change Management Team asks key expectation questions such as:

a. What are the stakeholder's business goals and objectives?
b. What other business initiatives is the stakeholder involved in?
c. How will they impact their goals and objectives?
d. What experience does the stakeholder have with similar past initiatives?
e. What concerns does the stakeholder have about the project?
f. What suggestions do they have to manage change effectively?
g. What communication strategies do they recommend?
h. Who else should be consulted for further insights?

Expectations Management Matrix: *This tool is designed to clarify and manage stakeholder expectations by outlining key project success measures, priorities, and guidelines. It helps align team members and stakeholders on what defines project success, reducing misunderstandings and increasing project satisfaction. The matrix includes measurable criteria such as cost, schedule, quality, and stakeholder satisfaction, ensuring all parties have a shared vision of success.*

Change Readiness Assessment Survey

As part of the change management methodology, an employee survey is distributed to gauge overall readiness and risk levels within the company. This survey covers essential topics such as leadership and management effectiveness, past experiences with change, reactions to change, work environment, training, and communication needs. The results from this survey provides critical data, which are incorporated into the Change Readiness Assessment, to refine strategies and address any concerns.

Developing the Change Management Roadmap

Based on the information gathered through leadership interviews, stakeholder analysis, and the survey, key impacts and issues are identified for management. These are categorized according to change management best practices across several business capabilities, including:

    a. Process
    b. Systems
    c. Organizational Structure
    d. Governance
    e. Skills and Competencies
    f. Leadership

For each key impact or issue, a corresponding action plan is developed to ensure proper resolution. Accountability is assigned to a specific person or team, and a timeframe for completion is established. These actions and activities are then integrated into the Change Management Roadmap. By conducting a thorough Change Readiness Assessment, the organization can proactively address potential challenges, align leadership and stakeholders, and develop a structured roadmap that ensures a smooth transition. This process not only mitigates risks but also strengthens the organization's ability to adapt to change, ultimately contributing to the successful implementation of the project.

CHANGE CONTROL PROCESS

Change management isn't just about guiding people through emotional or organizational shifts, it also plays a critical role in how we manage changes in scope throughout a project's lifecycle. As projects evolve, new requirements emerge, priorities shift, and unforeseen challenges arise. Without a structured approach, even small changes can disrupt timelines, inflate costs, and derail outcomes. That's where the change control process comes in. By integrating change management principles with formal scope change procedures, we can ensure that every change is evaluated, communicated, and implemented in a controlled and transparent way. Let's explore how this works in practice.

Project Change Control Process: *The formal, documented process that describes when and how official project documents may be changed.*

Any change in scope of the project as described in the Statement of Work, or changes that would affect the scope, timeline, resources, or cost would be processed using this Project Change Request (PCR) process. This could include:

a. Enhancement (Custom) Components like Interfaces, Custom Reports etc. Amendments
b. Additional Reporting
c. Other Changes

For each enhancement and extension that gets approved, the following must be provided:

a. Functional Design
b. Technical Design
c. Test Scripts

The PCR contains a description of the desired change, the business reason for the change, alternatives to the desired change, and estimates of resources, time, and/or cost to incorporate the change as well as any other pertinent information. This will allow the customer to make a decision whether to approve and incorporate the change into the project or not.

Change Control Board (CCB): *A formal group of people responsible for approving or rejecting changes on a project.*

A PCR will be the vehicle for communicating change to the CCB. The PCR must describe the change, the rationale for the change, and the effect the change will have on the project. It will also include the scope of the change, a description of the activities to be completed as part of the project change request, an outline of the responsibilities of the parties involved and the estimated level of effort (and cost) to complete.

a. Project Managers shall be authorized on behalf of Customer to approve Change Orders that do not increase the cost of the Project or delay the completion of the Project.

b. If a change request has an impact on budget or schedule, it will be presented to Customer steering committee for approval. The steering committee will determine whether the benefits of the proposed change merit the investment, and whether they are willing to provide additional funding. Resolution (acceptance or rejection) of the PCR will be documented on the PCR in the Resolution section.

c. If approved, a written PCR will be signed by both Service Provider and Customers Project Managers to authorize implementation of the requested change.

d. Approved PCR's will be incorporated into the project budget and the project work plan and assigned to the appropriate resources.

e. Upon receiving an approved Change Order, Service Provider shall promptly commence performing the Services described in the Change Order.

TECHNIQUES CRITICAL FOR PROJECT SELECTION

As our project integration journey comes full circle, we've explored a wide range of essential topics, from building strong charters and structured project plans to understanding the deeper nature of knowledge and the dynamics of change. Now, we shift from planning and execution to a critical decision-making point: how to select the right projects in the first place. At the heart of effective project integration is the ability to prioritize initiatives based on organizational needs, manage the triple constraints of scope, time, and cost, and ensure that every effort delivers real value to the business. This section introduces quantitative techniques for project selection, helping us make informed choices about where to allocate limited resources for the greatest strategic impact.

These financial techniques provide quantifiable, objective criteria for selecting the most financially sound projects. Without these accounting-based analytics, businesses risk investing in projects that consume resources but fail to generate sufficient returns. Using measurable procedures such as, net present value, NPV, internal rate of return, IRR, return on investment, ROI, and a cash flow analysis, organizations can:

1. Prioritize projects that maximize shareholder value
2. Assess risk versus return to ensure capital is invested efficiently
3. Align investments with strategic business objectives
4. Ensure financial sustainability by considering cost of capital and liquidity

Ultimately, data analysis techniques are not just accounting functions, they are vital decision-making tools that drive business success. Companies that apply these methodologies can confidently select projects that enhance profitability, reduce risk, and create long-term value.

The Role of Cash Flow in Project Selection

Cash Flow: *The net amount of money generated or spent by a business, calculated as total benefits minus costs or total income minus expenses.*

At the core of all these techniques is cash flow, the net amount of cash moving in and out of a business over a given period. Cash flow is essential because it reflects a company's liquidity and ability to finance operations, repay debts, and generate profits. Positive cash flow indicates financial health, while negative cash flow can signal potential risk. When evaluating projects, businesses must forecast expected cash inflows and outflows to determine whether an investment is financially sustainable and aligns with strategic goals.

Net Present Value (NPV) Analysis: *A financial method for evaluating the profitability of a project by discounting all future expected cash inflows and outflows to their present value.*

NPV is one of the most important financial analysis tools used in project selection. It measures the total value of projected future cash flows, discounted to their present value using a specified discount rate (typically the cost of capital or required rate of return). The NPV formula is:

$$NPV = \sum \frac{C_t}{(1 + r)^t} - C_0$$

Where:
- $C_tC\_tC_t$ = net cash inflow in period ttt
- rrr = discount rate (cost of capital or required return)
- ttt = time period
- $C_oC\_oC_o$ = initial investment

If **NPV > 0**, the project is expected to generate more value than its cost, making it a worthwhile investment. If **NPV < 0**, the project is likely to destroy value and should be reconsidered.

A project requiring an initial investment of $500,000 and generating future discounted cash flows totaling $700,000 results in an NPV of $200,000. Since the NPV is positive, the project manager can justify the investment as a value-generating initiative.

Return On Investment (ROI): *Return on Investment (ROI) is a financial metric used to evaluate the profitability of a project by comparing the net benefits to the total costs. It is calculated as (Total Benefits - Total Costs) ÷ Total Costs, expressed as a percentage.*

$$ROI = \frac{\text{Net Benefits – Total Costs}}{\text{Total Costs}} \times 100\%$$

If a business spends $50,000 on a marketing campaign that results in $80,000 in additional revenue, the ROI would be (80,000 - 50,000) ÷ 50,000 = 60%, indicating a strong return on the investment.

Required Rate of Return: *The required rate of return (RRR) is the minimum percentage of return an investment* *must achieve to be considered worthwhile. It accounts for factors such as the cost of capital, project risk, and alternative investment opportunities.*

If a company sets its RRR at 10%, any proposed project must generate at least a 10% return to be approved. A project expected to yield only 8% would likely be rejected, as it does not meet the minimum return threshold.

Payback Period: *The payback period is the time required for a project to recover its initial investment through net cash inflows. It is a simple way to assess the financial feasibility of a project by determining how quickly it will start generating positive returns.*

A company invests $100,000 in a new software system expected to generate $25,000 in annual savings. The payback period would be four years ($100,000 ÷ $25,000 = 4 years), meaning the company will break even on its investment after four years.

Cost of Capital*: The potential return an investor could earn by allocating capital to an alternative investment with similar risks.*

If a company's cost of capital is 8%, a project with a return of only 6% would not be justifiable, as the money could yield better returns elsewhere. As a project manager, understanding this helps in prioritizing projects that exceed the cost of capital.

Discount Factor: *A numerical value applied to future cash flows to adjust for the time value of money, derived from the discount rate and the specific year.*

A project generating $1 million five years from now won't have the same value in today's terms due to inflation and opportunity costs. If the discount factor for year five is 0.68, the present value of that future revenue is $680,000, helping the project manager make an informed investment decision.

Discount Rate: *The percentage rate used to convert future cash flows into their present value, also referred to as the capitalization rate or opportunity cost of capital.*

If a company uses a 10% discount rate, a project expected to generate $200,000 in profit five years from now will be worth much less today. Understanding this helps the project manager compare different projects on an equal footing.

Internal Rate of Return (IRR): *The discount rate at which the net present value (NPV) of a project equals zero, indicating the break-even rate of return.*

A construction project with an IRR of 12% compared to the company's cost of capital of 8% suggests a worthwhile investment. If the IRR were 5%, the project manager might recommend reconsidering the project.

Capitalization Rate: *Another term for the discount rate, representing the rate used to determine the present value of future cash flows, also known as the opportunity cost of capital.*

A real estate development project with an expected annual income of $100,000 and a capitalization rate of 5% implies a project valuation of $2 million ($100,000 ÷ 0.05). This helps the project manager determine whether the investment aligns with the organization's financial goals.

Opportunity Cost of Capital: *The rate of return an investor forgoes by choosing one investment over another with a similar risk profile. It is used to discount future cash flows and is also known as the capitalization rate or discount rate.*

If a company has $1 million to invest and can choose between Project A, which offers a 10% return, and Project B, which offers an 8% return, the opportunity cost of capital is 10% if they choose Project B. As a project manager, this helps in selecting the most financially beneficial project to maximize returns.

Weighted Scoring Model: *A weighted scoring model is a structured decision-making technique used to evaluate and prioritize projects based on multiple criteria, assigning different weights to each criterion based on its importance. This method ensures an objective and data-driven approach to project selection, allowing organizations to focus on initiatives that deliver the highest value.*

A company evaluating three potential IT projects may use a weighted scoring model with criteria such as cost (30%), expected ROI (40%), and alignment with company strategy (30%). Each project is rated against these factors, and the project with the highest weighted score is selected for implementation.

Balanced Scorecard: *A balanced scorecard is a strategic planning and management framework that enables organizations to translate their vision and strategy into measurable objectives across four key perspectives: financial, customer, internal processes, and learning & growth. By tracking performance across these dimensions, companies can ensure alignment between business activities and strategic goals while fostering continuous improvement.*

A retail company implementing a balanced scorecard may set financial goals such as increasing annual revenue by 15%, customer-focused objectives like improving satisfaction scores by 10%, internal process improvements such as reducing order fulfillment time by 20% and learning & growth targets like training 90% of employees on a new inventory system within six months. This holistic approach ensures balanced growth and success across all business functions.

DEVELOPING THE SWOT ANALYSIS

SWOT Analysis: *A SWOT analysis is a strategic planning tool used to evaluate an organization's Strengths, Weaknesses, Opportunities, and Threats. It helps organizations understand internal capabilities and external influences to develop informed strategies.*

Internal Strengths

Identify key internal advantages that benefit your organization. These can include tangible and intangible assets, policies, or capabilities that provide a competitive edge. If your organization has board-approved policies or statements, these must be considered strengths.

    Examples:
        a. Experienced and knowledgeable staff
        b. Well-established policies and procedures
        c. Upgraded technology, such as expanded servers

Internal Weaknesses

Recognize internal challenges or limitations that may hinder performance. These can be resource constraints, inefficiencies, or structural issues within the organization.

Examples:

    a. Outdated infrastructure, such as inadequate
       wiring for network access

    b. Poor communication or strained relationships
       between management and staff

    c. Lack of funding for staff training

External Opportunities

Identify external factors that could positively impact your organization. These opportunities can exist at local, state, national, or global levels and might include funding, partnerships, or market trends.

Examples:

    a. New state funding initiatives for technology and
       digital resources

    b. Public interest in data privacy and cybersecurity,
       creating a potential service niche

    c. Philanthropic support from local benefactors

External Threats

Consider external challenges or risks that could negatively impact your organization. These may stem from market shifts, policy changes, or global events beyond your control.

Examples:

    a. Regulatory changes affecting service delivery

    b. Cybersecurity threats and increased data privacy
       concerns

    c. Economic downturns impacting funding availability

LEVERAGING SWOT ANALYSIS FOR STRATEGIC OUTCOMES

The ultimate goal of conducting a SWOT analysis is to develop a strategic plan and a strategic outcome that ensures the long-term viability and success of an organization. A well-executed SWOT analysis identifies internal strengths and weaknesses, as well as external opportunities and threats, serving as the foundation for formulating strategic outcomes and actionable strategies. These strategic outcomes focus on achieving significant organizational improvements and aligning efforts with the vision and mission of the organization.

Strategic Planning: *Determining long-term objectives by analyzing the strengths and weaknesses of an organization, studying opportunities and threats in the business environment, predicting future trends, and projecting the need for new products and services.*

Developing Strategies and Support Statements

Begin with listing strategic outcomes, once defined, they must be supported by clear strategies that outline how these outcomes will be achieved. Each strategy should be concise and action-oriented, directly flowing from the strategic outcomes. For example, in support of the strategic outcome "Students succeed in a digital world," strategies might include:

a. Technology Infrastructure Enhancement: We will upgrade and expand digital resources to support learning and professional development.

    b. Digital Literacy Programs: We will provide
       training programs that empower students with
       essential digital skills.

Likewise, for the strategic outcome "Library services meet the diverse needs of students and the community," strategies may include:

    a. Community Engagement Initiatives: We will
       collaborate with local organizations to tailor
       library services to diverse populations.
    b. Inclusive Collection Development: We will ensure
       that our materials reflect the varied interests and
       backgrounds of our users.

These strategies establish a roadmap for achieving strategic outcomes while maintaining alignment with organizational priorities. They provide a structured approach to decision-making and resource allocation, ensuring that every initiative contributes to overarching goals.

From Strategy to Action

The final step in the strategic planning process is translating strategies into action plans. These plans break down strategies into specific, time-bound initiatives with clear responsibilities and performance indicators. Action plans ensure that strategies are not merely aspirational but are actively implemented and measured for success.

By continuously evaluating progress against these strategic outcomes and adjusting strategies as necessary, the organization can remain agile and responsive to emerging challenges and opportunities. In this way, a well-developed SWOT analysis serves as the backbone of a dynamic strategic plan, guiding the organization toward sustained success and relevance.

The next section provides a practical illustration of how we applied SWOT to a large retail organization turning strategy into action.

Strategic Outcomes:

  a. Agility to compete with lower cost competitors.
  b. Expand customer diversity.
  c. Enhance customer experience.

Strategies and Support Statements:

- **Strategy Area #1:** Diversity
  Supporting Statement: Grow the customer base's diversity through rebalancing the product mix and marketing to reflect local communities and cultures.
- **Strategy Area #2:** Customer Experience
  Supporting Statement: Create a more immersive, engaging customer experience.
- **Strategy Area #3:** Globalization
  Supporting Statement: Increase our global e-commerce capabilities, so that international guests will be able to shop from online store
- **Strategy Area #4:** Economics
  Supporting Statement: Expand the economic demographic profile to bridge gaps during macroeconomic slowdowns.
- **Strategy Area #5:** Sustainability
  Supporting Statement: Create environmentally friendly products, sustainable brands, and experience.

CHAPTER 4

Methodology: Five Little Steps, One Big Plan

HAROLD KERZNER (BORN 1940) is a key figure in contemporary traditional project management, often recognized for his comprehensive frameworks and educational impact. While not the "father" in a historical sense like Fayol or Gantt, Kerzner is a modern luminary who refined and popularized predictive project management practices from the late 20th century onward. As a professor, consultant, and author, he bridged academic theory with practical application, notably through his book *Project Management: A Systems Approach*,[32] which became a cornerstone for the Project Management Institute (PMI) and its Project Management Body of Knowledge (PMBOK).[33] His work emphasizes detailed planning, control systems, and maturity models, hallmarks of traditional methodologies making him a leader in formalizing structured project management for industries like construction, aerospace, and IT in its early phases, laying the groundwork for the methodologies that continue to shape how projects are planned and executed today.

Methodology: *How things should be done. A project management methodology is a structured set of principles, practices, tools, and processes designed to guide the planning, execution, monitoring, and completion of a project to achieve specific objectives within defined constraints (e.g., time, budget, scope). It provides a repeatable framework to ensure consistency, manage risks, allocate resources effectively, and deliver successful outcomes. Methodologies vary in approach, some are linear (e.g., Waterfall), others iterative (e.g., Agile), but all aim to systematize the chaotic nature of project work into an organized, predictable process.*

TRADITIONAL (PREDICTABLE) PROJECT MANAGEMENT VS. AGILE PROJECT MANAGEMENT

Predictability and control are the key characteristics for choosing traditional project methodologies. In project management, the traditional approach (Waterfall) and Agile methodology represent two fundamentally different ways of planning, executing, and delivering projects. Not every project is suitable for Agile methodologies; some projects benefit more from a structured, predictive approach. Organizations should recognize opportunities to leverage traditional project management methods that emphasize detailed planning, stability, and predictability. Traditional methodologies follow a linear progression, ensuring each phase is completed before moving to the next. Critical success factors include well-documented requirements, stable environments, and stakeholders who value predictability over adaptability. Agile methods may struggle in these situations as they lack the rigorous foresight needed for large-scale, long-term planning. For example, projects with well-defined requirements, regulatory constraints, and repetitive processes align well with predictive methodologies. These projects thrive on structured oversight, clear documentation, and upfront planning to minimize uncertainty and risk. Traditional project managers focus on following a structured, plan-driven approach with minimal changes, whereas Agile leaders embrace adaptability, continuous improvement, and customer value as their primary objectives.

The readiness of the team and stakeholders plays a crucial role in determining whether traditional methodologies should be applied. Traditional project management excels when roles, responsibilities, and outcomes are clearly defined, reducing ambiguity and ensuring efficiency. If the customer or stakeholders require a fixed scope, timeline, and budget, traditional methods provide the necessary structure. The rigid framework of predictive methodologies ensures accountability and consistency, preventing unnecessary deviations that could derail the project.

Projects that require compliance with industry regulations, safety standards, or government mandates are better suited for traditional approaches. These projects demand detailed documentation, thorough risk assessments, and strict adherence to guidelines. In such cases, Agile's iterative nature could introduce unnecessary risks and potential compliance issues. Similarly, infrastructure projects, construction, manufacturing, and large-scale enterprise system implementations benefit from a phased approach with clearly outlined milestones.

When determining whether to use a predictive approach, organizations must consider the many factors. The science of structured execution requires choosing projects that prioritize efficiency over flexibility and control over innovation. Traditional project management follows a systematic approach of initiating, planning, executing, monitoring, and closing phases, ensuring well-defined deliverables. The lower the uncertainty, the more suitable a project is for upfront planning and risk mitigation. Task-based projects with repetitive workflows align well with traditional methodologies, as they minimize disruption and maintain efficiency.

Traditional methodologies support detailed cost estimation, long-term scheduling, and milestone-based progress tracking. High-oversight plan-driven projects, like this, reduce risk by minimizing unexpected changes. Unlike Agile, which thrives on evolving requirements, predictive approaches ensure consistency through comprehensive documentation and controlled processes. While some may argue that change is inevitable, structured management mitigates risk by establishing clear guidelines from the outset. Finally, fostering precision and eliminating ambiguity enables teams to execute projects with confidence and reliability. These fundamental principles help project managers navigate complexity and ensure successful project completion.

Traditional (Predictive) Methodology: *A structured, sequential approach where the scope, time, and cost are defined early in the project lifecycle and carefully controlled throughout execution. Often known as the "Waterfall" model, this methodology follows a linear path through distinct phases such as initiation, planning, execution, monitoring, and closure.*

PROCESS GROUPS: TRADITIONAL (PREDICTIVE) APPROACH

In a traditional project management methodology, process groups represent the core phases that guide a project from start to finish.

They are not individual tasks or specific tools, but rather logical groupings of activities that reflect the natural flow of a project's lifecycle. Each process group serves a distinct purpose, laying the foundation, shaping the plan, driving execution, monitoring progress, and ultimately closing the effort. Together, they provide the substance and structure needed to manage complexity, align stakeholders, and ensure that every phase of the project is deliberate, traceable, and aligned with organizational goals. These groups form the operational backbone of traditional methodologies, emphasizing predictability, discipline, and control.

Project Management Process Groups: *The core framework that defines how projects are managed through- out their lifecycle. These group represent a logical sequence of activities that progress from initiation to planning, executing, monitoring and controlling, and closing.*

Project management processes are grouped into the following five Project Management Process Groups:

a. **Initiation**: This phase defines and authorizes the project. Key activities include identifying stakeholders, developing the project charter, and establishing high-level objectives. It ensures that the project has a clear purpose, alignment with business goals, and the necessary approvals to proceed.

b. **Planning**: The team creates a comprehensive roadmap for execution. This includes developing detailed plans for scope, schedule, cost, quality, resources, risk, communications, and procurement. Effective planning aligns expectations and sets a foundation for tracking performance. The planning processes focuses on the traditional triangle, where scope, schedule and budget are fixed, devising and maintaining a workable sequence to ensure that the project addresses the organization's objects.

c. **Execution**: This is where the work gets done, as per plan. Resources are mobilized, tasks are assigned, and deliverables are produced. Managing teams, coordinating resources, and ensuring quality outputs are central. Success depends on leadership, communication, and issue resolution.

d. **Monitoring & Controlling**: This group runs concurrently with execution. It involves tracking performance, managing changes, and ensuring the project stays aligned with the plan. Activities include scope verification, variance analysis, and risk response. The goal is to maintain control without stifling progress.

e. **Closure**: The final group focuses on formally completing the project or phase. This includes obtaining stakeholder acceptance, finalizing documentation, releasing resources, and conducting lessons-learned reviews. A strong close ensures organizational knowledge is captured and value is realized.

Challenges of the Predictive Approach

1. **Inflexibility to Changing Requirements or Market Shifts**

   The predictive approach locks in requirements early in the project lifecycle, assuming a stable environment where needs and market conditions remain constant. This rigidity makes it difficult to accommodate changes, such as new customer demands, technological advancements, or competitive pressures. Any deviation from the initial plan requires a formal change request process, which is often bureaucratic, time-consuming, and costly. For example, in software development, a client's request to add a new feature mid-project can disrupt the entire timeline and budget, as the process lacks mechanisms to seamlessly integrate evolving requirements. This inflexibility can result in delivering a product that no longer aligns with current market needs or stakeholder expectations

2. **Late Testing and Risk Discovery**

   Issues are often identified late in the process, making fixes costly. In the predictive approach, testing typically occurs late in the project lifecycle, often after development is complete. This delayed validation means that defects, design flaws, or misaligned requirements are frequently discovered only during the final stages, when addressing them is most expensive and disruptive. For instance, a critical performance issue in a software application might only surface during system testing, requiring significant rework that could have been mitigated with earlier feedback. This late risk discovery undermines the illusion of control that the predictive approach promotes, as unforeseen issues can derail budgets and timelines, leading to costly overruns or project failure.

3. **Heavy Documentation Requirements**
The predictive approach emphasizes comprehensive upfront documentation, including detailed requirement specifications, design documents, and project plans. While intended to ensure clarity and alignment, this focus on documentation can slow down project execution, diverting resources from actual development or innovation. For example, creating and maintaining extensive documentation for a complex infrastructure project can consume significant time, especially if requirements change, rendering parts of the documentation obsolete. This burden not only delays progress but also creates frustration among teams who must navigate cumbersome processes to update or revise documents, reducing overall efficiency.

4. **Illusion of Predictability and Control**
The predictive approach fosters a misleading sense of certainty by prioritizing strict adherence to predefined budgets, timelines, and scopes. Management often perceives this structure as a guarantee of predictability, assuming that risks can be fully mitigated through detailed planning. However, this illusion ignores the reality of dynamic project environments where change is inevitable. For instance, in industries like construction or IT, external factors such as supply chain disruptions or shifting client priorities

can invalidate initial assumptions, yet the predictive model resists adaptation. This overconfidence in control can lead to poor decision-making, as managers may overlook emerging risks or opportunities in favor of sticking to the original plan.

5. **Failure to Address Stagnation in Kanban-Like Workflows**

When predictive projects attempt to incorporate elements of Kanban (e.g., visualizing work in progress), they often fail to address bottlenecks and stagnation effectively. Everything gets stuck in the execution phase. The predictive approach's rigid phase-based structure clashes with Kanban's emphasis on continuous flow and adaptability. For example, tasks may get stuck in a particular phase (e.g., waiting for approval or resource allocation) due to the lack of iterative feedback loops or flexible prioritization. This stagnation can lead to delays, as work items pile up without clear mechanisms to resolve blockers quickly. Unlike agile methodologies, which use Kanban to promote flow and rapid response to issues, the predictive approach's strict sequencing exacerbates inefficiencies, leaving teams unable to address bottlenecks until the next phase or formal review.

When to Use the Predictive Approach

The predictive approach is best suited for projects where stability, structure, and regulatory adherence are paramount, despite its challenges with flexibility and adaptability. It excels in environments with clearly defined and stable requirements, such as developing a standardized software system for a mature industry where user needs are well-established and unlikely to shift. For instance, creating a payroll processing system with fixed functional requirements benefits from the predictive approach's linear structure, ensuring all specifications are meticulously planned and executed without mid-process deviations. Similarly, industries like aerospace, healthcare, and finance, where strict regulatory compliance is non-negotiable, rely on this approach to meet rigorous standards. In aerospace, for example, building an aircraft component demands precise adherence to safety and regulatory protocols, with detailed documentation and sequential processes to ensure compliance with bodies like the FAA. Large-scale infrastructure projects, such as constructing bridges or highways, also align well with the predictive approach, as their sequential execution, moving from design to procurement to construction, minimizes risks associated with overlapping phases in highly physical and resource-intensive environments. However, the decision to use this approach should be tempered by an understanding of its limitations, particularly in dynamic settings where change is frequent. Dynamic opportunities should refer to the chapters, Agile: The Magic Thread, and Information Gathering: You're Doing it Wrong!, where we explore other alternatives that can be used independently or unified with the traditional approach. The following section will provide a comprehensive analysis of how to optimize the predictive approach methodology.

COMPREHENSIVE ANALYSIS OF THE CLOUD APPLICATION SERVICES PROJECT METHODOLOGY

This section provides a sweeping analysis summarizing each phase and detailing a comprehensive set of tasks to form the Work Breakdown Structure, (WBS) for a predictive project. By integrating the full guidance from the document to illustrate their practical application. The following example can be used for a baseline for implementing cloud-based applications, designed to leverage out-of-the-box functionality and best practices. Its Work Breakdown Structure (WBS) organizes tasks into five phases: Initiate, Plan, Execute, Monitor and Control, and Close, offering a detailed framework for project execution.

Work Breakdown Structure (WBS): *A hierarchical decomposition of the total project work into manageable, deliverable-oriented sections, ensuring clarity in scope and responsibilities. A website redesign project may have a WBS structured into categories like design, development, content creation, and testing, each further divided into specific tasks.*

This section provides a comprehensive analysis of the predictive project management approach, outlining a detailed Work Breakdown Structure (WBS) that serves as a customizable framework for executing projects, particularly those involving cloud-based applications. The WBS organizes tasks into five distinct phases, Initiate, Plan, Execute, Monitor and Control, and Close, offering a structured roadmap to ensure systematic progression and alignment with project objectives. Each phase is meticulously detailed, integrating best practices and out-of-the-box functionality to streamline implementation while adhering to the predictive methodology's emphasis on upfront planning and sequential execution. This baseline WBS, grounded in industry-standard practices, can be tailored to your specific project by adjusting tasks to reflect unique requirements, such as compliance needs or integration with existing systems. Use this framework as a starting point, adapting its tasks and deliverables to align with your project's scope, timeline, and resources. The following sections will guide you through customizing this WBS, providing practical steps to apply it effectively to your cloud-based or other predictive projects.

Phase A: Initiate

The Initiate phase establishes the project's foundation, aligning scope, resources, and customer readiness through task groups like Project Launch, Prepare Project Team, and Functional and Technical Design Workshops.

Detailed Task Breakdown:

- **A.01 Review Statement of Work, Scope Statement, Workplan and Budget**
  In this task, the project manager reviews the executed statement of work and bid materials post-assignment, participating in a sales team handoff if feasible. The focus is on confirming scope, creating a Project Workplan, staffing resources, and validating the budget.
  - *Task / Summary Task:* A.01.01 Project Launch
  - *Work Product: Reviewed SOW, Contract, Scope, Workplan and Budget* — Includes reviewed bid material, contract, confirmed scope, requested resources, staffed project, baseline workplan, and confirmed budget.
  - *Formats: Project Workplan* (MS Project), *Reviewed and Analyzed Bid Material* (MS Word)
  - *Prerequisites: Executed Contract* — Signed statement of work, scope definition, costing financials, assumptions, and terms of agreement.

- *Activity:* Meet with proposal team, review contract estimates and terms, understand scope and objectives, document assumptions, create workplan, staff project, validate budget, resolve disconnects, identify center of excellence, create a timeline calendar.
- *Task Owner:* Implementation team has primary responsibility.

- **A.02 Collaborate Approach with Customer, Confirm Readiness, Socialize**

Socialize & collaborate, the project manager contacts the customer to assess readiness, confirming provisioned cloud environments, project approach, scope, objectives, assumptions, and resource commitments.

  - *Task / Summary Task:* A.02.01 Project Launch
  - *Work Product: Confirmed Customer Readiness* — Mutual understanding of next steps, scope, proposed schedule and customer ability to start.
  - *Formats: Readiness Checklist* (MS Word) Timeline (Visio)
  - *Prerequisites: Executed SOW/Contract* — Provides scope, assumptions and obligations.
  - *Activity:* Meeting with customer, review scope, timeline and approach, assess environment readiness, confirm resources, document readiness.
  - *Task Owner:* Shared, Project Leadership, Managers.

- **A.03 Establish Stewardship, Governance, Communication and Infrastructure**

Begin stewardship, establish project governance, build infrastructure, defining management policies and setting up supporting systems.

  - *Task / Summary Task:* A.03.01 Project Launch

- *Work Product*: *Project Management Plan and Establish Project Infrastructure* – Governance policies, Project plan and documents repository, systems/procedures.
- *Formats*: *Project Management Plan* (Word), *Summarized Project Management Plan bullet points* (PowerPoint), *Risk/Issue/Problem Log* (Excel, SharePoint)
- *Prerequisites*: *Reviewed SOW/Contract, Scope Statement, Project Workplan and Costing Budget* – Baseline for governance.
- *Activity:* Define governance policies, set up tracking systems (e.g., risk logs), establish communication protocols, review with stakeholders.
- *Task Owner*: Shared, Project Leadership, Managers.

- **A.04 Conduct Kickoff Meeting**
  Conduct a kickoff meeting to orient the project team and communicate objectives and structure.
  - *Task / Summary Task:* A.04.01 Mobilize Project Team
  - *Work Product*: *Kickoff Meeting* – Executed meeting with team orientation.
  - *Formats*: *Project Kickoff Presentation* (PowerPoint)
  - *Prerequisites*: *Collaborate Approach with Customer* – Ensures team alignment.
  - *Activity:* Perform meeting introduction, prepare agenda, present scope and objectives, outline roles, facilitate discussion, document outcomes, prepare for next steps.
  - *Task Owner*: Project team leaders. Executive Sponsorship.

- **A.05 Schedule Client Discovery Workshops**
  Schedule workshops to gather setup information and address technical in scope needs.
  - *Task / Summary Task:* A.05.01 Mobilize Project Team

- *Work Product*: *Workshop Schedule* — Lists workshops with dates, times, durations, objectives, and participants, integrated into the Project Workplan.
- *Formats: Workshop Schedule* (Excel, SharePoint)
- *Prerequisites*: *Collaborate Approach with Customer* — Fully Communicated Scope; *Kickoff Meeting* — Team orientation.
- *Activity:* Build agenda and sub-topics, sequence workshops, determine number per process area, identify cross functional areas, match customer resources to topics, CM review timing, secure customer availability, approve schedule.
- *Task Owner*: Shared Project team leads.

- **A.06 Conduct Functional & Technical Design Workshops**
  Conduct workshops to speculate functional & technical designs for the cloud application.
  - *Task / Summary Task:* A.06.01 Mobilize Project Team
  - *Work Product*: *Functional Design* — Requirement Documentation Matrix.
  - *Formats: Functional Design* (Excel, Word, SharePoint)
  - *Prerequisites*: *Workshop Schedule* — Scheduled sessions.
  - *Activity:* Facilitate discussions, capture requirements, align with leading practices, document high level approaches to requirements, model basic designs based on foundation needs and use cases.
  - *Task Owner*: Service provider team leads.

- **A.07 Conduct Phase Gate Review**
  In this task, you review phase work products and secure approval to proceed.

- *Task / Summary Task:* A.07.01 Phase Gate Review
- *Work Product: Phase Gate Review Meeting/Approval to Proceed* – Approval documentation.
- *Formats: Phase Gate review* (Word)
- *Prerequisites: Project Team Mobilization* – Phase outputs.
- *Activity:* Review outputs, confirm objectives, plan next steps, secure approval.
- *Task Owner:* PMO Center of Excellence.

Phase B: Planning

The Planning phase sets up the application, with task groups like Initial Configuration.

Detailed Task Breakdown:

- **B.01 Setup Applications (CRP1: Conference Pilot 1)**
  In this task, applications are configured based on validated designs.
  - *Task / Summary Task:* B.01.01 Initial Configuration
  - *Work Product: Configured Applications* – Setup per documentation.
  - *Prerequisites: Setup Documentation* – Detailed parameters.
  - *Activity:* Use tools (e.g., application accelerators), configure, review with customer.
  - *Task Owner:* Shared responsibility.

- **B.02 Prepare Validation Scenario's & Scripts**
  In this task, you prepare Scenarios & Scripts to validate configurations.
  - *Task / Summary Task:* B.01.02 Initial Configuration

- *Work Product*: *Validation Scripts* – Scenarios to be Tested, Test scripts.
- *Formats: Validation Scripts* (Word)
- *Prerequisites*: *Configured Applications* – Setup to test.
- *Activity:* Develop scenarios & scripts, align with requirements, review for coverage.
- *Task Owner*: Team leads.

- **B.03 Conduct Dry Run System Readiness**

In this task, you validate configurations through walk throughs.
  - *Task / Summary Task:* B.03.01 Initial Configuration
  - *Work Product*: *Validated Configuration* – Confirmed setups.
  - *Prerequisites*: *Validation Scripts* – Testing basis.
  - *Activity:* Facilitate workshops, test configurations, document results.
  - *Task Owner*: Shared responsibility.

- **B.04 Perform CRP1: Conference Room Pilot**

Team members perform limited testing of scenario use cases in a non-production environment.
  - *Task / Summary Task:* B.04.01 Team members perform limited scenarios.
  - *Work Product*: *Clean Non-Production Environment* – Approved Test Scripts.
  - *Prerequisites*: *Fully provisioned environment, entitlements, subscriptions* – Provisioned system.
  - *Activity:* Service provider led application system testing, log defects.
  - *Task Owner*: Shared responsibility, client led, service provider supported.

- **B.05 Perform Retrospect & FIT/ GAP Analysis**

  Analyze the results of Iteration 1 and identify gaps between con-forming requirements and standard out of the box functionality.

  - *Task / Summary Task:* B.05.01 Analyze Iteration 1 & defect log
  - *Work Product: Test Results & Defect Log* – Cross Analyzed Gap Matrix.
  - *Formats: Defect Log* (Word, SharePoint)
  - *Prerequisites: Scenario output* – Testing logs.
  - *Activity:* Load via templates, reconcile, validate, log actions.
  - *Task Owner:* Shared responsibility.

- **B.06 Conduct Phase Gate Review**

  Review phase work products and secure approval to proceed.

  - *Task / Summary Task:* B.06.01 Phase Gate Review
  - *Work Product: Phase Gate Review Meeting/Approval to Proceed* – Approval documentation.
  - *Formats: Phase Gate review* (Word)
  - *Prerequisites: Retrospective Complete* – Phase outputs.
  - *Activity:* Review outputs, confirm objectives, plan next steps, secure approval.
  - *Task Owner:* Executives, Project Management, Center of Excellence.

Phase C: Execute

The Execute phase showcases enhanced application functionality, leveraging insights and expertise gained from Iteration 1 to prepare for Iteration 2 and Systems Integration testing.

Detailed Task Breakdown

- **C.01.01 Setup Applications (Conference Room Pilot 2)**
  Refine application setups in the validation environment.
  - *Task / Summary Task:* C.01.01 Perform application configurations.
  - *Work Product: Configured Applications* – Advanced setup document.
  - *Prerequisites: Validated Configuration* – Prior setups.
  - *Activity:* Adjust configurations to CRP1 findings, verify functionality.
  - *Task Owner:* Service provider team leads responsibility.

- **C.02.01 Update Validation Scripts**
  Update initial scenarios with detailed scripts based on feedback.
  - *Task / Summary Task:* C.02.01 Prepare for Conference room pilot.
  - *Work Product: Updated Validation Scripts* – Updated detail test scripts.
  - *Prerequisites: Validation Scripts* – Original scenarios, scripts, retrospective.
  - *Activity:* Refine scripts, incorporate feedback, added gap resolutions.
  - *Task Owner:* Service provider team leads responsibility.

- **C.03.01 Load & Validate Data – Not Reconcile***
  In this task, you load and validate data in the validation environment.

---

*   The reconciliation process is performed by the customer, is separate and distinct from validating, and is the first step in beginning the testing process.

- *Task / Summary Task:* C.03.01 Load Master & Transactional Data
- *Work Product*: *Validated Data* – Source extracts & target output data files.
- *Formats: Varies Data* (Templates, XLM, CSV, Other)
- *Prerequisites*: *Prepared Data* – Extracted data.
- *Activity:* Load data, validate transmission, do not reconcile, document results.
- *Task Owner*: Shared responsibility.

- **C.04.01 Publish User Manuals**

  Publish first draft of user guide for end users to be used in train the trainer.
  - *Task / Summary Task:* C.04.01 Training Documentation
  - *Work Product*: *User Manual* – Job aid for trainers and end users.
  - *Prerequisites*: *Configuration Setup* – System stability for basis.
  - *Activity:* Compile visual guide, align with processes, distribute to users.
  - *Task Owner*: Training team leads.

- **C.05.01 Prepare for Training**

  Prepare for train the trainer sessions.
  - *Task / Summary Task:* C.04.01 Prepare for Training
  - *Work Product*: *Training Preparations* – Prepare seed data for train the trainer.
  - *Prerequisites*: *User Manual* – Training content.
  - *Activity:* Arrange logistics, prepare materials, coordinate schedules.
  - *Task Owner*: Service Provider leads.

- **C.06.01 Conduct Train-the-Trainer Sessions**
  Train customer trainers.
  - *Task / Summary Task:* C.06.01 Prepare for Training
  - *Work Product: User Manuals* – Prepared trainers.
  - *Prerequisites: Prepare for Training* – Available systems setup complete.
  - *Activity:* Conduct sessions, train on system use, evaluate readiness.
  - *Task Owner:* Shared responsibility.

- **C.07.01 Perform Iteration 2 (CRP2: Conference Room Pilot)**
  Team members reconcile data and perform advanced testing of use cases in a non-production environment.
  - *Task / Summary Task:* C.07.01 Team members perform advanced scenarios.
  - *Work Product: Clean Non-Production Environment* – Approved Test Scripts.
  - *Prerequisites: Fully provisioned environment, entitlements, subscriptions* – Provisioned system.
  - *Activity:* Reconcile data and perform hands on application system testing, log defects.
  - *Task Owner:* Shared responsibility, Service provider supported, Customer execution.

- **C.08.01 Perform System Integration Technical Readiness**
  Assess technical readiness for system integration testing.
  - *Task / Summary Task:* C.08.01 System Technical Readiness
  - *Work Product: Technical Readiness Assessment Recommendations* – Assessment findings.

- *Prerequisites*: *Configured Applications* — Systems and connectivity to assess.
- *Activity:* Evaluate infrastructure, document recommendations, review with team.
- *Task Owner*: Shared responsibility.

- **C.09.01 Conduct System Integration Testing**
Users review the system holistically, point to point, linked to CRP2 execution.
  - *Task / Summary Task:* C.09.01 Systems integration Testing
  - *Work Product*: *Conference Room Pilot Execution* — Technical Validation findings.
  - *Formats: System Integration Results* (Word, Excel, Various)
  - *Prerequisites*: *Configured Applications, Validated Data* — Test inputs.
  - *Activity:* Conduct end to end or point to point integrations, ensure consistency, verify transmission protocols, non-production data, document outcomes.
  - *Task Owner*: Shared responsibility.

- **C.10.01 Perform CRP2/SIT Retrospect & FIT/ GAP Analysis**
Analyze the results of Iteration 2 & SIT and identify gaps between conforming requirements and expected functionality, technical and data gaps.
  - *Task / Summary Task:* C.10.01 Analyze Iteration 2, SIT & defect log
  - *Work Product*: *Test Results & Defect Log* — Cross Analyzed Gap Matrix.
  - *Formats: Defect Log* (Word, SharePoint)
  - *Prerequisites*: *Test result output* — Testing summary logs.

- *Activity:* Compile testing results, gap mitigation.
- *Task Owner:* Shared responsibility.

- **C.11.01 Specify Cutover Strategy**

  Define the strategy for transitioning to production.
  - *Task / Summary Task:* C.11.01 Prepare for Cutover
  - *Work Product: Cutover Strategy* Documents – Cutover plan.
  - *Formats: Cutover Strategy* (Word, Excel, MS Projects, SharePoint)
  - *Prerequisites: CRP2/SIT Retrospective* – Basis for cutover.
  - *Activity:* Outline steps, timelines, roles, review with customer.
  - *Task Owner:* Shared responsibility.

- **C.12.01 Conduct Phase Gate Review**

  Review phase work products and secure approval to proceed.
  - *Task / Summary Task:* C.12.01 Gate Review
  - *Work Product: Phase Gate Review Meeting/Approval to Proceed* – Approval documentation.
  - *Formats: Phase Gate review* (Word)
  - *Prerequisites: CRP2/SIT Retrospective* – Phase outputs.
  - *Activity:* Review outputs, confirm objectives, plan next steps, secure approval.
  - *Task Owner:* Executive Leadership, Project Management, Center of Excellence.

Phase D: Monitoring & Controlling

The Monitoring & Controlling phase moves the system to final transitioning steps, with task groups like Perform User Acceptance Testing and Final Validation.

Detailed Task Breakdown:

- **D.01 Setup Applications (User Acceptance Configuration)**
  In this task, applications are configured based on validated designs.
  - *Task / Summary Task:* D.01.01 UAT Configuration
  - *Work Product:* *Configured Applications* – Setup per documentation.
  - *Prerequisites:* *Setup Documentation* – Detailed parameters.
  - *Activity:* Use tools (e.g., application accelerators), configure, review with customer.
  - *Task Owner:* Service provider responsibility.

- **D.02.01 Load, Validate Data, Connect Integrations in Non-Production**
  Load and validate production data in non-production environment for testing.
  - *Task / Summary Task:* D.02.01 Prepare for User Acceptance testing
  - *Work Product:* *Validated Data* – Loaded and verified data, connected protocols.
  - *Formats:* *Validated Data* (Word, Excel, CSV, XML, varies)
  - *Prerequisites:* *Configured Applications* – Prior ETL data prep.
  - *Activity:* Load data, validate, log actions.
  - *Task Owner:* Shared responsibility.

- **D.03.01 Perform User Acceptance Testing**
  Perform User Acceptance Testing in a non-production environment.
  - *Task / Summary Task:* D.03.01 End Users Perform Accepting Testing
  - *Work Product:* *Clean UAT Non-Production Environment* – Approved Test Scripts.

- *Prerequisites*: *Fully converted data with connected integrations* — Final Validated system.
- *Activity:* Customer led application business system testing.
- *Task Owner*: Client leads end users, service provider supported.

- **D.04.01 GO/NO GO Final Decision Review with Users and Stakeholders**
  Time to make a decision to begin cutover & move to production environment for use.
  - *Task / Summary Task:* D.04.01. Final Decision
  - *Work Product*: *Production Readiness Assessment* — Final review decision.
  - *Prerequisites*: *User Acceptance Testing results* — Decision Information
  - *Activity:* Executive meeting, review risks, make a decision to move to production.
  - *Task Owner*: Shared responsibility.

- **D.05.01 Migrate Configuration to Production**
  Migrate validated configurations to production.
  - *Task / Summary Task:* D.05.01 Execute Cutover Plan
  - *Work Product*: *Configured Production Environment* — Production setups.
  - *Prerequisites*: *Setup Documentation, Production Readiness Assessment* — GO decision
  - *Activity:* Execute Cutover Strategy, apply setups to production, review accuracy, involve customer.
  - *Task Owner*: Shared responsibility depending on risk and skill set.

- **D.06.01 Migrate Integrations and Extensions to Production**

  In this task, you migrate validated integrations and extensions.
  - *Task / Summary Task:* D.06.01 Execute Cutover Plan
  - *Work Product: Integrations and Extensions in Production* – Deployed components.
  - *Prerequisites: Production Readiness Assessment* – GO decision
  - *Activity:* Enable integrations/extensions, verify functionality.
  - *Task Owner:* Shared responsibility.

Phase E: Closure

The Closure phase stabilizes and closes the project, with task groups like Begin Production Use, GO LIVE, Stabilization and Project Closure.

Detailed Task Breakdown:

- **E.01.01 Employ Hypercare Production Support**

  Activate support mechanisms post go live.
  - *Task / Summary Task:* E.01.01 Hypercare Support
  - *Work Product: Production Support* – Support systems procedures.
  - *Prerequisites: Production Support Plan* – Procedure for managing change.
  - *Activity:* Rehearse procedures, test support channels, ensure awareness of processes.
  - *Task Owner:* Hypercare period begins, Service Provider responsibility.

- **E.02.01 GO LIVE Begin Production Use**

  You are Live, start production operations.
  - *Task / Summary Task:* E.02.01 Live Production Use
  - *Work Product:* *System in Production* — Operational system.
  - *Prerequisites:* *Production Readiness Verification, Support Plan* — Readiness confirmed.
  - *Activity:* Control initial transactions, sequence rollout, stabilize operations.
  - *Task Owner:* Customer leads.

- **E.03.01 Manage Transition to Stabilization**

  Monitor transition to routine operations.
  - *Task / Summary Task:* E.03.01 Stabilization
  - *Work Product:* *Daily-State Operations* — Stable system use.
  - *Prerequisites:* *System in Production* — Operational baseline.
  - *Activity:* Establish issue reporting, plan enhancements, improvements.
  - *Task Owner:* Shared responsibility.

- **E.04.01 Post Go-Live Support (Optional)**

  Provide contracted post-production support, if agreed after hypercare period ends.
  - *Task / Summary Task:* E.04.01 Extended Support
  - *Work Product:* *Extended Support* — Issue resolution.
  - *Prerequisites:* *System in Production* — Operational system.
  - *Activity:* Monitor, respond to issues, maintain system per contract.
  - *Task Owner:* Separate Service Provider Support Model.

- **E.05.01 Execute Handoff to Customer Transition Owner**

  Hand off to a customer transition owner.
  - *Task / Summary Task:* E.05.01 Transition to Customer Owner

- *Work Product*: *Customer Manager Handoff* – Project documentation.
- *Formats*: *Customer Manager Handoff* (All Work Products)
- *Prerequisites*: *System in Production, Hypercare ends* – Operational system.
- *Activity*: Migrate closure documentation, provide project overview, suggest enhancements.
- *Task Owner*: Shared Responsibility

- **E.06.01 Gain Acceptance Approvals Close Project**
  Validate scope delivery close project processes and contract.
  - *Task / Summary Task:* E.06.01 Project Closure
  - *Work Product*: *Final Acceptance Certificate Approval* – Scope verification approval.
  - *Formats*: *Acceptance Criteria, Acceptance Certificate, Project Acceptance Report* (Word)
  - *Prerequisites*: *Production Use* – Scope basis.
  - *Activity*: Validate delivery, secure acceptance, document outcomes, lessons learned.
  - *Task Owner*: Shared responsibility.

FROM TRADITION TO UNIFIED

The comprehensive and meticulously crafted Work Breakdown Structure (WBS) and phased progressions provided offers a disciplined framework one can use as a baseline for starting a new projects. However, some projects do not necessitate such a strict linear path and demand additional variations. In contexts where responsiveness, iterative refinement, or bold experimentation are critical, this method may struggle to deliver optimal value or keep pace with rapid change. The following section introduces three alternative and unifying methodologies, Solution-Driven, Requirements-Driven, and Innovation-Driven approaches, that reframe project execution. These strategies emphasize outcome-focused problem-solving, stakeholder-guided evolution, and pioneering creativity, respectively, offering pathways to navigate complexity and deliver impactful results in environments where predictability alone is insufficient.

Solution-Driven, Requirements-Driven, and Innovation-Driven Project Approaches

When managing projects, choosing the right approach is crucial for success. The three primary methodologies, Solution-Driven, Requirements-Driven, and Innovation-Driven, each cater to different business needs, project constraints, and technological landscapes. As a project manager, understanding their differences helps in selecting the most effective strategy for delivering value efficiently.[34]

1. Solution-Driven Approach

The solution-driven approach revolves around leveraging predefined solutions to meet business objectives with minimal customization. It is best suited for cloud-based SaaS applications and standardized business processes, where organizations adopt best practices embedded in pre-configured systems rather than building from scratch.

> *Example:*
> A company implementing a Cloud ERP system may opt for a solution-driven approach by using Modern Best Practices and out-of-the-box configurations. Rather than defining every requirement from scratch, the organization maps its business functions to existing features, refining configurations through iterations.

This reduces risk, accelerates deployment, and ensures alignment with industry standards.

Key Characteristics:
a. Predefined configurations and embedded best practices
b. Minimizes customization to reduce complexity and cost
c. Uses iterative refinement rather than starting from zero
d. Best for business process standardization and efficiency

However, the downside is that organizations must adapt their processes to fit the software, rather than tailoring the software to their specific workflows.

2. Requirements-Driven Approach

The requirements-driven approach is structured, focusing on detailed requirement gathering before designing and developing a tailored solution. It is best suited for AWS, Azure, OCI (Oracle Cloud Infrastructure), custom development applications, or highly regulated industries where compliance is critical.

Example:
A financial institution needing a customized risk management dashboard would follow a requirements-driven approach. The project begins with detailed interviews, workshops, and documentation of compliance and security needs. Only after completing the full requirement analysis, design, and documentation does development begin.

Key Characteristics:

a. Structured, contract-driven, and documentation-heavy
b. Best for custom solutions, regulatory compliance, and complex integrations
c. Follows Waterfall-like sequential phases (Analyze, Design, Build, Test, Deploy)
d. High predictability but limited flexibility for mid-project changes

The challenge with this approach is that late-stage changes can be costly and time-consuming, making it less suited for fast-changing environments.

3. Innovation-Driven Approach

The innovation-driven approach is highly Agile, focusing on rapid experimentation, iterative development, and user-driven evolution. It is ideal for dynamic markets like tech startups, software development, and emerging AI or IoT-based projects.

Example:

A health-tech company developing an AI-powered virtual assistant for patient diagnostics would use an innovation-driven approach. The team would start with a Minimum Viable Product (MVP), release early versions for feedback, and continuously refine the model based on AI learning and user data.

Key Characteristics:

a. Iterative, user-centric, and highly adaptable
b. Encourages continuous experimentation and rapid prototyping

    c. Prioritizes quick feedback loops over rigid planning

    d. Best for cutting-edge technology, digital transformation, and market disruptors

The trade-off is that the approach requires a culture of risk-taking, adaptability, and strong cross-functional collaboration, making it challenging for highly regulated industries.

Choosing the Right Approach as a Project Manager

Approach	Best For	Strengths	Challenges
Solution-Driven	SaaS-based cloud solutions, standard business processes	Fast implementation, minimal customization, industry best practices	Limited flexibility, organizations must adapt to predefined processes
Requirements-Driven	Regulatory-compliant projects, complex enterprise solutions, custom software development	Well-documented, structured, predictable outcomes	Rigid, change-resistant, long timelines
Innovation-Driven	AI, emerging tech, software startups, disruptive products	High adaptability, user feedback-driven, rapid market responsiveness	High risk, requires continuous experimentation

As a project manager, aligning the project approach with business needs, risk tolerance, and agility requirements ensures optimal outcomes. Some organizations even adopt a hybrid model, blending elements of all three to balance efficiency, flexibility, and innovation. By understanding the strengths and constraints of each methodology, teams can deliver projects on time, within scope, and with the highest possible business value.[35]

SIX SIGMA METHODOLOGIES

A chapter on methodology without commenting on the six Sigma methodology would be careless. Although we don't delve into significant details on this topic it's important to note that this approach is committed to using mathematical facts and excluding biases and judgments of human beings. If you are looking to become a Six Sigma black belt I would recommend researching the references noted in the following conclusion.

Six Sigma Methodologies: *Statistical approach for implementation. Define, Measure, Analyze, Improve, and Control (DMAIC) is used to improve an existing business process, and Define, Measure, Analyze, Design, and Verify (DMADV) is used to create new product or process designs.*

The Six Sigma approach to managing is about helping you identify what you don't know, emphasizing what you should know, and taking action to reduce the errors that cost you time, money, opportunities, and customers. Six Sigma translates that knowledge into opportunities for business growth. With Six Sigma, you can eliminate most errors, reduce costs, and satisfy your customers better. Six Sigma is a philosophy of management that emphasizes the elimination of defects through practices that emphasize understanding, measuring, and improving processes. The vital few factors that directly explain the cause-and-effect relationship of the process and output being measured in relation to the inputs that drive the process. Typically, data shows that there are six or few factors for any process that most affect the quality of outputs in any process even if there are hundreds of steps in which a defect can occur the vital few. When you isolate these factors, you know what basic adjustments you need to improve the output of the process effectively and reliably.[36] Six Sigma is based on a few key concepts defect, variation, critical to quality, process capability, and the cost of poor quality.

CHAPTER 5

Agile: The Magic Thread

Microsoft's shift from Waterfall to Agile for the development of Windows and Office 365

For decades, Microsoft leaned heavily on the Waterfall methodology to craft its flagship products like Windows and Office, a process rooted in a bygone era of software development. This approach was all about structure: teams would spend months, sometimes years, meticulously mapping out every detail, requirements, design, coding, testing, before a single line of code was written. Only after this exhaustive planning phase would development begin, culminating in a grand, polished release that might not see the light of day for two or three years. In the 1980s and 1990s, when software shipped on floppy disks or CDs and updates were a rare event, this made sense. Customers were willing to wait, and the tech landscape moved at a slower pace. Windows 95, for example, took years to build but landed as a monumental, era-defining release.[37]

But as the 2000s rolled in, the ground shifted. The rise of the internet, cloud computing, and mobile technology rewrote the rules. Customers didn't just want software, they wanted it fast, flexible, and constantly improving. Competitors like Google and smaller startups were churning out updates weekly, even daily, while Microsoft was still stuck in its multi-year cycles. The problems piled up: by the time a new Windows or Office version hit shelves, it risked feeling stale, unable to address emerging security threats or user needs that hadn't existed when planning began. Development teams, siloed and locked into rigid plans, couldn't pivot midstream without derailing timelines. The company's flagship products started to lose their edge, and Microsoft found itself playing catch-up in a world that demanded speed and adaptability.

The wake-up call came loud and clear. To stay relevant, Microsoft had to rethink everything. Starting around the early 2010s, they began shifting to Agile and DevOps methodologies, with Office 365 and Windows 10 becoming the proving grounds for this transformation. The old Waterfall playbook, build it all, then ship it, was scrapped for a continuous development and deployment model. Instead of dropping a massive update every few years, they rolled out smaller, bite-sized improvements on a regular cadence. Security patches could drop within days of a threat, new features could launch monthly, and bugs could be squashed without waiting for the next big release. For Office 365, this meant a cloud-based service that evolved in real time; for Windows 10, it meant a "Windows as a Service" approach that kept the OS fresh without the old reboot-everything mentality.

How did they pull it off? Microsoft broke their teams into Scrum units, small, cross-functional groups empowered to tackle specific goals. These teams worked in short, iterative sprints, often just two or three weeks long, delivering usable increments of software at every step. Gone were the days of planning everything years in advance; now, priorities could shift based on what was happening in the market or what users were clamoring for. Real-time customer feedback became a lifeline, funneled through telemetry data and direct input, letting Microsoft fine-tune features or ditch ones that didn't click. DevOps brought development and operations teams together, smoothing out the handoff from code to deployment and ensuring updates hit users seamlessly. Take Office 365's evolution: features like real-time co-authoring in Word or AI-driven insights in Excel didn't wait for a "Version 2.0", they rolled out as they were ready, keeping users engaged and the product competitive.

The shift wasn't just technical, it was cultural. Microsoft had to dismantle a decades-old mindset of perfection-before-release and embrace a world where "good enough, now" beat "perfect, later." The payoff was huge. Office 365 morphed into a subscription powerhouse, outpacing traditional Office sales, while Windows 10 stayed nimble enough to fend off rivals in a post-PC era. By solving the problems of sluggish cycles, inflexibility, and disconnect from users, Microsoft didn't just survive the tech revolution, they found a way to thrive in it.

So, if it worked for Microsoft, an undisputed leader in technology, what is Agile? Why is it the Magical Thread? and Why is it so Mysterious?

WHAT IS AGILE?

Agile is a philosophy and set of practices for software development that prioritizes flexibility, collaboration, and iterative progress over rigid, plan-heavy approaches. As Martin Fowler, a pioneer of the Agile movement, emphasized, Agile is about embracing adaptability, valuing people over processes, and delivering working software incrementally. It emerged from the *Agile Manifesto* (2001),[38] co-authored by Fowler and others, which outlined four core values:

- **Individuals and interactions** over processes and tools.
- **Working software** over comprehensive documentation.
- **Customer collaboration** over contract negotiation.
- **Responding to change** over following a plan.

At the heart of Agile lies a bold rejection of the illusion that software projects can be fully planned from the outset. Traditional approaches, like the waterfall model, assume that requirements can be locked in early, offering managers a comforting sense of control. But Martin Fowler recognized that this predictability is a mirage in the dynamic world of software development. Projects rarely unfold as planned, clients change their minds, new technologies emerge, and unforeseen challenges crop up. Agile embraces this reality, encouraging teams to expect and welcome change rather than resist it.

Imagine a ship navigating a stormy sea: a rigid course plotted in calm waters won't hold when the winds shift. Agile methodologies equip teams to adjust their sails, responding nimbly to new conditions. Fowler's insight was that adaptability isn't just a coping mechanism, it's a competitive advantage. By prioritizing responsiveness, Agile ensures that software evolves in step with real-world needs, delivering value even as requirements shift. This contrasts sharply with traditional methods, where rigid plans often lead to costly rework when assumptions inevitably falter.

Agile Methodology: *Quick and coordinated movement; a method based on iterative and incremental development, in which requirements and solutions evolve through collaboration.*

Think of Agile as a GPS for software development: instead of a fixed map plotted before the journey, it recalculates the route as new roads or obstacles appear, guiding teams to their destination through continuous course corrections. Let's explore a more in-depth analysis of what each of the manifesto bullet points mean in context.

THE AGILE MANIFESTO

In February 2001, a group of 17 software developers, including Jim Highsmith, gathered at a ski resort in Utah to address their frustrations with the rigid and inefficient Waterfall software development methods.[39] Recognizing the need for a more adaptable and value-driven approach, they developed the Agile Manifesto, a guiding philosophy for modern software development. The manifesto emphasizes flexibility, collaboration, and continuous delivery, shaping how Agile project managers lead their teams. At its core, the Agile Manifesto presents four key values, contrasting traditional methods with a more dynamic, people-centric approach. These values prioritize what truly drives project success, rather than adhering to rigid processes:

1. Individuals and Interactions Over Processes and Tools

Agile project managers understand that people, communication, and teamwork drive success, not just tools or procedures. While processes and tools provide structure, they should support collaboration, not replace it. Encouraging frequent feedback, open dialogue, and shared accountability among developers, stakeholders, and customers fosters an adaptive and high-performing environment. Agile isn't just about building better software, it's about empowering the people who build it. Picture a jazz band improvising a performance: each musician brings their flair, responding to the group's rhythm while contributing something uniquely their own. Fowler's vision challenges the outdated notion that processes alone can drive success, proving that human ingenuity is the true engine of progress.

2. Working Software Over Comprehensive Documentation

Traditional project management often emphasizes extensive documentation before development begins, but Agile prioritizes delivering functional software as early and frequently as possible. Teams could spend months crafting detailed plans and diagrams, only to discover during implementation that their assumptions were flawed. Why obsess over perfect blueprints when building and testing reveal gaps far sooner? Agile's focus on early construction, often guided by lightweight tools like unified modeling language, allows teams to prototype and iterate quickly. Agile project managers leverage iterative development and continuous testing to refine products based on real user feedback. This approach is cost-effective because, in software, building is relatively inexpensive compared to the sunk costs of over-designing. By starting with a rough but functional product, teams can test ideas, gather feedback, and refine their work iteratively. This not only accelerates delivery but also ensures the software aligns with actual user needs, not hypothetical plans.

3. Customer Collaboration Over Contract Negotiation

Requirements evolve, and Agile project managers recognize that engaging customers throughout the project lifecycle leads to better outcomes than rigid contracts. Rather than locking teams into static agreements, Agile fosters an ongoing partnership with stakeholders.

This focus on collaboration builds trust and shared ownership. Customers aren't just distant clients waiting for a final product; they're active participants, offering insights that shape the project from start to finish. Think of it like a dance: developers and customers move together, adjusting to the music of changing priorities. Frequent feedback loops ensure that teams align with real customer needs rather than outdated assumptions.

4. Responding to Change Over Following a Plan

While traditional project managers focus on sticking to the plan, Agile leaders embrace change as a competitive advantage. Regular check-ins and incremental deliveries mean that misalignments are caught early, preventing the dreaded scenario where a finished product misses the mark and SOW's require addendums and change orders. Using the Envision, Speculate, Explore, Adapt, and Close methodology, Agile teams develop a flexible roadmap that evolves as new insights emerge. By adapting quickly, Agile project managers ensure their teams remain resilient, innovative, and aligned with business goals.

Conclusion

The Agile Manifesto is not just a set of principles, it's a mindset shift that empowers project managers to lead with agility, foster collaboration, and prioritize customer value. By embracing people-first leadership, iterative development, and adaptive planning, Agile project managers drive projects to deliver meaningful results in a rapidly changing world. So, what makes this the magic thread to successful engagements?

WHY IS AGILE THE "MAGICAL THREAD"?

The term "magical thread" suggests Agile's ability to unify diverse teams, projects, and challenges into a cohesive, effective process. Here's why Agile feels like a magical thread, drawing from fundamental insights and themes:

1. **It Weaves Adaptability into Chaos**: Agile transforms the unpredictability of software development into an asset. Fowler noted that traditional methods, like waterfall, assume stable requirements, but in reality, needs shift constantly. Agile's iterative cycles and frequent testing allows teams to pivot quickly, delivering **Value** even when requirements evolve. This adaptability feels magical because it turns uncertainty, a project manager's nightmare into a strength, producing software that stays relevant.

2. **It Connects People Over Processes**: Agile's emphasis on individuals and interactions, as Fowler championed, creates a collaborative magic. By prioritizing communication between developers, customers, and stakeholders, Agile forms a shared sense of purpose. We point out how Agile rejects Taylorism's view of workers as "plug-and-play" resources.[40] Instead, it empowers teams to innovate, making them feel like alchemists turning ideas into output through creativity and autonomy.

3. **It Delivers Value Early and Often**: Agile's focus on working software over exhaustive documentation feels like a magic trick because it delivers usable results quickly. Instead of waiting months for a complete product, customers see functional pieces early,

offering feedback that shapes the final outcome. This iterative delivery builds trust and aligns projects with real needs, making Agile a thread that ties customer expectations to developer efforts seamlessly.

4. **It Unifies Diverse Methodologies**: Fowler explored how methodologies like Extreme Programming and Scrum share a common thread: responding to change. Agile acts as a universal framework, flexible enough to adapt to different project sizes, industries, and teams. This universality makes it "magical," as it connects seemingly disparate approaches into a cohesive philosophy that works across contexts.

In essence, Agile is the "magical thread" because it binds adaptability, human creativity, and customer needs into a dynamic process that consistently delivers results, even in complex, unpredictable environments. Yet it still remains mysterious. If you don't believe me, try bringing it up to a client that isn't ready to break free of the chain of traditional methods.

WHY IS AGILE SO MYSTERIOUS?

Agile's "mysterious" reputation stems from its unconventional approach and the challenges of mastering it. Here's why it feels elusive:

1. **It Defies Traditional Logic**: Traditional project management, rooted in predictability and control, feels intuitive: plan thoroughly, then execute. Agile's embrace of uncertainty, expecting and welcoming change, as we note, can seem counterintuitive or even

chaotic. Fowler's insight that stable requirements are rare challenges conventional wisdom, making Agile feel like a mysterious departure from the norm. Teams accustomed to rigid plans may struggle to trust a process that thrives on flexibility.

2. **It's More Art Than Science**: Agile's reliance on human interactions and iterative experimentation feels less like a formula and more like an art form. Agile prioritizes people-oriented communication and collaboration with customers. This human-centric focus, unlike the mechanistic processes of Taylorism, requires emotional intelligence, adaptability, and context-awareness, which can feel intangible and hard to pin down.[41] Mastering Agile demands practice and intuition, adding to its mystique.

3. **It Varies by Context**: Agile isn't a one-size-fits-all solution. Frameworks like Scrum, Extreme Programming, and Crystal have different iteration lengths and practices. This variability makes Agile mysterious because there's no single "right" way to implement it. Teams must tailor Agile to their project, team dynamics, and customer needs, which requires experience and judgment, leaving newcomers puzzled about where to start.

4. **It Challenges Measurement**: Traditional methods measure success through adherence to a plan, but Agile measures it through **Value**, working software and customer satisfaction. Agile's frequent testing contrasts with waterfall's late-stage testing, which often reveals defects too late. This shift in how progress is evaluated, through iterative feedback

rather than milestones, can feel foreign and abstract, contributing to Agile's enigmatic aura.

5. **It Requires Cultural Shift**: Adopting Agile often demands a mindset change, which can feel like stepping into uncharted territory. Fowler's emphasis on empowering individuals over rigid processes means organizations must foster trust, autonomy, and collaboration, qualities that may clash with hierarchical or control-driven cultures. This cultural transformation, as your essay suggests, makes Agile seem mysterious because it's not just a process but a philosophy that reshapes how teams think and work

DOES IT FIT?

How should an organization determine which projects to use Agile Project Management on and which ones not to use it on? Every project may not be a fit for a comprehensive Agile project management approach however we should be looking for opportunities to use the Agile concepts and themes that are productive and add value. For example, projects with a low amount of uncertainty, or task-based projects would not meet the response-to-change approach that distinguishes Agile projects. Attitudes of the people is critical to Agile success, getting the right people that have the desire to innovate and respond quickly. Evaluating the readiness of the customer, Agile relies on encouraging customer collaboration, without support it would not be a great fit. Clunky bureaucratic plan-based management with heavy oversight suppress innovative and creative thinking. Agile projects are exciting and vibrant because they are in a constant state of change and evolution. Product development, for example, is a good example where new features and functions add value upon delivery.

Complexity and uncertainty are the key characteristics for eligibility for Agile project methodology. Finding a project that fits with an agile method; however, it primarily depends on the people. Agile projects are broken down into smaller, manageable pieces and delivered incrementally within a constant feedback loop. Critical success factors incorporates team members and customers ready and willing to engage that can respond to change and adjust as needed. Established predictive planning approaches provide management comfort but cannot adapt and pivot over time. With an emphasis on working software over comprehensive documentation, Agile posits that following specific diagrams and designs will not recognize the requirement gaps until construction begins. Qualifying Agile projects exist when the probability of stable requirements at the start of a project is limited, projects with traditional repetitive tasks and activities are not good fits.

When determining to use an agile approach on a project, one must consider the following information to make a decision. The science of adaptation requires us to choose projects that promote flexibility over predictability and innovation over efficiency. The character of an Agile project reflects an organic evolutionary envision, explore, and adapt lifecycle, whereas optimizing projects begin with a single solution. In addition, the higher the uncertainty, the more suitable the projects become for multiple experiments and simulated fitness tests. Task-based projects would not meet the response-to-change approach that distinguishes Agile projects. Heavy bureaucratic plan-based projects have higher iteration costs with greater anticipatory work. We would be looking for concurrently evolving designs with low-cost iterations. Never listen to the naysayers; attitudes of people that place artificial barriers to success can be persuaded and turned into opportunities through continuous integration and automated testing. Finally, fostering innovation and encouraging experimentation enables teams to respond to changes quickly and inexpensively. These fundamental differences help Agile project managers make sense of the world.

Imagine managing the development of a new mobile banking app. A traditional project manager would begin by defining all requirements upfront, locking them into a detailed project plan, and following a strict sequence of phases, requirements gathering, design, development, testing, and deployment. Any change requests late in the process would be costly and difficult to implement. If, after months of development, market trends shift or a competitor launches an innovative feature, the team might struggle to pivot.

By contrast, an Agile project manager would approach the same project with flexibility in mind. Instead of waiting months to deliver a final product, they would break down the work into small, iterative cycles (sprints), continuously releasing working versions of the app with core functionalities. This allows for frequent customer feedback, quick adaptations to market changes, and a focus on delivering value early and often.

HOW AGILE AND SCRUM TRANSFORMED A STRUGGLING TEAM

At TechNova Solutions, a fast-growing software company, the development team was drowning in missed deadlines, unclear priorities, and constant rework. Stakeholders were frustrated, developers felt overworked, and every product release seemed to create more problems than solutions.

THE PROBLEM: A LACK OF STRUCTURE AND FOCUS

Without a clear process, the team struggled with:

- **Unclear priorities** – Developers were unsure what to work on first.
- **Frequent scope changes** – Requirements shifted daily, leading to wasted effort.
- **Poor visibility** – Stakeholders were in the dark until the final product was delivered.
- **No process for improvement** – Mistakes kept repeating because the team never stopped to reflect on what was working and what wasn't.

Something had to change. That's when they adopted Scrum, an Agile Methodology that encourages collaboration and coordination within a team involving several key practices, including daily standup meetings, ongoing interaction with product teams, and stakeholder coordination.

Scrum Master: *A Scrum Master is a servant leader and coach responsible for ensuring that a Scrum team follows Agile principles and practices effectively. They facilitate Scrum ceremonies (such as daily standups, sprint planning, and retrospectives), remove impediments that block progress, and foster collaboration between team members, stakeholders, and other departments. Unlike a traditional project manager, a Scrum Master does not dictate tasks but instead empowers the team to be self-organizing and high performing. Their* *primary goal is to create an environment where the team can deliver value efficiently while continuously improving their processes.*

Scrum Team: *A cross-functional team of five to nine people who organize themselves and the work to produce the desired results for each sprint.*

DAILY STANDUP MEETINGS

Daily Scrum: *A short meeting in which the team shares progress and challenges.*

Daily standup meetings serve as a platform for peer-to-peer coordination and information exchange. These meetings follow structured guidelines: they occur at the same time and place each day, last no more than 15 minutes, and require the attendance of all core team members. Product and project leaders participate as peers, while other managers typically do not attend. A designated team member, often an iteration or project leader, facilitates the discussion.

The primary goal of these meetings is to surface issues and obstacles, not to resolve them. Each participant is encouraged to answer three key questions:

    a. What are you working on today?
    b. What did you accomplish yesterday?
    c. What obstacles are in your way?

Standup meetings are not meant for problem-solving but for identifying issues. When a problem is raised, the relevant team members collaborate separately after the meeting to find a solution. The facilitator plays a supportive role, helping the team coordinate and manage their work efficiently.

DAILY INTERACTION WITH THE PRODUCT TEAM

Product Owner: *The person responsible for the business value of the project and for deciding what work to do and in what order when using a Scrum method.*

Regular engagement with the product team ensures that the development process stays aligned with customer needs and expectations. Frequent, if not daily, interactions provide a continuous flow of information and decision-making support from the product manager, helping the project maintain momentum and stay on track.

Product Backlog: *The product backlog is a dynamic, prioritized list of capabilities, features, and user stories that drive product development. It serves as the foundation for both release and iteration planning, containing just enough detail to enable effective decision-making.*

Key aspects of backlog management include defining who is responsible for maintaining and refining it and establishing best practices for identifying backlog items. This process involves understanding customer personas and breaking down functionality hierarchies to ensure alignment with user needs. The backlog evolves iteratively, expanding from the product vision into a refined set of features and stories through continuous feedback and collaboration. During the Speculate phase, the backlog is refined from its initial version in the Envision phase, incorporating insights from feasibility analysis, market research, and requirements gathering. The Product Manager owns and maintains the backlog, ensuring it remains the primary input for release wave and iteration planning. Each feature is translated into one or more user stories, which include essential descriptive details and estimation for execution.

SPRINTS: BRINGING FOCUS AND PREDICTABILITY

Instead of trying to deliver the entire product at once, the team broke work into Sprints, each lasting two weeks. This gave them short, achievable goals and forced them to prioritize. Now, instead of reacting to chaos, they were delivering small, working pieces of the product with each sprint.

Sprint: *a time-boxed development cycle, typically lasting two to four weeks, during which a Scrum team works on a defined set of tasks aimed at delivering incremental value to the product. The goal of each sprint is to complete a potentially shippable product increment, ensuring continuous progress toward the overall project objectives. Sprints promote predictability, adaptability, and iterative* *improvement, allowing teams to refine their work based on feedback and changing requirements.*

SPRINT BACKLOG: CLARITY ON WHAT MATTERS

Before, developers would grab tasks randomly, leading to misalignment. The Sprint Backlog solved this by ensuring that only the most important and highest-priority items were worked on. Now, every sprint had a clear purpose, and developers knew exactly what to focus on.

Sprint Backlog: *The Sprint Backlog consists of the highest-priority tasks pulled from the Product Backlog, selected for completion within the sprint. It serves as the team's workload for the sprint, providing a clear and focused plan to achieve the sprint goal. The backlog is owned by the development team and is flexible enough to allow for adjustments, ensuring that high-impact work is completed effectively. It evolves throughout the sprint as tasks are refined, completed, or reprioritized.*

SPRINT PLANNING: NO MORE GUESSWORK

Previously, the team would start coding without a plan, leading to wasted effort. During Sprint Planning, they now sat together and:

- Selected user stories from the **Product Backlog.**
- Broke them down into actionable tasks.
- Estimated effort and set realistic goals.

This eliminated confusion and unrealistic expectations, setting them up for success.

Sprint Planning Session: *A collaborative meeting held at the start of each sprint, where the Scrum team, including the Product Owner, Scrum Master, and Development Team, selects work from the Product Backlog to complete during the sprint. This session consists of two key parts:*
- **What will be done?** *The team reviews the backlog and defines the sprint goal.*
- **How will it be done?** *The team breaks down selected items into actionable tasks.*

By the end of the planning session, the team has a clear understanding of the work scope, objectives, and delivery expectations for the sprint.

SPRINT REVIEWS: KEEPING STAKEHOLDERS ENGAGED

Stakeholders used to be frustrated because they only saw the product at the end, often too late to make changes. With **Sprint Reviews**, the team demoed their work every two weeks, gathering feedback early. This meant:

- Faster course corrections instead of waiting months for a fix.
- Stakeholders felt heard and involved in the process.
- The team felt motivated, seeing their work appreciated.

Sprint Reviews: *a collaborative feedback session held at the end of each sprint where the development team demonstrates the completed work to the Product Owner, stakeholders, and other team members. This session serves as an opportunity to:*
- *Showcase working software or completed features.*
- *Gather stakeholder feedback for potential refinements.*
- *Align expectations and confirm whether the sprint goal was met.*

Unlike a formal approval meeting, the Sprint Review is meant to be interactive and iterative, ensuring that the team delivers what truly meets user needs.

Sprint Burndown Chart*: A burndown chart is an essential Agile tool that visually tracks work completed versus work remaining within a given timeframe. It provides a clear graphical representation of project progress, showing how much work is left compared to the time available for completion. Regularly updating the chart, preferably daily, ensures a real-time view of the project's status. This helps teams identify potential issues early, make necessary adjustments, and refine their planning. Additionally, a burndown chart serves as a predictive tool, allowing teams to estimate when the project will be completed based on current progress trends.*

SPRINT RETROSPECTIVE: LEARNING FROM MISTAKES

The biggest problem before Scrum? The team kept making the same mistakes, and no one stopped to ask why. With Sprint Retrospectives, they built a habit of reflecting on what went well, what didn't, and how to improve.

For example, they discovered that:

- Too much time was wasted waiting on approvals → They streamlined the approval process.
- Developers were often blocked by unclear requirements → They improved communication with Product Owners.
- Testing was left until the last minute → They introduced test automation to speed things up.

Sprint Retrospectives: *A post-sprint meeting where the team reflects on the sprint process, identifies challenges, and discusses opportunities for improvement. Unlike the Sprint Review, which focuses on the work delivered, the retrospective focuses on how the team worked together. The team typically addresses three key questions:*

- **What went well?** Identify successful processes and practices.
- **What didn't go well?** Recognize blockers or inefficiencies.
- **What can be improved?** Develop action items for future sprints.

This continuous feedback loop helps the team refine their work-flow, strengthen collaboration, and enhance efficiency over time.

USER STORIES: FOCUSING ON THE CUSTOMER

Before, requirements were long, complicated, and hard to understand. With User Stories, they shifted their mindset from "What features do we need?" to "What problems are we solving for the user?" User stories drive Agile development by ensuring that features prioritize user needs, enhance usability, and deliver real value. They are often broken down into smaller tasks, estimated, and included in sprints.

User Stories: *A concise, user-centric description of a software feature, written from the perspective of the end user. It helps teams understand what the user wants to achieve and why.*

A typical user story follows the format:

"As a [user role], I want [goal or feature] so that [benefit or value]."

For example: Instead of writing,

"Implement a password reset feature", they wrote:

"As a customer, I want to reset my password via email so that I can regain access to my account easily."

This made it clear who the feature was for, why it was important, and how success should be measured.

THE RESULT: A HIGH-PERFORMING TEAM

Within a few months, the team saw massive improvements:

- ✓ **Faster delivery** – Every sprint delivered value instead of waiting months for a release.
- ✓ **Happier stakeholders** – They saw progress regularly and could give feedback early.
- ✓ **Better teamwork** – Developers collaborated more, and problems were solved proactively.
- ✓ **Higher quality** – Continuous feedback loops meant fewer defects and less rework.

Most importantly, the team felt in control rather than constantly reacting to chaos. What was once a frustrated, disorganized team became a focused, motivated, and high-performing group, all thanks to embracing Agile and Scrum principles.

AGILE PROJECT MANAGEMENT (APM) PHASES

We've covered the Maximum Delivery Concepts for running an Agile project to build a foundation for the reader to understand the elements in building an Agile plan. Planning phases for Agile projects are different than traditional projects. The following section breaks down each of the phases and their purposes.

1. Envision Phase

The Envision phase establishes the product vision, project objectives, and constraints while defining the project community and team collaboration framework. This phase clarifies what needs to be built, who is involved, and how the work will be accomplished. The product vision is captured through artifacts such as the vision box and elevator test statement, providing stakeholders with a high-level concept of the product. Additional deliverables include the product roadmap, product skeleton architecture, guiding principles, and product data sheets, all of which set the foundation for the project.

2. Speculate Phase

The Speculate phase focuses on developing a feature-based release plan that aligns with the product vision. Since Agile embraces uncertainty, this phase involves hypothesizing and refining broad requirements, defining the backlog, estimating workload, and integrating risk management strategies. The primary outcome is a release plan based on capabilities and user stories, rather than traditional activity-based project plans. Key components of this iterative approach include short time-boxed iterations and feature-driven planning to ensure flexibility and responsiveness to change.

3. Explore Phase

The Explore phase is where execution begins, with the goal of delivering tested, working stories in short iterations while continuously reducing project risk and uncertainty. This phase includes three critical activities:

- Delivering planned stories by managing workloads, employing technical best practices, and mitigating risks.
- Fostering a self-organized, collaborative team where accountability is shared.
- Managing stakeholder interactions, ensuring alignment between customers, product managers, and development teams.

By focusing on these areas, the team ensures incremental delivery of value while maintaining adaptability.

4. Adapt Phase

The Adapt phase emphasizes continuous improvement and responsiveness to change over rigid adherence to a plan. The team conducts regular reviews of delivered results, project status, and team performance, making necessary adjustments. Key activities include:

- Customer feedback sessions to assess how well the product meets requirements.
- Technical reviews to evaluate architecture, testing, integration, and design practices.
- Iteration-based team retrospectives, ensuring ongoing reflection and improvement.
- Status reporting on value, scope, quality, schedule, risks, and agility metrics.

This phase ensures that each iteration enhances product quality and team efficiency.

5. Close Phase

Closing the project involves finalizing deliverables, capturing key learnings, and celebrating successes. Agile mitigates the risk of poor closure through continuous collaboration, ensuring all stakeholders have visibility into the project's progress. Closing activities include:

- Resolving outstanding issues from the issue log.
- Documenting work products, including process flows, user tests, configurations, and technical deliverables.
- Conducting a project retrospective, analyzing what worked well, what didn't, and lessons learned for future projects.
- A well-executed closure ensures the project's success is sustained, knowledge is transferred, and the team is prepared for future initiatives.

Comprehensive Analysis of an Innovative Agile Project Methodology

The following example can be used for a baseline for implementing agile eligible projects, designed to leverage innovation and best practices. Its Work Breakdown Structure (WBS) organizes tasks into five phases: Envision, Speculate, Explore, Adapt, Close, offering a detailed framework for project execution. This section provides a sweeping analysis by summarizing each phase and detailing a comprehensive set of tasks from the WBS, integrating their full guidance from the document to illustrate their practical application. This template can be used as a baseline; your specific project may be different and require changes for your project specific needs.

Phase A: Envision

Detailed Activities Breakdown:

- **A.01 Review Statement of Work, Scope Statement, Workplan and Budget**

  In this task, the project manager reviews the executed statement of work and bid materials post-assignment, participating in a sales team handoff if feasible. The focus is on confirming scope, creating a Project Workplan, staffing resources, and validating the budget.

  - *Activity / Summary Activity:* A.01.01 Project Launch
  - *Work Product: Reviewed SOW, Contract, Scope, Workplan and Budget* — Includes reviewed bid material, contract, confirmed scope, requested resources, staffed project, baseline workplan, and confirmed budget.
  - *Formats: Project Workplan* (MS Project), *Reviewed and Analyzed Bid Material* (MS Word)
  - *Prerequisites: Executed Contract* — Signed statement of work, scope definition, costing financials, assumptions, and terms of agreement.
  - *Activity:* Meet with proposal team, review contract estimates and terms, understand scope and objectives, document assumptions, create workplan, staff project, validate budget, resolve disconnects, identify center of excellence, create a timeline calendar.
  - *Task Owner:* Implementation team has primary responsibility.

- **A.02 Build the Project Community**

  Collaborate & Socialize the team, getting the right people.
  - *Activity / Summary Activity:* A.02.01 Participant Identification
  - *Work Product: Venn diagram–* Crossing the end user customer with the product team and the development team.
  - *Formats: Talent Community* (MS Word, PowerPoint, Visio)
  - *Prerequisites: Stakeholders Analysis –* Provides talent resource pool.
  - *Activity:* Create a diagram that depicts the product teams and product manager with the customers collaboratively working with the development team and the project manager.
  - *Task Owner:* Shared, Project Leadership, Managers.

- **A.03 Establish Communication, Collaboration and Coordination**

  Encouraging collaboration and coordination, daily standup meetings, daily interaction with product teams, stakeholder coordination.
  - *Activity / Summary Activity:* A.03.01 Communication Launch
  - *Work Product: Communication Management Plan –* Meeting cadences and guidelines.
  - *Formats: Communication Management Plan* (Word), *Summarized Communication Management Plan bullet points* (PowerPoint), *Risk/Issue/Problem Log* (Excel, SharePoint)
  - *Prerequisites: Reviewed SOW/Contract, Scope Statement, Project Workplan and Costing Budget –* Baseline for governance.

- *Activity:* Daily interaction with product team, help the development team efforts, stay on track and meet the needs and expectations of the customers.
- *Task Owner:* Shared Project Teams.

- **A.04 Conduct Kickoff Meeting**

  Conduct a kickoff meeting to orient the project team and communicate objectives and structure.
  - *Activity / Summary Activity:* A.04.01 Mobilize Project Team
  - *Work Product: Kickoff Meeting* — Executed meeting with team orientation.
  - *Formats: Project Kickoff Presentation* (PowerPoint)
  - *Prerequisites: Collaborate Approach with Customer* — Ensures team alignment.
  - *Activity:* Perform meeting introduction, prepare agenda, present scope and objectives, outline roles, facilitate discussion, document outcomes, prepare for next steps.
  - *Task Owner:* Project team leaders. Executive Sponsorship.

- **A.05 Product Vision Box & Elevator Statement**

  Documented in a single page project data sheet conveys the essence on how the project will deliver the product vision, articulate business objectives, quality objectives, and a defined set of capabilities that bind the scope of the releasable product.
  - *Activity / Summary Activity:* A.05.01 Product Architecture
  - *Work Product: Product Vision* — The product vision creates a concise, visual, and short textual form defined by the vision box and elevator test statement. These two artifacts and the product

roadmap provide a high concept of the product for stakeholders.

- *Formats: Product Vision* (Design Studio, Visio, Draw)
- *Prerequisites: Collaborate Approach with Customer* — Fully Communicated Scope; *Kickoff Meeting* — Team orientation.
- *Activity:* The task is to design the product box front and back. This involves coming up with a product name, a graphic, three to four key bullet points on the front to sell the product, and a detailed feature description on the back with operating requirements. The elevator statement is a few sentences that indicate the target customer, key benefit, and competitive advantage.
- *Task Owner:* Shared Project team leads, Product Owners.

- **A.06 Product Data Sheet**

  Documented in a single page project data sheet conveys the essence on how the project will deliver the product vision, articulate business objectives, quality objectives, and a defined set of capabilities that bind the scope of the releasable product.

  - *Activity / Summary Activity:* A.06.01 Product Data Sheet
  - *Work Product: Functional Design* — Requirement Documentation Matrix.
  - *Formats: Functional Design* (Excel, Word, PowerPoint, SharePoint)
  - *Prerequisites: Workshop Schedule* — Product Vision Box.
  - *Activity:* Create a single page summary of key business and quality objectives, product capabilities, and project management information.

- *Task Owner*: Shared Project team leads, Product Owners.

- **A.07 Conduct Phase Gate Review**

  In this task, you review phase work products and secure approval to proceed.
  - *Activity / Summary Activity:* C.07.01 Phase Gate Review
  - *Work Product*: *Phase Gate Review Meeting/Approval to Proceed* – Approval documentation.
  - *Formats: Phase Gate review* (Word)
  - *Prerequisites*: *Project Team Mobilization* – Phase outputs.
  - *Activity:* Review outputs, confirm objectives, plan next steps, secure approval.
  - *Task Owner*: PMO Center of Excellence.

Phase B: Speculate

Detailed Activities Breakdown:

- **B.01 Product Backlog**

  In this task, you prepare an evolutionary requirement definition process into a feature list or backlog.
  - *Activity / Summary Activity:* B.01.01 Product Backlog
  - *Work Product*: *Product Backlog* – List of capabilities, features
  - *Formats: Features List* (Word)
  - *Prerequisites*: *Product Vision* – Initial Product Vision
  - *Activity:* Expand the product vision through an evolutionary requirement definition process into a feature list or backlog
  - *Task Owner*: Product Owners

- **B.02 Build Feature Story & Story Cards**

  In this task, defined as a piece of a product that delivers some useful and valuable functionality to the customer.
  - *Activity / Summary Activity:* B.02.01 Feature Story
  - *Work Product*: *Story Card* – Small piece of functionality.
  - *Prerequisites*: *Product Backlog* – Detailed features.
  - *Activity:* Produce a small piece of a specific persona activities, gathering basic information about stories recording high level requirements that delivers useful functionality but may not deliver a complete function.
  - *Task Owner*: Shared responsibility.

- **B.03 Estimate & Assign Story Points or Value Points**

  In this task, define a unit of work size rather than work effort, different unit of measure than time, can be story points or value points..
  - *Activity / Summary Activity:* B.03.01 Story or Value Points
  - *Work Product*: *Story Points* – Estimated Story or Value Metric
  - *Prerequisites*: *Story Card* – Detailed Information.
  - *Activity:* Create a new unit of measure called story/value points to represent sizing or relative value. Understanding the value and cost in relative numbers of stories and capabilities that improve the team's ability to deliver the highest value stories early.
  - *Task Owner*: Shared responsibility.

- **B.04 Timebox**

  In this task, identify development approach in short iterative timeboxes

- *Activity / Summary Activity:* B.04.01 Development Efforts
- *Work Product: Timelines* – Estimated efforts with specific deadlines.
- *Prerequisites: Product Backlog* – Detailed features.
- *Activity:* Setting a fixed time limit to overall development efforts and allowing other characteristics such as scope.
- *Task Owner:* Shared responsibility.

- **B.05 Release Plan**

  Create a road map of how the team intends to achieve the product vision within the project objectives and constraints identified in the project data sheet
  - *Activity / Summary Activity:* B.05.01 Preliminary Release Plan
  - *Work Product: Release Plan* – Stories driven feature breakdown structure
  - *Formats: Release Plan* (MS Projects, Smart Sheet, Task, Activities List)
  - *Prerequisites: Timebox* – Development Efforts
  - *Activity:* Allocate work to iterations in a release plan using stories involving the product team in the process that don't relate to technical tasks
  - *Task Owner:* Executives, Project Management, Center of Excellence.

- **B.06 Preparation Iteration 0**

  Preparation to find some middle ground between diving in and building code and requirements gathering
  - *Activity / Summary Activity:* B.06.01 Establish a solid foundation.

- *Work Product*: *Foundation Key* — A skeleton architecture or diagram
- *Prerequisites*: *Backlog, Stories, Timebox* — All Speculate activities.
- *Activity:* Clarify requirements, set expectations, identify risks, plan for resources, align stakeholders set up the environment and curate an application architecture.
- *Task Owner*: Project Management.

Phase C: Explore

Detailed Activities Breakdown

- **C.01 Iteration Planning**

  In this task, the project the team develops a detailed plan for the next iteration.
  - *Activity / Summary Activity:* C.01.01 Detailed Release Plan
  - *Work Product*: *Iteration Plan* — Iteration Theme Activities
  - *Prerequisites*: *Prelease Plan, Story Cards* — Overall releases plan, stories.
  - *Activity:* The team takes each story card from the release plan and identifies a list of technical and other tests required to implement the story and record the tasks.
  - *Task Owner*: Iteration manager

- **C.02 Workload Management Iteration 1 (N+)**

  The objective of workload management is to have team members themselves manage assignments of day-to-day task required to deliver stories at each iteration.
  - *Activity / Summary Activity:* C.02.01 Perform testing.

- *Work Product*: *Testing results* – Delivered Stories
- *Prerequisites*: *Iteration 0* – Foundation Setup, Iteration Planning.
- *Activity:* Each iteration plan team member determine the task required to deliver planned stories, tests themselves, monitoring their own progress and making necessary adjustments.
- *Task Owner*: Iteration Team Owners.

- **C.03 Ruthless Automated Testing & Feedback Loops**
  The objective of ruthless testing is to ensure the product quality remains high throughout the development process. Early feedback on delivery linking customers and features.
  - *Activity / Summary Activity:* C.03.01 Constant Testing & Feedback
  - *Work Product*: *Updated Development* – Updated quality development, customer feedback loop, continuous testing.
  - *Prerequisites*: *Workload Management* – Continuous testing results.
  - *Activity:* Software engineers refine development, team perform constant unit tests integrating quality assurance tests in each iteration, includes acceptance testing and challenges the teams to face the reality of how the design actually works.
  - *Task Owner*: Iteration Team Owners.

- **C.04 Iteration Retrospective**
  Each iteration gives the opportunity to reflect on what is working and what is not.
  - *Activity / Summary Activity:* C.04.01 Retrospective
  - *Work Product*: *Status Reporting* – Lesson Learned

- *Formats: Results Summary* (Word, PowerPoint, SharePoint)
- *Prerequisites: Ruthless Testing & Feedback Loop* – Quality Testing Logs.
- *Activity:* Reflect on the outcome of the iteration and areas for improvement
- *Task Owner:* Shared responsibility.

- **C.05 Participatory Decision Making**
  Provide the project community with specific practices to frame, analyze, and make decisions that arise during the project.
  - *Activity / Summary Activity:* C.05.01 Decision Framing & Decision Making,
  - *Work Product: Action Plan* – Decision Gradient.
  - *Formats: Varies Data* (Templates, Checklist, XLS, Word, Other)
  - *Prerequisites: Iteration Retrospective* – Feedback Loop
  - *Activity:* Team members move from having individual opinions to having a unified position and path forward.
  - *Task Owner:* Shared responsibility.

Phase D: Adapt

Detailed Activities Breakdown:

- **D.01 Team Performance Evaluation**
  Measure teams oriented towards outcomes, the business value created, productivity.
  - *Activity / Summary Activity:* D.01.01 Team participants performance

- *Work Product: Team Structures* – Team activities assignments.
- *Formats: Team Groups* (Stakeholders, Smart Sheet, Task, Activities List)
- *Prerequisites: Iteration Retrospective* – Delivery Reflection
- *Activity:* Measuring concepts must go beyond budgeting, team dynamic, adoption of agile concepts and methods.
- *Task Owner:* Executives, Project Management.

- **D.02 Focus Group Sessions**
  Sessions demonstrating ongoing versions of the final product to the product team to get periodic feedback on how well the product meets customer requirements
  - *Activity / Summary Activity:* D.02.01 Focus Group Sessions
  - *Work Product: Tested Applications* – Testing Scenarios.
  - *Prerequisites: Iteration Retrospective* – Delivery Reflection
  - *Activity:* Product team members, review the product itself not the documents, focus on discovering and recording desired changes but not on gathering detailed requirements.
  - *Task Owner:* Product Team Members.

- **D.03 Technical Reviews**
  Address key technical practices of simple design, continuous integration, ruthless testing, and refactoring to ensure that they are being effectively implemented.
  - *Activity / Summary Activity:* D.02.01 Practice Review
  - *Work Product: Code Review* – Various code packages, workflow changes
  - *Formats: Varies* (Word, Excel, CSV, XML, varies)

- *Prerequisites*: *Iteration Retrospective* — Delivery Reflection
- *Activity:* Adherence to standards and quality, update comments, code optimization, consistency and design.
- *Task Owner*: Shared responsibility.

- **D.04 Update Product Backlog**

  In this task, update he evolutionary requirement definition process into a feature list or backlog.
  - *Activity / Summary Activity:* B.01.01 Updated Product Backlog
  - *Work Product*: Updated *Product Backlog* — List of capabilities, features
  - *Formats: Features List* (Word)
  - *Prerequisites*: *Iteration (N)* — Explore Phase Completed
  - *Activity:* Expand the product vision through an evolutionary requirement definition process into a feature list or backlog
  - *Task Owner*: Product Owners

- **D.05 Updated Stories & Story / Value Points**

  In this task, defined as a piece of a product that delivers some useful and valuable functionality to the customer.
  - *Activity / Summary Activity:* D.05.01 Updated Stories
  - *Work Product*: *Story Card* — Small piece of functionality.
  - *Prerequisites*: *Updated Product Backlog* — Detailed features.
  - *Activity:* Produce a small piece of a specific persona activities, gathering basic information about stories recording high level requirements that delivers useful functionality but may not deliver a complete function.
  - *Task Owner*: Shared responsibility.

- **D06 Workload Management Iteration (N+)**

  The objective of workload management is to have team members themselves manage assignments of day-to-day task required to deliver stories at each iteration.
  - *Activity / Summary Activity:* D.06.01 Perform testing.
  - *Work Product: Testing results* – Delivered & Updated Stories
  - *Prerequisites: Iteration (N)* – Iteration (N) Results.
  - *Activity:* Each iteration plan team member determine the task required to deliver planned stories, tests themselves, monitoring their own progress and making necessary adjustments.
  - *Task Owner:* Iteration Team Owners.

- **D.07 Iteration Retrospective**

  Each iteration gives the opportunity to reflect on what is working and what is not.
  - *Activity / Summary Activity:* D.07.01 Retrospective
  - *Work Product: Status Reporting* – Lesson Learned
  - *Formats: Results Summary* (Word, PowerPoint, Share-Point)
  - *Prerequisites: Ruthless Testing & Feedback Loop* – Quality Testing Logs.
  - *Activity:* Reflect on the outcome of the iteration and areas for improvement
  - *Task Owner:* Shared responsibility.

- **D.08 Final Release Plan**

  Create a road map of how the team intends to achieve the product vision within the project objectives and constraints identified in the project data sheet
  - *Activity / Summary Activity:* D.08.01 Final Release Plan

- *Work Product*: *Release Plan* – Stories driven feature breakdown structure
- *Formats: Final Release Plan* (MS Projects, Smart Sheet, Task, Activities List)
- *Prerequisites*: *Preliminary Release Plan* – Development Efforts
- *Activity:* Allocate work to a final release plan for deployment.
- *Task Owner*: Executives, Project Management, Center of Excellence.

Phase E: Close

Detailed Activities Breakdown:

- **E.01.01 Final Validation**

  Run end-to-end tests (e.g., usability, performance, security).
  - *Activity / Summary Activity:* E.01.01 Final Results
  - *Work Product*: Acceptance *Testing Results* – Team Acceptance
  - *Prerequisites*: *Workload Management* – Fully tested system.
  - *Activity:* Perform final testing & gain user acceptance.
  - *Task Owner*: Shared responsibility, emphasis on Customer.

- **E.02 GO/NO GO Final Decision Review with Users and Stakeholders**

  Time to make a decision to begin cutover & move to production environment for use.
  - *Activity / Summary Activity:* E.02.01. Final Decision
  - *Work Product*: *Production Readiness Assessment* – Final review decision.

- *Prerequisites*: *Final Validation* – Decision Information
- *Activity*: Executive meeting, review risks, make a decision to move to production.
- *Task Owner*: Shared responsibility.

- **E.03 Document Process**

  Provide contracted post-production support, if agreed after hypercare period ends.
  - *Activity / Summary Activity*: E.03.01 Final Code ready for deployment.
  - *Work Product*: *Release Code* – Varies depending.
  - *Prerequisites*: *Final Validation* – Bug fixes resolved.
  - *Activity*: Write user documentation or onboarding guide. Train stakeholders or support teams.
  - *Task Owner*: Development Team

- **E.04 Deploy to Production**

  Monitor transition to routine operations.
  - *Activity / Summary Activity*: E.04.01 Stabilization
  - *Work Product*: *Daily-State Operations* – Stable system use.
  - *Prerequisites*: *System in Production* – Operational baseline.
  - *Activity*: Establish issue reporting, plan enhancements, improvements.
  - *Task Owner*: Shared responsibility.

- **E.05 GO LIVE Begin Production Use**

  You are Live, start production operations.
  - *Activity / Summary Activity*: E.05.01 Live Production Use
  - *Work Product*: *System in Production* – Operational system.

- *Prerequisites*: *Production Readiness Verification*, *Support Plan* – Readiness confirmed.
- *Activity:* Control initial transactions, sequence rollout, stabilize operations.
- *Task Owner*: Customer leads.

- **E.06 Execute Handoff to Customer Transition Owner**
  Hand off to a customer transition owner.
  - *Activity / Summary Activity:* E.06.01 Transition to Customer Owner
  - *Work Product*: *Customer Manager Handoff* – Project documentation.
  - *Formats: Customer Manager Handoff* (All Work Products)
  - *Prerequisites*: *System in Production* – Operational system.
  - *Activity:* Migrate closure documentation, provide project overview, suggest enhancements.
  - *Task Owner*: Shared Responsibility

- **E.07 Final Closure & Retrospective**
  Validate scope delivery close project processes and contract.
  - *Activity / Summary Activity:* E.07.01 Project Closure
  - *Work Product*: *Final Acceptance Certificate Approval* – Scope verification approval.
  - *Formats: Acceptance Criteria, Acceptance Certificate, Project Acceptance Report* (Word)
  - *Prerequisites*: *Production Use* – Scope basis.
  - *Activity:* Validate delivery, secure acceptance, document outcomes, lessons learned.
  - *Task Owner*: Shared responsibility.

THE VALUE OF ITERATIONS

Agile projects expect uncertainty and manage for it through iterations, anticipation, and adaptation. Iterations help teams answer the question, what defines a releasable product, rather than looking at a detailed requirements checklist. The process involves breaking down the project into small, manageable chunks, called iterations or sprints, where tests are performed and completed in a fixed amount of time, typically two to four weeks. The backlog, maintained by the product manager, is the major input for release wave and iteration planning. Iterations provide a structured framework for the development team to work on a small set of requirements at a time with the intent of continuous improvement. By focusing on smaller, more manageable portions of the project, the team can achieve a better understanding of the project's requirements, identify potential issues early, and make necessary adjustments to the project scope or direction. Iterations provide a vehicle for teams to receive feedback from stakeholders, customers, and end-users. At first feasible deployment strategy is the first iteration in which the product could potentially be deployed.

Iterations are the heartbeat of agility, the ability for the team to create a working, tested, value-added delivered product in short sprints.[42] Continuous innovation emerges from iterations by providing feedback loops, promoting teamwork, and enabling the project team to adapt to changing requirements. The format structure starts with responsible parties presenting stories, followed by discussions with the stakeholders and product owners moving stories to an acceptable state.[43] This feedback helps the team identify areas for improvement and make adjustments for the next iteration. The teamwork exhibited during the iteration encourages collaboration, enabling shared knowledge and expertise to identify areas of progress in working together to solve problems. Finally, as compared to traditional development methodologies, the Agile method incubates adaptability allowing organizations to respond quickly to changing market conditions and remain competitive.

CHAPTER 6

Scope: Lock It Down

IT OFTEN BEGINS with a single accommodation. A customer requests a small tweak, and it seems harmless, you give an inch, thinking it's just this, it's only that. In his book "Principles," Ray Dalio warns, nothing is isolated; everything is threaded throughout many unnoticed connections.[44] That small string you pull unravels into a tangled web. What starts as a minor adjustment, adding a feature or modifying a deliverable, quickly leads to another request, then another. Before you know it, you're 50% deep into developing a solution you thought would take mere minutes. This is the essence of scope creep: a death by a thousand cuts, where each small change compounds into a gaping wound, jeopardizing the project's timeline, budget, and ultimate acceptance.

Dalio emphasizes the importance of clear decision-making and understanding the cascading effects of our choices, particularly in complex systems like businesses or projects. One of his key insights is the idea that "the second consequence is always worse than the first consequence."[45] This principle is especially relevant when managing scope creep, a phenomenon where small, seemingly innocuous decisions spiral into larger, unintended problems. By integrating Dalio's principles with the psychology of "starting with no," concentrating on one thing at a time, and understanding the subtle links between our actions, we can manage scope creep and ensure successful project outcomes.

Starting with "no" is a powerful antidote to this trap, easier said than done. By beginning with a clear boundary, identifying only the core elements within the agreed-upon scope (for instance, the four corners of an agreement), you establish a firm foundation. Saying "no" upfront doesn't mean rejecting the customer outright; it means protecting the project's integrity so you can deliver what was promised. Customers may push for more, and it's tempting to accommodate them to keep them happy. After all, the bottom line is that they need to accept the final product upon delivery and sign off on it. But as Dalio's second-consequence principle highlights, the cost of saying "yes" too easily is far greater down the line than the discomfort of saying "no" at the start.

Consider the scenario: you intend to keep the scope tight, but a customer's request seems reasonable, so you agree to a small change. That first consequence might be a few extra hours of work, manageable, you think. But the second consequence is dire: those hours multiply as the change ripples through the project, requiring additional resources, testing, and adjustments. Suddenly, you're in a hole you didn't intend to dig, facing a change order that could have been avoided. This is where Dalio's advice to "focus on long term outcomes" comes in, tackle the toughest, most essential decision (saying "no" to scope expansion) right away, before it festers into a bigger problem.[46]

Focusing on one thing at a time, you protect the project from undesirable consequences. Instead of juggling multiple small requests, address the primary objective: delivering the agreed-upon product and avoiding a ripple effect. When you try to accommodate every minor suggestion, you lose sight of the core goal. It's not that those suggestions lack merit, but they often pull you away from the finish line. By starting with "no" and sticking to the defined scope, you maintain clarity and momentum, ensuring that the customer's ultimate satisfaction, accepting the final product, remains achievable.

In practice, this means setting expectations early. Define the scope with precision, communicate it clearly, and resist the urge to bend when "it's just this" creeps in. The consequences of not doing so are predictable: you find yourself in a position where acceptance becomes much harder because the project has morphed beyond recognition. Dalio's principles remind us that small decisions are rarely small; they're the first domino in a chain. By embracing "no" as a starting point and anticipating the second consequence, you can navigate scope creep effectively, delivering a product that meets its original intent without drowning in a sea of unintended obligations.

USE CASE: DEVELOPMENT OF A UNIVERSITY LEARNING MANAGEMENT SYSTEM

In the realm of project management, scope serves as the foundation upon which successful outcomes are built. A well-defined scope ensures that all stakeholders align on objectives, deliverables, and boundaries, while effective project scope management keeps the project on track by controlling what work is included or excluded. However, when scope is poorly managed, the consequences can ripple through a project, leading to delays, cost overruns, and dissatisfied stakeholders. Let's explore a specific use case, the development of a university-wide Learning Management System (LMS), where scope became a significant problem.

Project Scope Management: *The systematic process of defining, managing, and controlling what work is included* *(or excluded) from a project. It ensures alignment with business objectives and prevents unnecessary work from being performed. Effective project scope management minimizes risks, optimizes resource allocation, and keeps the project within budget and schedule constraints.*

Scope: *Refers to the total work required to create a project's deliverables, as well as the processes used to achieve them. It defines the project's boundaries, ensuring that all necessary tasks are completed while avoiding unnecessary work. A well-defined scope is critical for managing time, costs, and resources effectively.*

SOLVE THE PROBLEM: SCOPE CREEP TAKES HOLD

The project in question was an ambitious initiative to design and implement a custom LMS for a mid-sized university. The initial project scope statement outlined clear objectives: create a platform to host course materials, facilitate online assessments, enable student-teacher interaction, all within a 12-month timeline and a $500,000 budget. The scope was defined as the development of core functionalities, course management, a user-friendly interface, and basic analytics, along with integration into the university's existing IT infrastructure. A scope baseline was established, including a Work Breakdown Structure (WBS) that detailed tasks such as software design, testing, and deployment, and a WBS dictionary specifying deliverables like a functional login portal and gradebook module.

Project Scope Statement: *A comprehensive document that provides a detailed description of the project, including its objectives, justification, deliverables, constraints, and acceptance criteria. It serves as a critical reference throughout the project lifecycle to ensure all stakeholders share a common understanding of the project's goals and expectations.*

Scope Baseline: *The approved reference point for project scope, consisting of the project scope statement, Work Breakdown Structure (WBS), and WBS dictionary. The scope baseline serves as a benchmark against which project performance is measured and helps prevent deviations from the original objectives.*

However, as development progressed, the project succumbed to scope creep. Faculty members, excited by the potential of the LMS, began requesting additional features such as real-time virtual classrooms, plagiarism detection tools, and advanced data analytics for student performance tracking. Meanwhile, the IT team identified the need for enhanced cybersecurity features to comply with new regulations, which had not been anticipated in the original plan. These requests, while valuable, were introduced without formal approval processes, gradually expanding the project's boundaries beyond the agreed-upon scope baseline. By the sixth month, the project was 20% over budget and two months behind schedule, with developers juggling an ever-growing list of tasks.

Scope Creep: *The gradual expansion of a project's scope due to additional requests, new requirements, or unforeseen*

*changes, often without proper approval. Scope creep can
lead to increased costs, extended timelines, and resource
overuse if not properly controlled through effective scope
management practices.*

WHY THE PROBLEM OCCURRED: A FAILURE IN SCOPE MANAGEMENT

The root cause of this issue lay in inadequate project scope management. The project team failed to enforce the processes necessary to
define, manage, and control the work included in the project. While
the initial project scope statement was comprehensive, it lacked a
robust change management protocol to handle new requests. Stakeholders, including faculty and administrators, were not sufficiently
educated on the importance of adhering to the scope baseline,
leading to ad-hoc demands that blurred the project's boundaries.
Additionally, the team did not conduct regular scope validation
checkpoints to ensure deliverables aligned with the original plan,
allowing deviations to accumulate unnoticed.

Scope Validation: *The formal review and acceptance of
completed project deliverables by key stakeholders, ensuring
they meet the predefined requirements and expectations.
Scope validation involves testing, inspections, and reviews
to confirm that deliverables align with project goals before
they are officially approved.*

The absence of a disciplined approach to managing scope meant
that the project drifted away from its business objectives, delivering

a functional LMS within time and budget constraints, and instead chased an idealized vision of a feature-rich platform. This misalignment exemplifies how scope creep can erode a project's focus, straining resources and jeopardizing success.

THE BUILD: HOW THE PROBLEM MANIFESTED

As the project unfolded, the build process became increasingly chaotic. Developers, initially tasked with coding the core LMS features, found themselves pulled in multiple directions. For instance, the addition of a virtual classroom feature required integrating third-party video conferencing tools, a task not accounted for in the original WBS. Meanwhile, the cybersecurity enhancements demanded extensive rewriting of the backend architecture, further delaying milestones like user testing. The team's attempt to accommodate these changes without revising the scope baseline or securing additional resources led to burnout and compromised quality. By the ninth month, the LMS was still in beta, with critical bugs in the gradebook module and incomplete integration with the university's systems.

THE CORRECTION AND PAYOFF: RESTORING CONTROL THROUGH SCOPE MANAGEMENT

Recognizing the project's trajectory toward failure, the university appointed a new project manager with expertise in project scope management. The first step was to halt development and conduct a thorough review of the scope baseline. The team revisited the project scope statement, reaffirming the original objectives and identifying which new features aligned with them. A formal change request process was established, requiring stakeholders to justify additions based on cost, time, and strategic value. Non-essential features, such as advanced analytics, were deferred to a future phase, while critical updates like cybersecurity enhancements were prioritized and formally integrated into a revised scope baseline.

Next, the team implemented scope validation through structured testing and stakeholder reviews. Each deliverable, such as the login portal and course management module, was rigorously evaluated against the updated scope criteria, ensuring alignment with expectations before approval. This process restored clarity and discipline, allowing the developers to focus on completing the core LMS within a revised 15-month timeline and a slightly adjusted budget of $600,000.

The payoff was significant. By the project's end, the university launched a stable, user-friendly LMS that met its primary goals: enabling online learning and integrating with existing systems. Faculty and students praised its reliability, and the project team regained credibility. While the final product lacked some of the bells and whistles initially envisioned, its success in delivering on the core scope demonstrated the value of disciplined project scope management. The deferred features were later incorporated into a Phase II project, planned with a separate budget and timeline, ensuring sustainable growth without compromising the initial effort.

CONCLUSION

The university LMS project illustrates how scope, when poorly managed, can derail even the most well-intentioned initiatives. Scope creep, fueled by uncontrolled stakeholder requests and a lack of scope validation, pushed the project beyond its boundaries, threatening its viability. However, by reasserting control through a refined project scope statement, an updated scope baseline, and rigorous management practices, the team turned the project around. This case underscores a critical lesson: effective project scope management is not just about defining what's included, it's about protecting the project's integrity, optimizing resources, and delivering value that aligns with the original vision.

THE BLUEPRINT FOR SUCCESS: REQUIREMENTS MANAGEMENT PLAN

A clear and well-defined scope is essential to any project's success, but scope doesn't exist in a vacuum, it is built directly from the project's requirements. To ensure the scope is accurate, aligned, and stable throughout the project lifecycle, we need a structured approach to managing those requirements. This is where the Requirements Management Plan is introduced to capture, document, prioritize, and monitor requirements throughout the project lifecycle.

Requirements Management Plan: *A structured document that details the processes and methodologies used to identify, analyze, prioritize, track, and manage project requirements throughout the lifecycle. It outlines roles and responsibilities, tools for requirement documentation, approval workflows, change control mechanisms, and strategies to address evolving requirements. This plan helps prevent scope creep, miscommunication, and overlooked stakeholder expectations.*

The Requirements Management Plan (RMP) is the cornerstone of effective requirements gathering, providing a structured framework to identify, document, and maintain project needs. It outlines how requirements will be elicited, analyzed, prioritized, and validated throughout the project lifecycle. For example, in developing a payroll system, the RMP might specify that requirements must be gathered via a JAD workshop, documented in a centralized repository, and approved by key stakeholders within one week. It could define roles, such as the project manager as the requirements owner and end users as validators and establish traceability to ensure every requirement links to a business objective, like "ensure tax compliance." Additionally, the RMP addresses change management, detailing how scope adjustments (e.g., adding mobile access) are proposed, evaluated, and integrated. By setting these ground rules, the RMP ensures that the subsequent JAD workshop operates within a clear, controlled framework, maximizing efficiency and focus.

Requirement: *A defined expectation, condition, or functionality that a project, product, or service must achieve to meet stakeholder expectations, legal regulations, business objectives, or technical constraints. Requirements can be functional (describing what the system must do) or non-functional (defining performance, security, or usability constraints). Effective requirement gathering and documentation are critical for project success, ensuring alignment between stakeholder needs and final deliverables.*

Deliverable: *A tangible or intangible output produced as part of a project, which can include reports, training materials, hardware components, software modules, or completed* *services. Deliverables are key milestones that indicate project progress and fulfillment of objectives.*

THE WORKSHOP: LEVERAGING JOINT APPLICATION DESIGN (JAD)

Joint Application Design [JAD]: *Joint Application Development (JAD) / Collaborative Design Workshops / Facilitated Design Sessions — A structured, intensive workshop approach that brings together key project stakeholders, such as sponsors, end-users, business analysts, and developers, to collaboratively define, design, and refine information systems. These sessions promote efficient decision-making, stakeholder alignment, and accelerated system development by fostering direct communication and consensus-driven solutions.*

In the world of project management and systems development, success hinges on one critical factor: understanding what needs to be built. This clarity doesn't emerge in isolation, it begins with collaboration, discussion, and a structured process to capture requirements. One of the most effective ways to kick off this journey is through a workshop, specifically using Joint Application Design (JAD). Whether employing a top-down approach, a bottom-up perspective, or a use-case-driven analogy, JAD brings stakeholders together to define project scope and requirements swiftly and accurately. By integrating tools like the Work Breakdown Structure (WBS), WBS Dictionary, and work packages, JAD transforms abstract ideas into actionable plans. This section explores how JAD serves as the starting point for successful projects, detailing its methodologies and tools to capture requirements based on scope

JAD APPROACH OPTIONS: THE WORKSHOP CATALYST

Joint Application Design (JAD) is a collaborative workshop technique that unites project stakeholders, end users, developers, managers, and subject matter experts, in a focused, facilitated session. Unlike traditional requirement-gathering methods that rely on lengthy interviews or isolated documentation, JAD accelerates the process by fostering real-time dialogue. The goal is simple yet powerful: get to the requirements as quickly as possible while ensuring alignment across all parties. A typical JAD session begins with defining the project scope, moves into brainstorming and analyzing needs, and concludes with documented deliverables, such as a requirements list or system design outline.

The strength of JAD lies in its inclusivity and immediacy. By gathering everyone in one room (or virtual space), miscommunication is minimized, assumptions are challenged, and consensus is built on the spot. This workshop-driven approach sets the stage for subsequent planning, ensuring that the project starts with a shared vision.

Top-Down vs. Bottom-Up: Analogies for Structuring JAD

Top-Down Approach: *A hierarchical project planning technique that starts with the highest-level project goal or deliverable and progressively breaks it down into smaller, more manageable components. This approach provides a*

structured way to develop a Work Breakdown Structure (WBS), ensuring alignment with strategic objectives before focusing on specific tasks. It is commonly used in large-scale, enterprise-level projects where high-level planning guides resource allocation and execution.

Bottom-Up Approach: *A planning methodology where individual team members identify specific tasks or deliverables first, which are then grouped into broader categories to develop a structured Work Breakdown Structure (WBS). This approach allows for a highly detailed and accurate project plan, leveraging the expertise of subject matter experts and ensuring that all necessary activities are considered. It is particularly useful in Agile and iterative project environments, where team collaboration drives planning and execution.*

When capturing requirements in a JAD session, two conceptual approaches often come into play: top-down and bottom-up. These can be likened to building a house. In a top-down approach, you start with the blueprint—the big picture of the house (project scope)—and then break it into rooms, walls, and fixtures (specific requirements). In a JAD session, this might begin with leadership defining high-level objectives, such as "improve customer service efficiency," followed by participants drilling down into detailed needs, like "reduce call wait times by 30%" or "integrate a chatbot."

Conversely, a bottom-up approach is like assembling a house from individual bricks. Participants first identify granular needs, say, "users need a password reset feature"—and then aggregate these into broader categories, such as "enhance user account management." In JAD, this might involve frontline employees sharing day-to-day pain points, which are then synthesized into a cohesive system scope by the facilitator.

Both approaches have merits. Top-down ensures alignment with strategic goals, while bottom-up captures real-world usability. A skilled JAD facilitator often blends the two, starting with a high-level scope to set boundaries and then encouraging participants to fill in details organically. For example, in designing a payroll system, the top-down scope might dictate compliance with tax laws, while bottom-up input ensures employees can easily submit overtime hours.

Use-Case Approach: Bringing Requirements to Life

Use Case Modeling: *A technique used in software and systems engineering to define and analyze interactions between users (actors) and a system. It captures functional requirements by identifying key business events, describing the system's expected behavior, and specifying conditions for success or failure. Use case models help developers, designers, and business analysts understand user workflows and ensure that the system meets real-world usage scenarios.*

Another powerful analogy in JAD is the use-case approach, which focuses on how users will interact with the system. Imagine scripting a play: each use case is a scene describing an actor (user), their goal, and the steps to achieve it. During a JAD session, participants might define a use case like "Employee submits expense report," detailing preconditions (e.g., logged into the system), actions (e.g., upload receipts), and outcomes (e.g., manager approves within 24 hours).

This method bridges abstract requirements with tangible scenarios, making it easier to spot gaps. For instance, discussing the expense report use case might reveal a need for mobile access, something overlooked in a purely top-down list. By role-playing these scenarios in the workshop, JAD participants ensure the scope reflects real-world needs.

Analogy Approach: Leveraging the Past for the Present

Analogy Approach: *A method for developing a Work Breakdown Structure (WBS) by referencing and adapting the structure of a similar past project. This technique leverages historical project data to streamline planning, improve accuracy, and reduce effort in defining deliverables and tasks. It is particularly useful when managing projects with similarities in scope, industry, or technology.*

A lesser-known but equally valuable method in JAD is the analogy approach, particularly when developing the Work Breakdown Structure (WBS). This technique involves referencing and adapting the structure of a similar past project to streamline planning. Picture a chef using a trusted recipe as a starting point for a new dish: the analogy approach leverages historical project data, such as a previous payroll system rollout, to define deliverables and tasks efficiently. For instance, if a past project included a WBS with activities like "data migration" and "user training," the JAD team can adapt these to the current scope, adjusting for new requirements like "cloud integration." This method improves accuracy, reduces planning effort, and is especially useful for projects with similarities in scope, industry, or technology, ensuring the team benefits from lessons learned without reinventing the wheel.

WORK BREAKDOWN STRUCTURE (WBS): MAPPING THE PATH FORWARD

Once requirements emerge from the JAD session, they must be organized into an actionable plan. This is where the Work Breakdown Structure (WBS) takes shape. The WBS is a hierarchical decomposition of the project into manageable deliverables. Think of it as a family tree: the project scope is the root, major deliverables are branches, and smaller tasks are leaves.

For a JAD-derived payroll system, the WBS might look like this:

1.0 Payroll System Development
- 1.1 Requirements Gathering
- 1.1.1 Conduct JAD Workshop
- 1.1.2 Document User Needs

1.2 System Design
- 1.2.1 Create Database Schema
- 1.2.2 Design User Interface

1.3 Implementation
- 1.3.1 Code Core Functions
- 1.3.2 Test System

Each level breaks the scope into smaller, trackable units, ensuring nothing is missed. The WBS provides a visual roadmap, directly traceable to the JAD outputs.

WBS Dictionary: Defining the Details

WBS Dictionary: *A document that provides detailed descriptions of each Work Breakdown Structure (WBS)* *element, including scope, deliverables, responsibilities, resources, and cost estimates. A software development project's WBS dictionary may include details on the "User Authentication Module", specifying its functionality, responsible team, estimated budget, and dependencies.*

The WBS alone isn't enough, it needs context. Enter the WBS Dictionary, a companion document that describes each WBS element in depth. For "1.1.1 Conduct JAD Workshop," the dictionary might specify:

- Description: Facilitated session with stakeholders to define payroll system requirements.
- Deliverables: Requirements list, use-case diagrams.
- Responsible Party: Project Manager and Facilitator.
- Resources: Conference room, whiteboard, JAD facilitator guide.
- Duration: 2 days.

This clarity ensures everyone understands what each WBS item entails, preventing scope creep and aligning expectations with the JAD outcomes.

Work Packages: The Building Blocks

Work Package: *The smallest unit in a WBS, representing a specific, well-defined task that can be assigned, estimated, and tracked independently. Within the "Backend Development" section of a WBS, a work package might be "Develop user login API", with detailed requirements, assigned developers, and a timeline.*

At the lowest level of the WBS are work packages, discrete tasks that can be assigned and completed. A work package for "1.2.2 Design User Interface" might include:

- Task: Mock up payroll dashboard.
- Input: JAD requirements (e.g., "easy overtime entry").
- Output: Wireframe approved by stakeholders.
- Effort: 20 hours by UI designer.

Work packages translate JAD discussions into executable steps. They're small enough to manage yet tied directly to the scope, ensuring the workshop's vision becomes reality.

Capturing Requirements Based on Scope

The magic of JAD lies in its ability to capture requirements within a defined scope. The facilitator begins by presenting the project's boundaries, say, "build a payroll system within 6 months and $200,000." From there, top-down goals set the tone, bottom-up input fills in details, and use cases test feasibility. The WBS, dictionary, and work packages then structure these requirements into a plan. For instance, if the scope excludes mobile apps, JAD participants focus only on desktop features, and the WBS reflects this constraint.

This process isn't linear, it's iterative. A JAD session might reveal scope gaps (e.g., missing tax compliance needs), prompting adjustments. The WBS and dictionary evolve accordingly, keeping the project grounded in the workshop's insights.

UNDERSTANDING DECOMPOSITION AND MICROPRODUCTIVITY

Efficiency and structure are crucial to ensuring that complex tasks are manageable, trackable, and successfully executed. Two important concepts that contribute to project success are **decomposition** and **microproductivity**. These approaches help teams break down work into smaller, more achievable units, leading to improved organization, accountability, and overall productivity.

Stop trying to swallow the ocean, explore microproductivity or decomposition mixtures that turn information into knowledge. For example, a global IT implementation project might seem overwhelmingly complex, but breaking it into chapters, write the story where elements of the project can work independently and be available when needed, or parallel, with separate release dates as in the supply and demand planning challenge. Microproductivity is an outcome of accountability beyond project planning process groups, such as information gathering, testing, and deployment. Decomposition reveals information patterns designed to enlighten clear and manageable structures.

Decomposition: Breaking Down Complexity

Decomposition*: Decomposition is the process of subdividing project deliverables into smaller, more manageable components. It is a core technique in Work Breakdown Structure (WBS) development, where a large project is broken into progressively smaller work packages. This hierarchical structure allows for better resource allocation, clearer task ownership, and easier progress tracking.*

In a software development project, the creation of a "Mobile App" could be considered a single deliverable or broken down through decomposition into smaller tasks such as UI/UX design, backend development, API integration, testing, and deployment. Each of these tasks can be further subdivided into specific subtasks, ensuring a structured, organized, and systematic approach to project execution.

The key benefits of decomposition include:

    a. Enhanced clarity by defining each task clearly.
    b. Improved project control, as smaller tasks are easier to monitor.
    c. Better risk management, since identifying potential issues is easier when tasks are well-defined.
    d. More accurate cost and time estimates, leading to better planning.

Microproductivity*: The practice of breaking work into very small, focused tasks that can be completed in short bursts of time. Unlike decomposition, which focuses on project structure, microproductivity is more about individual efficiency. This approach helps workers maintain focus, overcome procrastination, and build momentum by achieving small wins throughout the day.*

Instead of assigning "Write project proposal" as a single task, microproductivity would divide it into actionable steps such as outlining key sections, drafting the executive summary, researching data, and formatting the final document. Each step takes less time, making the work feel more achievable and reducing the mental burden of large tasks.

Key advantages of microproductivity include:

    a. Increased motivation by providing frequent, measurable progress.
    b. Reduced cognitive overload, making work more manageable.
    c. Greater flexibility, allowing workers to make progress even in short time blocks.
    d. Improved focus, as smaller tasks reduce distractions and mental fatigue.

HOW TO STRUCTURE THE OUTPUT: WORK PRODUCTS

Once we've completed the workshops, such as Joint Application Development (JAD) sessions, and captured the requirements, the next step is to translate those discussions into tangible work products. These work products are the documented outputs that serve as evidence of the work completed and form the foundation for the next phases of the project. This transition from collaborative dialogue to formal documentation ensures that everyone has a clear, shared understanding of what needs to be delivered, and creates a traceable link between stakeholder input and the final project scope.

Requirements Traceability Matrix (RTM): *A comprehensive table or mapping tool that connects each requirement to its origin (such as business needs or regulatory standards),* *stakeholders, associated risks, test cases, and status. The RTM ensures that all requirements are accounted for, properly validated, and aligned with project deliverables. It is particularly useful in complex projects, where maintaining visibility on requirement fulfillment is critical for compliance and quality assurance.*

Artifact: *Refers to any tangible output or document that is created, used, or maintained throughout the project lifecycle. Artifacts serve as evidence of work performed and decisions made, and may include items such as requirements documents, design specifications, test plans, code, user manuals, or reports. They provide a foundation for communication, traceability, and accountability among stakeholders. Far from being static, artifacts often evolve with the project and play a central role in ensuring quality, transparency, and successful delivery.*

The MoSCoW Method*: A prioritization technique used in project management and business analysis to determine the importance of various project requirements. It helps teams and stakeholders categorize features or tasks based on their necessity and feasibility within a given timeframe. The acronym MoSCoW represents four levels of priority: Must have, Should have, Could Have, Won't have.*

STEP BY STEP GUIDE USING THE MOSCOW METHOD

In this section, we're going to walk through a step-by-step guide to building a Requirements Matrix using the MoSCoW method, a popular technique for prioritizing requirements based on business need. We'll begin by defining what each of the MoSCoW acronyms are, and how they apply to requirement categorization. Then, we'll break down how to structure the matrix itself, including which columns to include, what each column represents, and how to fill in each field accurately and consistently. The section will conclude with a practical example to demonstrate how the matrix comes together in action.

It's important to note that while the MoSCoW method is a widely used approach, it's just one of many ways to organize and manage requirements. The core objective isn't which format you choose, it's that your requirements are clearly captured, traceable, and aligned with project goals. A well-constructed matrix allows you to "cross-foot" each element, ensuring that every requirement (row) has a clear connection to key attributes (columns) like priority, source, acceptance criteria, and ownership. This creates a living document that drives clarity, accountability, and successful delivery.

Definitions

M - MUST: These are non-negotiable requirements that must be included for the project or solution to be successful. If any MUST requirement is not met, the project is considered a failure. These typically include core functionalities, legal requirements, or critical system operations that the solution cannot function without.

S - SHOULD: These are high-priority requirements that are not critical to the project's success but should be included if possible. They are important for enhancing usability, efficiency, or user satisfaction but can be deferred to a future phase if necessary.

C - COULD: These are desirable but not essential requirements. They serve as enhancements that can improve the project but will only be implemented if time and resources allow. These may include minor features, additional UI improvements, or non-essential integrations.

W - WON'T: These requirements are explicitly agreed upon by stakeholders as not being included in the current scope but might be considered for future versions or releases. Identifying WON'T items early helps prevent scope creep and sets clear expectations for deliverables.

How to Build the MoSCoW Matrix

a. Begin by gathering all potential requirements and entering them into the matrix.
b. Classify each requirement based on business and technical needs using the MoSCoW framework. M, S, C, W.
c. Assess the feasibility of each requirement by performing a FIT/GAP analysis.
d. Prioritize based on business value, complexity, and dependencies.
e. Track progress and update the status as the project evolves.

Below is a detailed explanation of each column and how to fill it out effectively:

Columns and How to Fill Them

1. **MoSCoW.ID** – A unique identifier for each
    requirement in the matrix. Typically, this follows a
    numbering format like REQ-001, REQ-002, etc. for
    easy tracking.
2. **Source** – The origin of the requirement. This can be a
    stakeholder request, business need, regulatory com-
    pliance, customer feedback, or technical necessity.
3. **MoSCoW Classification** – The priority classification
    based on the MoSCoW method:
    *   **MUST** – Critical requirement that the project
        cannot succeed without.
    *   **SHOULD** – Important but not essential; can be
        deferred if necessary.
    *   **COULD** – Desirable but non-essential; implemented
        if resources allow.
    *   **WON'T** – Not included in the current scope but
        may be considered later.
4. **Requirement Description** – A clear and concise
    explanation of what the requirement is and why it
    is needed. This should include enough details for
    implementation teams to understand its purpose.
5. **Requirement Owner** – The individual or team
    responsible for defining and ensuring the imple-
    mentation of the requirement (e.g., Business Analyst,
    Product Owner, Project Sponsor).
6. **FIT/GAP** – A Fit/Gap analysis to determine whether
    the requirement aligns with existing systems or if new
    development is required:
    *   **FIT** – The requirement can be met with the current
        system functionality.

- **GAP** – The requirement requires additional development or customization.

7. **Category** – Categorization of the requirement, such as:
   - Functional (related to system features or business processes)
   - Non-functional (performance, security, compliance, usability)
   - Technical (related to infrastructure or integrations)

8. **Complexity** – An assessment of how difficult the requirement is to implement. This can be labeled as **Low, Medium, or High** based on factors like development effort, dependencies, and risks.

9. **Priority** – The relative urgency of the requirement within the classification. Even within MUST or SHOULD, some requirements may be **High, Medium, or Low priority** based on business needs.

10. **Module** – The specific system or functional area that the requirement applies to, such as CRM, Finance, HR, Reporting, etc.

11. **Scope Phase** – The phase in which the requirement will be addressed:
    - Phase 1 (Immediate implementation)
    - Phase 2 (Future enhancement)
    - Phase 3 (Long-term roadmap)

12. **High-Level Approach** – A brief description of how the requirement will be implemented, such as:
    - Custom development
    - Configuration change
    - Third-party integration
    - Business process change

13. **RICE ID** – If using the **RICE Scoring Model**, this field references the unique identifier for a **RICE (Reach,**

Impact, Confidence, Effort) analysis**, which helps prioritize requirements based on their impact and feasibility.

14. **Test Case ID** – A reference to test cases that will be used to validate whether the requirement has been successfully implemented.

15. **RAID ID** – If applicable, a reference to associated **Risks, Assumptions, Issues, and Dependencies (RAID)** that may impact the requirement's implementation.

16. **Status** – The current state of the requirement, such as:
    - Pending
    - In Progress
    - Completed
    - On Hold
    - Rejected

17. **Comments** – Additional notes or clarifications, such as dependencies, blockers, or decisions made regarding the requirement.

Output

MoSCoW ID	Source	MoSCoW Classification	Requirement Description	Requirement Owner	FIT/GAP	Category	Complexity	Priority	Module	Scope Phase	High-Level Approach	RICE ID	Test Case ID	RAID ID	Status	Comments
REQ-001	Business Need	MUST	The system must support multi-factor authentication for all users.	Security Team	GAP	Security	High	High	Authentication	Phase 1	Custom Development	RICE-101	TC-001	RAID-005	In Progress	Required for compliance with ISO 27001.
REQ-002	Customer Feedback	SHOULD	Add a dark mode option for better user experience.	UX Team	FIT	UI/UX	Medium	Medium	Frontend	Phase 2	Configuration Change	RICE-102	TC-002	RAID-010	Pending	Can be deferred if development resources are limited.
REQ-003	Regulatory	MUST	Generate automated tax reports in PDF format.	Finance Dept.	GAP	Compliance	High	High	Reporting	Phase 1	Third-Party Integration	RICE-103	TC-003	RAID-015	Not Started	Required for tax law compliance.
REQ-004	Internal IT	COULD	Enable single sign-on (SSO) with Google accounts.	IT Team	GAP	Authentication	Medium	Low	Security	Phase 3	Third-Party Integration	RICE-104	TC-004	RAID-020	On Hold	Nice-to-have, but not essential.
REQ-005	Business Decision	WONT	Develop a mobile app for iOS and Android.	Product Owner	GAP	Mobile	High	High	Mobile	Future Scope	New Development	RICE-105	TC-005	RAID-025	Rejected	Not in the current project scope, may be revisited later.

Leveraging Benchmarking to Master Project Scope at Kerzner's Level 4 Maturity

At Level 4 of Harold Kerzner's Project Management Maturity Model (PMMM), an organization reaches a sophisticated stage of project management maturity, characterized by a dedicated project management office (PMO) that actively benchmarks its processes against industry standards and best practices.[47] This level emphasizes both quantitative and qualitative approaches, tracking metrics, refining methodologies, and nurturing adaptive cultures, while prioritizing continuous improvement. Unlike lower maturity levels, where scope management might be reactive or haphazard, Level 4 organizations proactively seek out new ways to enhance effectiveness, drawing insights from both similar and non-similar industries. When applied to the challenge of controlling project scope, this benchmarking-driven approach offers a disciplined framework to prevent scope creep and ensure successful delivery.

Benchmarking: *A process of evaluating and improving project performance by comparing specific practices, processes, or product attributes against those from other projects, organizations, or industry standards. By analyzing best practices and identifying gaps, benchmarking helps organizations refine strategies, enhance efficiency, and drive continuous improvement.*

At Level 4, benchmarking becomes a strategic tool for scope management, enabled by the PMO's systematic evaluation of internal processes against external standards.[48] The organization doesn't just execute projects, it measures performance through hard data, such as schedule adherence rates or scope change frequencies, and soft insights, like team dynamics or client feedback. This dual focus allows the PMO to identify patterns of scope creep, those insidious expansions that start small but balloon into major disruptions. By comparing its practices to competitors in the same sector (e.g., other tech firms) and high-performing industries outside it (e.g., manufacturing or logistics), the organization builds a robust methodology that anticipates and mitigates scope-related risks. The PMO's role is not just to collect this information but to translate it into actionable protocols that keep projects aligned with their original intent.

Imagine a hypothetical software development firm tasked with delivering a customer relationship management (CRM) system. The initial scope is clear: core features like contact management, sales tracking, and basic reporting, to be completed in six months for $500,000. Midway through, the client requests additional features, custom dashboards and third-party integrations, framing them as minor tweaks. In an organization at a lower maturity level, these might be accepted without scrutiny, leading to delayed timelines and budget overruns. However, at Level 4, the PMO's benchmarking practices provide a safeguard. Historical data from past projects might show that each scope change increases delivery time by 20%, while qualitative feedback reveals client dissatisfaction when expectations diverge from the agreed plan. Armed with this insight, the project manager declines the additions unless formalized through a change order, preserving the original scope and timeline.

This disciplined approach is enhanced by the PMO's commitment to continuous improvement, a hallmark of Level 4 maturity.[49] Benchmarking against a similar industry might uncover a tech firm's practice of using agile sprints to limit scope drift, short, focused cycles where only predefined features are developed. Meanwhile, a non-similar industry, like automotive manufacturing, might offer a "stage-gate" process, locking scope at critical milestones to prevent late-stage changes. The PMO synthesizes these findings into a hybrid methodology tailored to software projects. Quantitatively, it sets targets like "80% rejection rate for out-of-scope requests" or "delivery within 5% of the original timeline." Qualitatively, it fosters a team culture where developers feel empowered to flag scope risks early, ensuring alignment with the CRM project's goals. This blend of hard metrics and soft insights keeps the project on track, delivering a focused product without unnecessary bloat.

The PMO's benchmarking efforts also create a structured decision-making framework. For instance, when the client pushes for a custom dashboard, the project manager consults a protocol informed by benchmarked data: Does it fit the original scope? (No.) Does it risk the timeline? (Yes, by three weeks, based on historical trends.) Is the client willing to adjust the budget? (Not yet.) The decision to defer is clear, grounded in evidence rather than guesswork. This systematic approach extends to regular benchmarking cycles, perhaps quarterly reviews against Project Management Institute (PMI) standards or lean principles from other sectors, allowing the PMO to refine its scope management tactics continually.[50] Over time, this builds a repository of best practices that prevent scope creep from taking root.

The CRM project's outcome highlights the payoff. By resisting scope expansion, the team delivers the agreed features on time and within budget, achieving a 95% scope adherence rate (versus an industry average of 75%) and a client satisfaction score of 4.8/5. Post-project analysis feeds back into the PMO's benchmarking process, identifying areas for further improvement, perhaps tightening change request thresholds or enhancing client scope education. This cycle of execution, evaluation, and refinement ensures that lessons from one project strengthen the next, a key advantage of Level 4 maturity.

However, benchmarking's effectiveness hinges on execution. While gathering data from competitors or industry standards is relatively straightforward, embedding those insights into everyday practice can be challenging. Project managers and teams must internalize the PMO's protocols, requiring a culture that values data-driven discipline over ad hoc flexibility. For the software firm, this means training staff to see scope control as a collective responsibility, not a barrier to client pleasing. When done well, the organization not only delivers the CRM system successfully but also establishes a scalable framework for future projects.

At Level 4 of the Kerzner PMMM, benchmarking transforms scope management into a proactive, evidence-based discipline. By leveraging quantitative metrics and qualitative insights from diverse industries, the PMO equips project teams to define, defend, and deliver within scope boundaries. The CRM example illustrates how this maturity level turns potential chaos into predictable success, ensuring that projects meet their goals without succumbing to the creeping demands that derail lesser-prepared organizations. Through continuous improvement and a commitment to learning from the broader ecosystem, Level 4 maturity offers a blueprint for scope mastery that adapts and endures.[51]

CHAPTER 7

Information Gathering: You're Doing it Wrong!

Y OU WON'T HEAR the truth from many implementation service providers, they're too busy seeking the next starburst opportunity to focus on delivering a successful project. They are stuck in the past with traditional models that superficially give the customer a false sense of security in predictability. Gathering requirements and building a wish list that will ultimately go unsatisfied leaves the customer frustrated. The problem is, it assumes requirements are fixed and can be fully captured upfront. In dynamic environments, user needs and business contexts change rapidly, making initial requirements outdated and unachievable. Conventional requirements gathering often results in exhaustive documentation, which may be disconnected from actual stakeholder needs or product usability. Your delivery becomes a library of word documents and PDF files that no one will read until they need to perform a referential search. In addition, requirements gathering often prioritizes technical functionality over user experience, potentially leading to products that meet technical specs but fail to delight users. A better approach is to incorporate research and information gathering to validate how the product solves real user problems. The ultimate goal is to provide working software the users see, touch and feel in their daily lives. The future is information driven, not requirements driven. The show and tell approach replaces the ask and do method.

Set the expectation that the goal is to focus on the desired end result of their processes, not the specific path to get there. Sequential thinking encourages a linear approach to project execution, which can delay feedback and make course corrections costly. Adopt a discovery-driven process, where hypotheses are tested iteratively, and features are prioritized based on real-world usage and value. This approach aligns with the principle of envisioning the outcome first and working backward to determine what is truly needed to achieve it. Static requirements are often subject to misinterpretation by implementation teams, leading to mismatched expectations. Replacing traditional requirements gathering with information gathering shifts the emphasis from collecting rigid, predefined needs to exploring the broader objectives and outcomes stakeholders aim to achieve. Unlike requirements gathering, which often fixates on detailed steps and static specifications, information gathering embraces flexibility, collaboration, and discovery. Once requirements are gathered, they can be treated as strict commitments, making it difficult to adapt when new insights or opportunities arise. You will see this boil over during the late stages of testing when the geniuses awake from their deep sleep during the project lifecycle and are alerted to the reality of acceptance and deployment. By under-standing the "why" behind the goals rather than just the "what," this approach fosters clarity, adaptability, and solutions better aligned with the ultimate vision.

Focus solely on gathering insights rather than attempting to address specific issues or redesign business processes. Start by setting clear expectations with stakeholders that the objective is to understand their desired outcomes and the high-level needs that support them. Prioritize and categorize the information gathered into clear groups: functionality included in the base system, needs that can be addressed through analytics, functionality provided by another application, and features not covered in the base system. Throughout this process, ensure that the identified needs and goals align with the company's overall mission and objectives, avoiding conflicts or misaligned priorities. This structured approach enables clarity, avoids scope creep, and ensures that the collected information serves as a strong foundation for delivering solutions aligned with organizational goals.

When gathering information during the envisioning phase, the work product moves beyond a MOSCOW list of must haves, should have, could haves and instead develop actionable, collaborative deliverables that align with the project's objectives and constraints. This approach emphasizes defining the product vision, identifying project objectives, and understanding the constraints that shape the project community and how the team will work together. The envisioning phase aims to clearly outline what needs to be done and how it will be accomplished, focusing on the "what," "who," and "how."

THE 5W1H FRAMEWORK

When preparing for workshops that involve information collection, it is crucial to approach the process methodically, ensuring that the chosen methods align with the investigation's purpose and objectives. A key first step is to carefully reason about the purpose of the study, the units of analysis, and the timeframe over which the data will be collected and analyzed. This foundational consideration lays the groundwork for selecting the most appropriate methods for examination and analysis. To frame the inquiry, and build the initial questionnaires, use the 5W1H framework—comprising What, Who, When, Where, Why, and How— this serves as a robust tool for facilitators. This framework allows the organizers to systematically dissect the investigation's objectives. For example:

- "What happens?" focuses on understanding the event or phenomenon in question.
- "Who does that?" identifies the actors involved.
- Similarly, "When and Where does it take place?" contextualizes the phenomenon temporally and spatially.
- "Why did that happen?" explores underlying causes or motivations.
- The "How did it happen?" question seeks to unravel the mechanisms or processes at play.

Workshops can target different goals, ranging from exploring new phenomena to understanding or explaining established ones. Focus on the future state vision, leaving unnecessary existing process analysis where it belongs, in the past. When exploring a new phenomenon, the objective is often to gain a basic understanding through qualitative insights or preliminary observations. Conversely, identifying when an established conventionality must remain static, typically this involves measuring well-defined fixed actualities, which contributes to a more comprehensive or nuanced understanding. If the aim is to explain an observed phenomenon, the focus shifts to uncovering causal relationships and mechanisms.

The unit of analysis, whether individuals, activities, or objects such as process flows—is another crucial factor. It determines the breadth of the analysis directly impacts the methods used for collection and examination. The unit of analysis is usually a system rather than an individual, actors or groups of individuals, note that there can be multiple units of analysis. Concentrate on the social network analysis method discussed later in the study. When driving a project to success it's important to always remember, people are more important than process.

INDUCTIVE VERSUS DEDUCTIVE APPROACHES

Two primary approaches to information gathering are the deductive and inductive methods, which represent inverse processes of reasoning. The deductive approach begins with a general theory or hypothesis and applies it to a specific case to test its validity or applicability. This structured, hypothesis-driven method aims to confirm or falsify existing theories by analyzing whether the case evidence supports or contradicts the theoretical framework. For example, applying a financial department and human capital hierarchy synchronization to a workplace scenario tests whether the theory holds in that context. In contrast, the inductive approach starts with specific observations or case studies and reasons toward broader generalizations or theories. This exploratory method focuses on uncovering patterns or themes in the data to build new theories, such as identifying bifurcated supply chain physical and logical flows, which are common strategies used by smart businesses to adapt economic opportunities. While the deductive approach refines or rejects pre-existing ideas, the inductive approach generates fresh insights. Both methods, though opposites, can complement each other by combining the development of new theories with their validation, enriching the overall research process.

ENVIRONMENTAL SCANNING

We define environmental scanning as the process of collecting and analyzing information about an organization's external environment, it reflects both the pursuit of information seeking and a commitment to organizational learning. How do we perform environmental scanning that can be used to gather information, interpret it, and use it to make informed decisions? The conditions include a wide range of factors such as competitors, economic trends, political and legal issues, social and cultural factors, and technological developments. The assessment is used for strategic planning as it allows facilitators to stay aware of needed changes to customer specific circumstances and adjust their strategies accordingly.[52]

The process involves four key components: acquisition, interpretation, dissemination, and use.[53] These components work together to create a cycle of learning that allows organizations to adapt to changes through abstract conceptualization. One of the key strengths is its emphasis on the importance of organizational learning in the examination process. Environmental scanning is not just about gathering information but also about using that information to improve the organization's knowledge and understanding of its environment. This is critical as it allows organizations to adapt to changes and make informed decisions that are aligned with their goals and objectives

The acquisition of information is the first step in the environmental scanning process. This involves gathering data from a variety of sources such as surveys, interviews, focus groups, data collection, industry reports, quantitative statistics, and qualitative social and cultural analysis. It is important for investigators to cast a wide net when gathering information to ensure that they do not miss any important trends or developments. See detailed qualitative and quantitative information gathering action items later in this chapter.

The second step in the environmental scanning process is interpretation. This involves analyzing the information that has been collected to identify patterns, trends, and potential implications for the organization. This step is critical as it allows organizations to move beyond simply collecting data to understanding what it means and how it might impact their operations. This requires a combination of analytical skills and knowledge of the organization's industry and market.

The third step in the environmental scanning process is dissemination. This involves sharing the information that has been collected and analyzed with relevant stakeholders within the organization. Effective dissemination is critical as it ensures that decision-makers have access to the information they need to make informed decisions. This can be achieved through a variety of methods such as reports, presentations, and meetings.

The final step in the environmental scanning process is use. This involves using the information that has been collected, analyzed, and disseminated to inform decision-making and strategic planning. This is where the real value of environmental scanning lies as it allows organizations to adapt to changes in their environment and stay competitive.

QUALITATIVE AND QUANTITATIVE INFORMATION GATHERING METHODS

Achieving Maximum Delivery requires a keen ability to stay connected to the pulse of emerging trends, stakeholder needs, and actionable insights. This is where strategic information gathering becomes the Toolkit cornerstone. Having established the "why" behind the need for robust data and the "what" of identifying key priorities, we now turn to the "how"—the practical, high-impact methods that drive transformative outcomes. The information gathering techniques we will explore are designed to help you move beyond outdated, static approaches that stifle progress. Instead, these dynamic methods empower you to harness real-time insights, foster adaptability, and propel projects toward meaningful, results-driven change. By leveraging these techniques, you'll not only keep pace with the demands of a fast-changing environment but also unlock the potential for innovation and sustainable growth, ensuring your initiatives deliver maximum value and impact.

Survey Research: *Save your organization service provider fees by forming an internal center of excellence that compiles pain points and areas of need before bringing the subject matter experts and advisors onboard.* **Survey research methodology** *involves collecting data from a predefined group of individuals through structured questionnaires or interviews to gather information on their attitudes, behaviors, or characteristics. The strategy is to use statistical analysis to identify patterns, trends, or correlations within the responses. This approach helps inform action plans or strategies by providing insights into public opinion, user satisfaction, or other key areas of interest, guiding decisions or policy development based on the survey results. Do this before opening the checkbook.*

Grounded Theory: *Grounded theory is a qualitative information gathering methodology aimed at developing theories* **grounded in data,** *rather than testing existing theories. The strategy involves systematic data collection and analysis through methods like coding, constants, and abstract sampling, which help generate insights and build a framework that emerges directly from the data. Consultants and team members using grounded theory aim to understand moored predeterminations such as legal entities in ERP systems. For example, a grounded theory would emerge that explains how the organization experiences ERP entities for consolidation,* *its impact on workflows, and factors that contribute to success or failure, ultimately providing a comprehensive understanding of ERP financial consolidation process in that context. A deductive approach of fact-based data can also be obtained during the prerequisite stage, such as a list of legal entities, % of ownership, intercompany relationships, eliminations and currency requirements. Utilization of data within an organization enlightens opportunities to future state modern best practices.*

USE CASE STUDIES

Use Case Study Research: *Use case research methodology involves analyzing real-world scenarios or specific user interactions with a product, system, or service to understand its functionality, performance, and user needs. The strategy focuses on identifying and documenting key tasks or problems users face, providing insights into how the product or system can be improved. This approach informs action plans or strategies by ensuring that design or development decisions are user-centered, addressing actual use cases and enhancing overall user experience.*

USE CASE EXAMPLE FOR LANDED COST MANAGEMENT

A use case study for landed cost management, for example, could focus on the process of accurately calculating and tracking all costs associated with importing goods, including duties, freight, insurance, and customs fees at various points of entry. Information gathering for this use case should involve collecting detailed data from various sources involved in the importation process. This includes freight charges, insurance premiums, and documentation related to the movement of goods. Key customs documents required for this use case at the port would typically include the commercial invoice, packing list, bill of lading (BOL), import declaration form, and certificate of origin. Additionally, the customs entry form (such as a CBP entry summary in the U.S. or equivalent in other countries) and proof of payment for duties and taxes would be necessary to ensure that the full landed cost is accounted for in the preferred costing method. The use case examples would be integrated into the system to provide a best practice alternative on how to better manage a comprehensive view of costs, enabling better financial planning, accurate cost allocation, and compliance with import regulations.

ACTION ANALYSIS METHOD

The Action Analysis Method starts by delving into organizational decision-making processes through carefully crafted questionnaires that capture diverse stakeholder perspectives. It further involves systematically examining actions, decisions, or processes from the persona of the individual or role assignment to understand their underlying mechanisms, impacts, and effectiveness. Identifying the relevant actors, user stories and their goals. It is a methodology that combines observation, evaluation, and reflection to develop strategies or plans for improvement. Analyzing the factors that limit or enable specific actions within a context. By analyzing specific actions in context, this method provides insights into their outcomes and helps design targeted, evidence-based interventions or strategies.

Action Research: *Action theory emphasizes the importance of understanding people's motives, goals, and desires when analyzing their behavior. It is a sociological approach that examines human actions by considering the subjective motivations, goals, and intentions behind them, essentially looking at how people actively interpret and respond to their environment when making decisions, rather than just observing behaviors as objective occurrences; it emphasizes the importance of understanding the "why" behind people's actions, not just the "what." At this juncture, defining a questionnaire is only the beginning, it is the follow-up questions that make the participant think and elaborate on the response. Ask "what makes you say that" when given absolute answers like it "won't work".*

Once the data is gathered, it is analyzed through the lens of **action theory**, which looks at the intentions behind actions, how those actions align with the goals of the overall SaaS system, and any obstacles that prevent effective action. In this context, actions might include system inputs (e.g., entering data), system outputs (e.g., generating reports), and intermediate steps (e.g., reviewing data or cross-checking with other departments). The analysis will uncover how well the system supports or hinders the users' ability to achieve their goals and areas where their goals may be in competition or conflict with the objectives of the organization, other departments or individuals.

APPLYING CONTENT ANALYSIS TO MASTER DATA MANAGEMENT (MDM)

We can apply content analysis to Master Data Management (MDM) as it is critical in ensuring the consistency, accuracy, and reliability of key organizational data, particularly customer and supplier site master data. Using the **content analysis method**, organizations can systematically examine and refine their MDM processes by identifying patterns, themes, and discrepancies in the data across various systems. Content analysis offers a structured approach to understanding the qualitative and quantitative aspects of master data, enabling actionable improvements in content quality and management practices.

Content Analysis*: The* **content analysis method** *is a systematic approach to analyzing text, images, or media to identify patterns, themes, or meanings within the data. It involves coding and categorizing the content to interpret underlying messages or trends, often combining qualitative and quantitative techniques. This methodology is used to develop strategies or plans by uncovering insights from communication materials, enabling evidence-based decision-making.*

Step 1: Data Collection and Preparation

To apply content analysis, the first step involves gathering master data from multiple sources, such as CRM systems, ERP modules, and supplier portals. For customer master data, this may include customer 360 records like company names, addresses, tax identification numbers, and communication preferences. For suppliers, key data points include vendor codes, payment terms, shipping locations, and certifications. Text fields, descriptions, and structured metadata serve as the primary dataset for content analysis.

Step 2: Categorization and Coding

The next step is to develop a coding framework to categorize the data, generally beginning with the target system requirements and data structure. This involves identifying recurring elements such as inconsistencies in naming conventions, missing or incomplete data fields, and discrepancies in site locations or payment terms. For instance, customer data might be coded for patterns in address formats (e.g., "Street" vs. "St.") or differences in tax identification numbers across regional systems. Supplier data could be analyzed for variations in payment terms, such as "Net 30" vs. "30 Days Due," and mismatches in site address details on purchase orders and invoices.

Step 3: Quantifying and Analyzing Themes

Always, always, always, ask for and use a metric identify the number occurrences before assigning time and resources to any problem, otherwise too often you will find the team wasting time and money focusing on exception and immaterial challenges. Using the coding framework, organizations can systematically quantify occurrences of specific categories, such as the frequency of missing email addresses in customer records or incorrect shipping addresses for suppliers. Themes might emerge around common errors, such as outdated contact information for customers or incorrect tax codes for suppliers. This quantification helps pinpoint systemic issues in how master data is collected, validated, or updated.

Step 4: Interpretation and Insights

Through interpretation, the organization can uncover insights into the underlying causes of data issues. For example, frequent mismatches in supplier shipping addresses may indicate a lack of synchronization between the procurement system and the MDM platform. Similarly, inconsistencies in customer naming conventions may highlight the absence of standardized data entry guidelines. Content analysis helps map these issues to their potential impacts, such as delayed shipments, compliance risks, or inaccurate reporting. This alone will improve your return on investment and can be quantified to management for justification of the changes.

Step 5: Actionable Improvements

The results of the content analysis guide actionable improvements in both content management and MDM practices. For customer master data, this might involve implementing validation rules for tax identification numbers or introducing mandatory fields for critical contact details. For supplier master data, the organization could establish workflows for verifying and updating site locations during the onboarding process. Additionally, the insights may drive the adoption of MDM tools with automated data cleansing and enrichment capabilities to minimize manual errors.

THE ETHNOGRAPHIC MODEL

Ethnography: *The ethnographic model is a qualitative research approach where the investigator immerses themselves in the cultural and social environments of a group to*

*understand behaviors, interactions, and experiences from
the perspective of that community. A "day in the life" walk-
through of the warehouse, docks or shop floors. This involves
detailed observation of daily practices, language, rituals,
and the unspoken nuances that influence how individuals
interact within their environment, receipts, work orders,
communications. The goal is to produce a narrative that
captures the cultural essence of the group while relating it
to broader operational frameworks. The* **ethnography
method** *focused on studying people in their natural
environments. The strategy is to develop a deep, nuanced
understanding of the studied group, enabling actions or
plans that are culturally informed and contextually relevant.*

THE ETHNOGRAPHIC CASE STUDY

Imagine a scenario where a company develops a platform for internal
team collaboration, like a messaging app with integrated project
management features. The aim of the ethnographic study would be
to understand how teams communicate within their work culture
and social context, going beyond surface-level feedback to uncover
deeper behavioral and cultural insights. Investigators would begin by
immersing themselves within the company environment, observing
how employees naturally interact with each other through existing
communication tools. This includes noting both formal communications (team meetings, project updates) and informal interactions
(casual chats, social discussions). Observations would focus on how
people use language, symbols (emojis, jargon), rituals (daily stand-
ups, reporting routines), and shared meanings (inside jokes, team
rituals) that define their communication practices.[54]

Through immersive observation, the observer would explore not just what is communicated, but how and why certain modes of communication are preferred. For instance, employees may use emojis and GIFs to add emotional context, signaling a shared culture that values informality and humor. Alternatively, hierarchical language may reveal cultural norms around authority and respect. The observer would note what is not said as much as what is vocalized, such as moments of silence in meetings indicating cultural discomfort or non-verbal cues signaling approval or disagreement.

For example, if you are building a interactive application for enabling better communication, the right assessment questions could be:

1. Why aren't you choosing off-the-shelf software for communication?
2. What software applications are you using currently?
3. What challenges do you face when interacting with the existing UI communication-based product?
4. How would you rate the user experience for the existing solution?
5. What improvements or enhancements do you suggest to the existing software?

Ethnography helps identify gaps in the current SaaS communication experience. For example, employees might circumvent the official SaaS platform using informal channels like WhatsApp for urgent messages, indicating a cultural need for more real-time, seamless communication that the existing tool does not provide. Alternatively, they may express frustration with rigid workflows that do not align with their team's dynamic, culturally fluid working style.

The objective is to identify the problem you are trying to solve and for whom, formulate what questions you want answers for, finalize a location, and determine the appropriate research type. You may begin with passive observation, but to immerse yourself in their regular activities, get involved, join a group and interact with them during the analysis through informal contextual intermingling.

SINGULARITY

Phenomenology: *The phenomenology method is a qualitative approach that explores and interprets individuals' lived experiences to uncover the essence and meaning of a particular phenomenon. This methodology involves in-depth interviews, reflective analysis, and thematic exploration to understand how people perceive and make sense of their experiences. The strategy focuses on gaining insight into subjective realities, guiding actions or plans that resonate deeply with human experiences and perspectives.*

PHENOMENOLOGY EXAMPLE IN PRACTICE

Imagine a SaaS company offering a team collaboration and communication workflow. The workshop reveals that users perceive the product as overly formal and disconnected from their dynamic, creative workflows. Through **free imaginative variation**, the team explores alternative approaches, such as adopting direct messaging and an immediate notifications alert. **Bracketing** helps facilitators set aside assumptions about the brand's professionalism to truly listen to user preferences. Change champions, like an engaged product manager and a trusted power user, advocate for these shifts, while a phased **change management approach** ensures a smooth transition, fostering both internal and external acceptance.

Step 1: Bracketing Personal Biases

Before beginning the workshop, facilitators engage in bracketing, a process of setting aside preconceived notions or biases about the SaaS brand. This ensures that the focus remains on participants' authentic experiences rather than assumptions or external influences. For example, if the internal team believes the brand is perceived as saddling, or even innovative, bracketing allows the facilitators to approach the workshop without projecting this belief onto participants, enabling a fresh and unbiased exploration of their perspectives.

Step 2: Gather Detailed Lived Experiences

During the workshop, facilitators would use interviews, open discussions, and interactive activities to gather rich, detailed accounts of users' experiences with the brand. For example, participants might be asked to describe how they feel about the product's founder, or when they encounter its logo, landing page, or user interface. They could share their thoughts on whether the branding conveys trust, innovation, or accessibility. Facilitators might also observe non-verbal cues and note commonalities in language, such as repeated words like "confusing," "reliable," or "modern," which reflect users' lived experiences with the brand.

Step 3: Free Imaginative Variation

Free imaginative variation is employed during the analysis phase to explore how the essence of the brand might change under different circumstances. This involves asking hypothetical questions to uncover the non-negotiable elements of the brand's identity. For example:

1. How would user perceptions change if the brand adopted a more casual mobile tone?
2. What if the product branding emphasized sustainability over innovation?
3. What core elements must remain to preserve the product identity (e.g., trustworthiness, simplicity)?

By varying different aspects of the product in these thought experiments, the team can distinguish the essential components of the user experience from those that are incidental or flexible.

Step 4: Identifying Change Management Champions

Change management champions are selected from key stakeholders, both internally and externally, to support and advocate for the implementation transformation. Internal champions might include marketing team leaders, UX designers, and executives who understand the brand's strategic goals. External champions could include trusted customers or user community members who have a strong connection to the brand and can provide authentic feedback during the change process. These champions ensure alignment, build trust, and help communicate the need for change effectively across teams and user groups.

Step 5: Developing and Applying the Change Management Approach

A structured change management approach ensures the transition to the new branding aligns with organizational goals and is accepted by users. This approach includes:

1. Assessing Readiness: Evaluate the current perception of the SaaS brand and organizational capacity for change using workshop findings.
2. Creating a Shared Vision: Collaborate with stakeholders and champions to define the objectives and desired outcomes of the branding changes, ensuring alignment with user needs identified during the workshop.
3. Engaging Stakeholders: Proactively involve employees, users, and champions in the change process through regular updates, feedback loops, and co-creation opportunities.
4. Executing Iterative Improvements: Implement branding changes in phases, such as updating messaging tone, redesigning visuals, or improving touchpoints like onboarding. Regularly measure the impact of these changes and refine based on user feedback.
5. Communicating Benefits: Use champions to communicate how the new branding reflects user needs and adds value, addressing any resistance with transparency and empathy.

Step 6: Measuring and Sustaining Change

After implementing branding updates, the organization monitors their impact through user surveys, focus groups, and performance metrics such as customer retention or engagement rates. Champions play a key role in sustaining momentum by ensuring that internal teams continue to align with the brand's revised identity and values.

USE OF LINGUISTICS

Discourse Analysis: *Discourse analysis is a qualitative research method that examines how language is used in communication to construct meaning, power dynamics, and social realities. This methodology involves analyzing texts, conversations, or media to uncover underlying structures, themes, and contexts influencing discourse. The strategy is to interpret how language shapes perceptions and interactions, enabling the development of informed actions or plans that address societal or organizational narratives effectively.*

NETWORK ANALYSIS IN CONTEXT

The objective of the network analysis is to depict the internal plumbing of the project, and early skeleton. An early skeleton guides both the technical work and the organization of people to carry out the technical work. It is not intended to communicate the logic context to the development team and not a lock in design. One might utilize technical block diagram conceptual models. Technical architectures utilize some combination of platform, component, interface, and module architectures. For example, a network topology map showing integration points for source and target systems with the named responsible parties, transmission methods, formats, tools and frequency.

Network Analysis: *Network analysis is a methodological approach that examines relationships and interactions within a network of individuals, organizations, or systems* *to uncover patterns, structures, and influences. It uses tools like mapping and statistical measures to analyze connections and the flow of information or resources. The strategy focuses on leveraging these insights to optimize networks, improve collaboration, or address inefficiencies for effective decision-making and planning.*

Another example of a network analysis involving supply chain procurement, distribution, shipping, and inventory management could be a company that sources raw materials from multiple suppliers, distributes them to manufacturing plants, and ships the finished products to retailers. The process flow includes initial procurement requestor and buyer of raw materials, inventory management and shop floor managers needed to track stock levels and distributed to production facilities, picking, packing and shipping of finished goods to various retail locations. The output of this system could be a **network process flow diagram** that visualizes the interconnected stages, showing the people and processes patterns of procurement, inventory updates, production, and distribution channels, with arrows indicating the flow of goods and information between each step.

HEURISTICS ANALYSIS

Heuristics are cognitive strategies that allow people to make quick, efficient judgments by focusing on the most relevant information while ignoring less critical details. They are practical approaches to problem-solving, though they may not always yield perfect or optimal solutions.

Heuristic Analysis: *Heuristic analysis is a problem-solving methodology that relies on practical, experience-based techniques or "rules of thumb" to evaluate systems, processes, or designs, particularly in usability studies. It involves experts systematically identifying issues by comparing the subject against predefined heuristics or modern best practices. The strategy is to uncover and address flaws efficiently, guiding improvements or action plans that enhance functionality and user experience.*

THE TEN USABILITY HEURISTICS

Jakob Nielsen's ten usability heuristics, developed with Rolf Molich in 1990 and refined in 1994, provide a framework for evaluating user interface design to ensure systems are intuitive, efficient, and user-friendly.[55] These principles are widely used in usability testing and human-computer interaction to identify potential issues and enhance user experience. Below is a concise explanation of each heuristic:[56]

1. **Visibility of System Status**: Keep users informed about what is happening through timely and clear feedback (e.g., progress indicators or status updates).

2. **Match Between System and the Real World**: Use language, concepts, and workflows familiar to users, aligning the system with real-world conventions (e.g., using a trash can icon for deletion).

3. **User Control and Freedom**: Provide options for users to undo or redo actions and easily exit unintended states (e.g., a clear "cancel" button).

4. **Consistency and Standards**: Maintain consistent design elements and follow platform conventions to avoid confusion (e.g., uniform button styles across the interface).

5. **Error Prevention**: Design interfaces to minimize errors by guiding users and eliminating error-prone conditions (e.g., form validation before submission).

6. **Recognition Rather Than Recall**: Make information and options visible or easily accessible, reducing the need for users to rely on memory (e.g., clear menu labels instead of cryptic icons).

7. **Flexibility and Efficiency of Use**: Cater to both novice and expert users with customizable or streamlined interactions (e.g., keyboard shortcuts for advanced users).

8. **Aesthetic and Minimalist Design**: Present only relevant information, avoiding clutter to keep the interface clean and focused (e.g., removing unnecessary graphics).

9. **Help Users Recognize, Diagnose, and Recover from Errors**: Offer clear error messages with actionable solutions (e.g., "File not found. Check the file name and try again.").

10. **Help and Documentation**: Provide accessible, concise, and task-focused help resources for users who need guidance (e.g., tooltips or a searchable help section).

HOW TO USE HEURISTICS IN THE CONTEXT OF A SAAS EVALUATION

During a user demo for a Warehouse Management System (WMS), these heuristics were systematically applied to evaluate various interfaces and processes, such as receiving, scanning with handheld tools, notifications, and picking with auto-selection of locations. Each heuristic informed the client of a different aspect of usability in these tasks.

For Visibility of System Status, when a user scans a package with a handheld tool, the system should immediately confirm the scan's success or highlight issues, such as a barcode error. Real-time feedback through visual indicators, sounds, or notifications ensures the user understands the system's current state and can proceed confidently.

Using Match Between System and the Real World, the WMS should employ terminology familiar to warehouse staff. For instance, instead of technical jargon, terms like "received," "in transit," or "picked" resonate with the operational language of warehouse workflows. This alignment reduces cognitive load and eases task comprehension.

User Control and Freedom is critical during tasks like auto-selection of picking locations. If a user disagrees with the suggested location, the interface should allow easy overrides, such as manually selecting a preferred location without restarting the task.

Applying Consistency and Standards, all interfaces across the WMS should follow the same visual and functional design patterns. For example, the placement of buttons like "Submit" or "Cancel" should be consistent, and scanning tools should behave uniformly across different workflows.

Error Prevention could involve proactive design, such as graying out unavailable locations in the auto-picking process or validating receipt data before final submission. This reduces the likelihood of mistakes, such as selecting an incorrect inventory bin.

To support Recognition Rather than Recall, the WMS should display relevant options and recent actions directly on the interface. For example, during the picking process, users should see a list of remaining items rather than relying on memory.

Flexibility and Efficiency of Use benefits experienced users by offering shortcuts. For instance, expert warehouse staff could use handheld tools with programmable quick actions to execute common tasks like confirming receipts or marking items as picked, speeding up their workflow.

An Aesthetic and Minimalist Design ensures that the interfaces are not cluttered with irrelevant information. Notifications should display only critical details, like shipment delays, without over-whelming users with excessive data.

In situations where users encounter issues, Help and Documen-tation can provide step-by-step guidance on performing tasks like troubleshooting a handheld scanner or adjusting auto-selection settings.

Finally, Recognition, Diagnosis, and Recovery from Errors could involve clear, actionable error messages, such as "Invalid barcode scanned. Please retry or check the label." These messages should avoid cryptic codes and guide users toward resolution.

By methodically applying Nielsen's heuristics during SaaS evalua-tion of the WMS, the user demo process can be optimized to enhance usability, reduce errors, and ensure a seamless experience for ware-house staff. This structured approach ensures that the application aligns with both technical expectations and user needs, fostering successful adoption and efficiency.

ORAL HISTORY

Oral History*: Oral analysis is a qualitative methodology that examines spoken communication, such as interviews, speeches, or conversations, to understand meanings, themes, or patterns in verbal expression. It involves collecting and interpreting oral data in its cultural, social, or contextual setting to gain insights into the speaker's perspective. The strategy is to use these findings to inform actions or plans that align with the observed communication dynamics and underlying narratives. One output could be a definitions glossary added to the end of a status report to dissolve any miscommunication and acronyms.*

NARRATIVE INQUIRY

Narrative Inquiry: *Narrative inquiry is a research methodology that focuses on collecting and analyzing stories or personal narratives to understand how individuals make sense of their experiences. The strategy involves deep engagement with the narratives, interpreting them in their social and cultural contexts to reveal themes and patterns. This approach helps develop action plans or strategies that reflect the complexities of lived experiences, and the meaning individuals attach to them.*

META ANALYSIS

Meta-analysis serves as a powerful tool for synthesizing findings from multiple studies to uncover broader patterns and more reliable conclusions. It involves a systematic process of reviewing relevant research, extracting key data, and using statistical methods to combine results, offering a clearer and more precise understanding of trends, relationships, or outcomes across diverse contexts.

Meta Analysis: *Meta-analysis is a quantitative research methodology that aggregates the results of multiple independent studies on a particular research question to draw more generalized conclusions. This method involves systematically reviewing relevant studies, extracting data, and applying statistical techniques to combine the results, thus providing a more precise estimate of effect sizes, relationships, or outcomes across different contexts. Meta-analysis is particularly valuable when studies on a topic yield varying or inconsistent results, as it helps identify broader trends and provide a clearer picture.*

META ANALYSIS: CONSTRUCT A FEATURE BREAKDOWN STRUCTURE (FBS)

A meta-analysis approach offers a powerful method to synthesize diverse data sources, ensuring a comprehensive and nuanced perspective on project needs. By leveraging this approach to construct a Feature Breakdown Structure (FBS), you can systematically dissect and prioritize features, transforming abstract goals into actionable components.. This involves blending and applying key insights from several groups to formulate a structured and holistic product architecture. The FBS serves as a bridge between the envision and speculate phases, effectively delineating features to communicate between customers and development teams while enabling a seamless transition from concept to execution. In the CRM example, the system integrates sales management, marketing functions, lead generation, advertisement tracking, call services, and territory management. Applying this use case as a blueprint allows for the systematic construction of an FBS that is adaptable to both hardware and software contexts.

Building an FBS

At the highest level, the FBS should mirror the overarching purpose of the CRM: to enhance customer relationship management and streamline operational workflows. This is achieved by breaking down the architecture into discrete, interrelated features:

1. **Sales Management**
    *   Lead Management: Systems for capturing, tracking, and nurturing leads.
    *   Pipeline Tracking: Tools for visualizing sales stages and progress.
    *   Forecasting: Analytics to predict revenue and identify opportunities.
2. **Marketing Integration**
    *   Campaign Management: Planning, execution, and analysis of marketing campaigns.

- Advertisement Tracking: Monitoring ad performance across platforms.
- Content Delivery: Personalized content creation and distribution tools.

3. **Customer Support**
   - Call Service: Integration of telephony systems for customer interaction.
   - Knowledge Base: Self-service resources and automated FAQs.
   - Ticketing System: Mechanisms for logging and resolving support requests.

4. **Territory Management**
   - Geographic Segmentation: Division of sales territories by region.
   - Resource Allocation: Assigning personnel and tools to maximize coverage.
   - Performance Analysis: Metrics to evaluate territory effectiveness.

5. **Platform Integration**
   - APIs and Extensibility: Tools for integrating third-party applications.
   - User Management: Role-based access control and permissions.
   - Custom Reporting: Dashboards tailored to user needs.

Meta-Analysis Findings

The CRM use case highlights several critical interactions between technical architecture, project organization, and planning. A key finding is the importance of cross-functional feature teams, comprising experts in software development, data analytics, and customer support working collaboratively to ensure feature alignment. This multi-disciplinary approach enhances adaptability and responsiveness to customer needs. Additionally, the division of features into manageable components enables incremental development and testing, aligning with Agile methodologies.

Guiding Principles

Guiding principles are integral to steering the FBS's development and ensuring alignment with customer preferences. These principles are conceptual and evolve alongside the project:

1. Customer-Centric Design: Features should prioritize end-user value and seamless interaction.
2. Scalability and Flexibility: The architecture must accommodate growth and adapt to changes.
3. Integration First: Emphasis on interoperability with existing systems and third-party tools.
4. Data-Driven Decisions: Features should leverage analytics to inform strategies and improvements.
5. Agility in Development: Rapid iteration and responsiveness to feedback are critical.

EXPERIMENTAL RESEARCH METHODOLOGY

Experimental Research: *The experimental research method involves manipulating one or more independent variables to observe their effect on dependent variables, typically through controlled conditions like a development* *or test environment, a field experiment. The strategy is to establish causal relationships by isolating variables and testing hypotheses with a high degree of control to minimize bias. This approach leads to action plans or strategies based on reliable cause-and-effect conclusions, such as improving product designs or implementing interventions that drive specific outcomes. This method is generally reserved for testing suggested approaches and solutions to pain points derived from the information gathering process.*

DO THE RESEARCH

Experimental research, in information gathering, focuses on systematically observing and analyzing user interactions, workflows, and system behaviors to collect data that informs future decisions. This study emphasizes understanding the process without delving into solution-building or speculation, ensuring that the data collected is unbiased and feasible. By conducting controlled experiments, such as A/B testing, usage pattern analysis, or small-scale user trials, researchers gain insights into customer needs, pain points, and the dynamics of the ecosystem. This disciplined approach establishes a foundation for informed decisions in subsequent phases, while clearly maintaining a distinction between observation and design.

Experimental research are prone to human error. Human errors in experimental research arise from a combination of cognitive, environmental, and procedural factors that compromise accuracy and reliability. Cognitive limitations, such as lapses in attention, memory failures, or cognitive overload, often lead to mistakes, especially under stress or fatigue, with error rates in complex tasks potentially reaching 20-30%.[57] Bias and subjectivity, like confirmation bias, can distort data interpretation or recording when researchers unconsciously favor expected outcomes, a problem well-documented in clinical trials without strict blinding.[58] Procedural complexity further increases error risks, as intricate protocols or unfamiliar equipment, such as miscalibrated tools, can result in missteps. Environmental distractions, poor training, and inadequate communication within research teams also contribute, amplifying the likelihood of oversights or miscalculations. These factors highlight the need for robust controls, clear protocols, and strategies like automation or double-checking to minimize human error in research settings.

COMMON CAUSES FOR HUMAN ERRORS

1. **People are by nature poor observers:**
    Human perception is inherently limited and often influenced by external factors such as distractions, emotions, or biases. For example, we might overlook details or fail to accurately interpret what we see, hear, or experience because our brains prioritize certain stimuli over others. This limitation can lead to misinterpretations or incomplete assessments of situations.

2. **People tend to overgeneralize from small samples of evidence or opinion:**
    Humans often draw broad conclusions from limited data, leading to inaccurate beliefs or decisions. For instance, encountering one rude individual from a particular group might lead someone to stereotype the entire group, despite the lack of substantial evidence. This tendency can skew judgment and perpetuate errors in thinking.

3. **We tend to notice those things that support our beliefs and ignore evidence that does not:**
Known as confirmation bias, this tendency causes people to focus on information that aligns with their preexisting beliefs while disregarding conflicting evidence. For example, someone who believes in a particular diet's efficacy might only pay attention to success stories while ignoring scientific studies that debunk its effectiveness.

4. **We sometimes make up information to support our beliefs, no matter how illogical it might appear to another person:**
When faced with a lack of evidence, people may fabricate justifications to defend their viewpoints. This cognitive defense mechanism often stems from the need to maintain consistency in beliefs and avoid admitting errors. For example, conspiracy theories frequently rely on unfounded or invented claims to support their narratives.

5. **Our ego is often involved in what we "know" and profess to be true:**
Pride and self-identity can influence how strongly people hold onto their beliefs, even in the face of contrary evidence. Admitting to being wrong may feel like a personal failure, leading individuals to double down on their positions rather than reconsider them. This resistance can perpetuate misunderstandings and errors.

6. **In the extreme case that we call "prejudice," we may simply close our minds to any new evidence about an issue:**

Prejudice involves forming rigid opinions or biases that exclude the possibility of reevaluation. This mental closure can prevent individuals from considering alternative perspectives or learning new information, further entrenching false or harmful assumptions.

7. **People are prone to mystify anything they don't understand:**

   When confronted with complex or inexplicable phenomena, humans often attribute them to mysterious or supernatural causes rather than seeking logical explanations. This inclination can lead to misunderstandings or the perpetuation of myths, as people prefer simplicity over the effort required to analyze and comprehend intricate issues.

CHAPTER 8

Scheduling: The Ticking Clock and Racing Feet

"This is the beginning of a new day. God has given me this day to use as I will. I can waste it or use it for good. What I do today is very important because I am exchanging a day of my life for it. When tomorrow comes, this day will be gone forever, leaving something in its place I have traded for it. I want it to be gain, not loss — good, not evil. Success, not failure in order that I shall not forget the price I paid for it."

— Paul "Bear" Bryant

THE PRIMARY OBJECTIVE of scheduling in project management is to orchestrate the effective use of time, ensuring that a project progresses smoothly from inception to completion within defined constraints. When I approach scheduling, my first instinct isn't to dive into sophisticated Gantt charts or modern project management software like Microsoft Project or Primavera. Instead, I reach for a simpler, more intuitive starting point: a traditional calendar and Visio timeline diagrams. While Gantt charts, pioneered by Henry Gantt in the early 20th century offer a visual breakdown of tasks over time, and software tools provide automation and scalability, I find these less effective for initial planning than the tangible clarity of a calendar and the flexibility of Visio's flowcharting capabilities. This preference stems from a belief that foundational scheduling should prioritize human intuition and experience over algorithmic complexity, at least in the early stages.

Scheduling is deeply intertwined with the classic triple constraints of project management: scope, schedule, and cost. These elements, first formalized in traditional methodologies like those underpinning the Project Management Body of Knowledge (PMBOK), are interdependent.[59] Scope defines what must be delivered, cost dictates the financial resources available, and the schedule ties these together by determining when deliverables will materialize. To create a schedule that balances these constraints, I treat scope and resources as critical inputs. The scope outlines the project's deliverables, its breadth and depth, while resources, including team expertise and availability, inform how long tasks will take and at what expense. Together, they shape a timeline that not only meets the project's objectives but also respects the budget, ultimately delivering value to the customer.

My scheduling process begins with a blank calendar and a Visio timeline, tools that allow me to visualize time in a straightforward, adaptable way. Drawing from experience, honed over years of managing diverse projects, I craft three distinct scenarios: a best-case scenario, a probable scenario, and a worst-case (or possible) scenario. Each scenario reflects different assumptions about risks, resource availability, and task complexity, providing a spectrum of possibilities to anticipate challenges and opportunities. Typically, I work backward from a targeted Go-Live date, a technique inspired by critical path methods but executed manually for greater control. For instance, if a software implementation must launch by December 31, I mark this endpoint on the calendar and reverse-engineer the timeline. Key milestones like requirements approval, prototype completion, or testing phases are plotted up to the present, creating a skeletal framework that captures the project's rhythm.

A milestone represents a significant project event or achievement that acts as a key progress indicator, much like a landmark on a road trip. Milestones help project teams monitor deadlines and assess performance by breaking the project into measurable checkpoints. By celebrating these moments, such as completing the system design or launching a prototype, the team stays motivated and aligned, ensuring the project remains on track within the framework.

Milestone: *A significant project event or achievement that serves as a key progress indicator. Milestones help project teams monitor deadlines and assess project performance.*

Next, I anchor the schedule in the project's scope, which I prioritize over cost because it directly drives customer value, an ethos echoing Fayol's principle of Subordination of Individual Interests to General Interest.[60] The scope, often detailed in a Statement of Work or contract (e.g., Review Contract, Scope, Workplan and Budget), dictates what must be achieved, such as delivering a fully functional application with specific features. To estimate activity durations, I collaborate with specialized resources, subject matter experts like developers, engineers, or analysts who bring practical insight. Together, we categorize tasks into three complexity tiers: complex (e.g., integrating legacy systems, 8-12 weeks), medium (e.g., configuring standard modules, 10–15 days), and low (e.g., data entry, 3–5 days). This classification not only refines the timeline but also informs resource allocation and preliminary costing.

At this stage, costing remains high-level. I estimate the number of resources needed per task tier, say, three developers for a complex task versus one for a low-complexity one and approximate effort in days, not yet tying it to named individuals or precise hourly rates. For example, a complex task requiring 25 days might need 75 person-days total (3 resources × 25 days), while a low task might need 5 person-days (1 resource × 5 days). This approach, akin to Kerzner's PMMM Level 2 (Common Processes),[61] establishes a baseline without locking into specifics too early, preserving flexibility as the project evolves. Later, these estimates feed into a detailed budget, but initially, they serve to validate that the schedule can deliver the scope economically.

This method adds value by grounding the schedule in reality, experience tempers optimism, scope ensures relevance, and tiered estimates balance precision with pragmatism. Unlike Gantt charts, which can overwhelm with detail, or software that risks over-automation, my calendar-and-Visio approach keeps the focus on strategic milestones and team readiness. For instance, a best-case scenario might assume full resource availability and no delays, finishing by November 30, the probable scenario might buffer for minor setbacks, hitting December 15; and the worst-case might account for supply chain issues, pushing to January 15, the subsequent year. Presenting these to stakeholders encourages informed decision-making, perhaps accelerating with extra resources or trimming scope to meet the deadline.

Scheduling is both an art and a science, blending intuition with structure to manage time effectively. By starting with a calendar and Visio, leveraging scope as the north star, and building scenarios with expert input, I craft a timeline that delivers value within constraints. This traditional yet adaptable approach ensures the project not only starts strong but sustains momentum toward a successful Go-Live, proving that sometimes, simplicity outperforms sophistication in laying the groundwork for success.

THE NEXT STEP: SEQUENCING ACTIVITIES

Crafting a timeline that delivers value within constraints requires a clear understanding of scheduling, but the process truly comes to life through the deliberate sequencing of tasks. By shifting focus from merely plotting dates to identifying critical activities and arranging them in a logical, efficient order, we ensure that each step builds on the previous one, maximizing productivity and minimizing bottlenecks. This transition from scheduling to sequencing tasks transforms a static timeline into a dynamic workflow, where the careful identification and prioritization of activities drive the project toward its goals with precision and clarity.

Activity: *A fundamental unit of work within a project, typically defined in the Work Breakdown Structure (WBS). Each activity is associated with specific duration estimates, costs, and required resources. Activities collectively contribute to the completion of project deliverables and must be carefully planned to align with the overall project objectives. Effective management of activities ensures timely completion and efficient resource allocation.*

Dummy Activities: *Placeholder activities with no duration or resource requirements, used in project scheduling to establish logical relationships between tasks. They help clarify dependencies in network diagrams without affecting the actual project timeline or workload.*

Sequencing: *Sequencing, in the context of scheduling, refers to the specific order in which tasks, activities, or operations are arranged and executed. Effective sequencing minimizes idle time, reduces bottlenecks, and enhances workflow efficiency.*

LET ME SHOW YOU

In project management and scheduling, sequencing tasks are often visualized using tools like an arrow-on-arrow diagram, which maps out the logical relationships between activities. These diagrams map out the logical relationships between activities, clearly illustrating how one task leads to another.

Activity-on-Arrow (AOA) / Arrow Diagramming Method (ADM) — *A project scheduling technique in which activities are represented by arrows, and nodes illustrate the logical relationships between them. This method is particularly useful in visualizing task sequences and identifying critical dependencies. It helps project managers analyze workflow efficiency and pinpoint areas where potential bottlenecks may occur.*

Follow these four steps and the accompanying guidance to confidently construct your arrow-on-arrow diagram.

AOA Step 1: Define Project Activities

Activity List — *A structured document outlining all tasks required for project completion. It ensures that every aspect of the project is accounted for, reducing the risk of overlooked work elements. The activity list provides a foundation for creating schedules and allocating resources, supporting transparency and accountability among project stakeholders.*

Activity Attributes: *Detailed characteristics associated with each activity, such as dependencies (predecessors and successors), constraints, required resources, scheduling relationships, and key assumptions. These attributes play a crucial role in sequencing tasks and ensuring that logical relationships are maintained throughout the project lifecycle. By defining activity attributes, project managers can accurately estimate timeframes, mitigate risks, and optimize workflows.*

Here's an example breakdown of key activities for a Software Development Project:

ID	Activity	Description	Predecessors
A	Requirements Gathering	Collect software requirements	None
B	System Design	Design system architecture	A
C	Database Setup	Create and configure database	B
D	Backend Development	Develop backend APIs and logic	B
E	Frontend Development	Develop UI and frontend logic	D
F	Integration Testing	Test system integration	C, D, E
G	User Testing	Conduct user acceptance testing	F
H	Deployment	Deploy software to production	G

AOA Step 2: Construct the AOA Diagram

1. Nodes (Circles) represent milestones (events).
2. Arrows represent activities and their dependencies.

DEPENDENCIES: CONNECTING THE DOTS

Dependencies define the logical sequencing of activities within a project, establishing the relationships between tasks like links in a chain. These relationships influence scheduling constraints, resource assignments, and workflow efficiency, ensuring tasks are executed in the right order.

Dependency: *The logical sequencing of activities within a project, defining the relationships between tasks. Dependencies dictate the order in which tasks must be completed and influence scheduling constraints, resource assignments, and workflow efficiency. Understanding dependencies is crucial for preventing bottlenecks and ensuring smooth project execution.*

Mandatory Dependencies: *Dependencies that are inherent to the nature of the project work, meaning certain tasks must be completed in a specific order due to technical or legal constraints.*

Internal Dependencies: *Task relationships that exist within the project scope and are controlled by the project team. Managing internal dependencies is crucial for maintaining workflow efficiency and ensuring coordinated task execution.*

External Dependencies: *Task relationships that involve external factors or entities outside the immediate project team. These dependencies may involve regulatory approvals, third-party vendors, or market conditions, requiring careful coordination to prevent schedule disruptions.*

Discretionary Dependencies: *Dependencies that are based on project team decisions, best practices, or workflow preferences rather than mandatory technical requirements. While these dependencies provide flexibility in project scheduling, they should be established carefully to avoid unnecessary constraints that may limit future scheduling options.*

Another such relationship is the Finish-to-Finish Dependency, where the completion of one activity is directly tied to the completion of another. Imagine two tasks, such as writing a software module and testing it. The testing phase can only finish once the coding is fully complete, even if testing begins earlier. In an arrow-on-arrow diagram, this dependency would be depicted with arrows indicating that the endpoint of the successor task (testing) hinges on the endpoint of the predecessor task (coding). This type of dependency is crucial for tasks that need to align closely in their final stages, ensuring that parallel efforts culminate together without leaving loose ends.

Finish-to-Finish Dependency: *A logical relationship in which one activity must be completed before another activity can finish. This dependency type is essential for coordinating tasks that must progress together within a project timeline.*

An alternative is the Finish-to-Start Dependency, a more traditional and widely used sequencing method in project timelines. In this case, one activity must be entirely finished before the next can even begin. For example, consider constructing a building: the foundation must be fully laid before the walls can start going up. In an arrow-on-arrow diagram, this is shown with an arrow extending from the end of the predecessor task (foundation) to the start of the successor task (walls), emphasizing a clear handoff point. This dependency is vital for maintaining order in projects where tasks cannot overlap, as it prevents downstream activities from starting prematurely and ensures that each phase builds on a completed prior step. Mastering this relationship is key to avoiding bottlenecks and keeping a project on track.

Finish-to-Start Dependency: *A common scheduling relationship where one activity must be completed before the next one can begin. Understanding this dependency is critical for sequencing tasks effectively and preventing project delays.*

Here's how the Arrow Diagramming Method (ADM) would structure the software project:

- Start Node (1) → Activity A → Milestone Node (2)
- Node (2) → Activity B → Node (3)
- Node (3) → Activity C → Node (4)
- Node (3) → Activity D → Node (5)
- Node (5) → Activity E → Node (6)
- Nodes (4, 5, 6) → Activity F → Node (7)
- Node (7) → Activity G → Node (8)
- Node (8) → Activity H → End Node (9)

AOA Step 3: Draw the Diagram

To visually represent this, here's an ASCII-like structure:

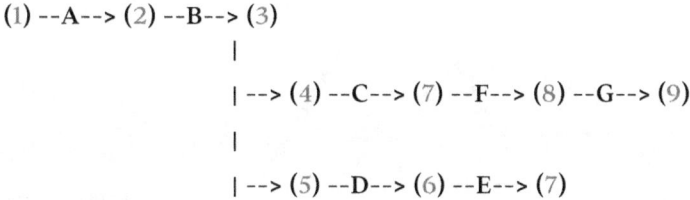

```
(1) --A--> (2) --B--> (3)
                |
                | --> (4) --C--> (7) --F--> (8) --G--> (9)
                |
                | --> (5) --D--> (6) --E--> (7)
```

Step 4: Identify the Critical Path

The Critical Path is the longest sequence of dependent activities, determining the project's minimum duration.

1. Path 1: A → B → C → F → G → H
2. Path 2: A → B → D → E → F → G → H

Whichever is longest is the critical path.

Critical Path: *The longest sequence of dependent activities that determines the minimum project duration. Since the critical path has zero slack, any delay in its activities directly impacts the overall project completion date. Monitoring and managing the critical path is essential for keeping the project on track and avoiding schedule overruns.*

Graphical representation of the Activity-on-Arrow (AOA) diagram

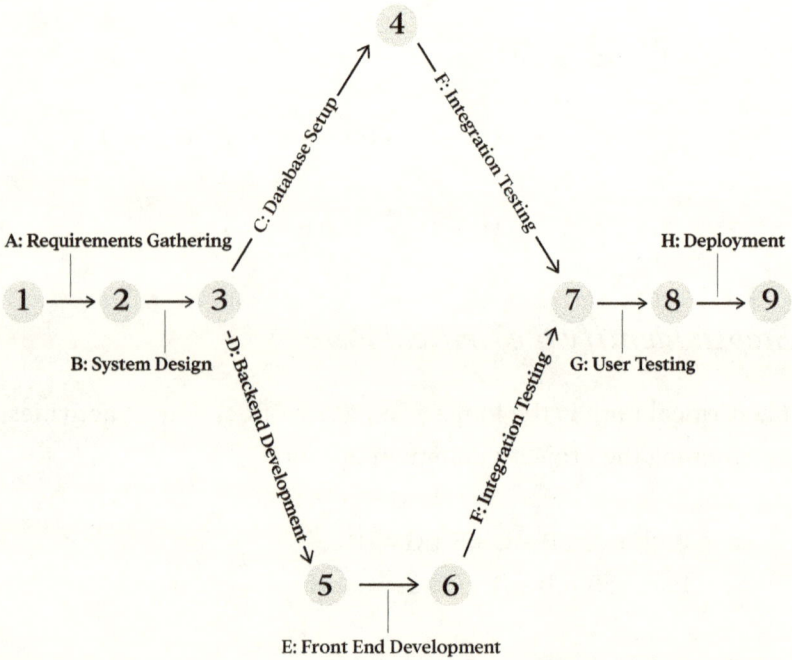

THE CRITICAL PATH AND ELI GOLDRATT

The Critical Path Method, developed in the 1950s, is a cornerstone of project management.[62] It identifies the longest sequence of dependent tasks, known as the critical path, that determines the minimum time required to complete a project. Any delay in these tasks directly impacts the project's completion date.

Critical Path Method (CPM): *A project management technique used to analyze and optimize the project schedule by identifying the longest path of dependent tasks. CPM helps*

in determining task priorities, assessing schedule risks, and
making data-driven decisions to enhance project efficiency.

Eliyahu M. Goldratt, a physicist turned management guru, revolutionized the way businesses approach operational efficiency and project management through his Theory of Constraints (TOC). The Critical Path Method is deeply rooted in Goldratt's broader Theory of Constraints, a methodology that views any system as being limited by a small number of bottlenecks. TOC posits that improving a system requires identifying its weakest link, the constraint, and subordinating all other processes to its optimization. The TOC's five focusing steps are: identify the constraint (e.g., a scarce resource), exploit it (maximize its use), subordinate other activities (align non-critical tasks), elevate the constraint (add capacity if needed), and repeat the process.[63] This systematic approach not only accelerates project completion but also aligns with TOC's core belief that local optimizations (e.g., padded task estimates) often undermine global performance. By embedding TOC into project management, Goldratt bridges the gap between manufacturing efficiency and the unpredictable nature of projects.

USE CASE OF TOC UNDER DURESS

The onset of the COVID-19 pandemic in 2020 placed unprecedented pressure on the Critical Path of supply chain networks. Disruptions influenced by the mandatory lockdowns produced an atmosphere of unknown unknowns for procurement managers and product delivery characterized as the perfect storm. By pinpointing the critical path, the sequence of activities most impacting the delivery schedule, we were able to identify the bottleneck and remodel the process. To accomplish this, first we asked what needed to change, what do we change to, and how do we make a smooth transition while managing according to the goal. The goal, in this case, was to maintain our delivery schedule.

We could not have idealized an environment under better conditions to test the principles of the Theory of Constraints.[64] The modern globalization era challenges the philosophy that there is only one constraint in a contemporary supply chain network. The intimacy between the predecessor and successor activities threatened the adage that a chain is only as strong as its weakest link. Identifying and exploiting the constraints would depend on the integration and elasticity, preventing maximization of the throughput. Bottlenecks in the fulfilment forced organizations to implement a continuous improvement process to balance stock flow in the "**new normal**" environment.

The cyclical semiconductor industry's sudden, unpredictable fluctuations triggered uncontrolled macroscale changes from the normal gluts and shortages. Examine the throughput of a new-age network solutions organization using an arrow-on-arrow diagram, from the moment a customer books an order to the time cash is received from the sale under these conditions.

The semiconductor input shortage caused a radical shifting of the drum, rope, and buffer efficiency model.[65] The lag time to secure commonly found raw materials instantly shifted to the drum and the constraint in the production. The material was no longer upstream from the bottleneck; it was the bottleneck. Waiting for the customer demand signal to begin production caused delays in estimated shipping delivery times. Limited supplier production from the lockdown sparked a ripple effect in downstream capacity and distribution shipping containers. Demand for finished products dried up, resources had stopped production, and the fully integrated global system felt an unprecedented stop in the machine. Suddenly, the pendulum would violently swing back.

An extreme surge in demand quickly followed, causing a V-shaped recovery in the economy. Significant behavioral shifts were evolving in the new normal of essential businesses, changes in work shifts, customer needs, and transport carriers, containers, and truckloads. Think of the global economy as a speeding racecar at 200 miles per hour hitting a brick wall, then asked to immediately maintain a 300-mile-per-hour increase in velocity from zero. Businesses needed to adapt, improve, and perform what-if analysis to survive.

We determined that semiconductors would need to be placed in the front of the line to control the speed of the march. Shaping how we should operate would be the new challenge. How do we procure materials without tying up money in inventory before receiving customer orders? Waiting to receive customer orders would be too late to procure the necessary materials needed for production. Unfortunately, most businesses do not have a mentor to lean on with all the correct answers to guide us in our decisions. Unlike in 1984, information technology systems from 2019 through 2022 could provide us with information to make better decisions, increase, productivity, and meet delivery promise dates.

Demand planning, what-if analysis enabled the business to simulate various scenarios by adjusting key triggers or changes to evaluate their impact on demand forecasts, inventory, and supply chain operations. These triggers included modifying sales data to account for anomalies, simulating demand shifts due to black swan events.[66] External factors like economic conditions, Covid regulation restrictions, as well as transportation disturbances, were also be tested. By using demand planning software to adjust these parameters, the business analyzed potential outcomes, compared scenarios, and made data-driven decisions, ensuring realistic assumptions and cross-functional collaboration for optimal results.

Information provided by these tools merged into a sales and operations planning process that aligns demand, supply, and financial planning. The product supervisor managed the company's master plan and supported executive decision-making on how to exploit the system constraint. Measurements provided by these tools helped identify inventory patterns that, when analyzed, changed behaviors that instituted new policies and procedures. The devil is in the details with these tools because we want to ensure we measure the right things. To be successful in this environment, we needed to challenge the assumption that all inventory was bad because it tied up money. Instead, we thought of it as an investment that we could capitalize on sooner by procuring contracts with Vendors at lower prices in an inflationary market.

Shock waves from the pandemic not only challenged the assumptions of business but challenged some of the principles laid out in the critical chain. The timing of the demand placed on the bottleneck had REVERSED!. To optimize the flow and balance the system as a whole, enterprise contracts with raw material vendors and contract manufacturers pre-assembly needed to be ordered up to 12 months in advance of customer sales orders. Congestion for shipping containers and freight carriers forced businesses to seek alternative methods that increased transportation costs. Even Amazon prime was unable to meet its delivery dates. Logistical scheduling at shipping distribution centers, stop-and-go's, ports, rail stations, airports, and bonded warehouses was obstructed and misaligned. Where is the bottleneck now, Mr. Goldratt?

To find the bottleneck, find the weakest link. Companies found the weakest link and started buying semiconductor chip plant capacity from the source instead of buying the inventory. An excess workforce at these plants was needed to create surplus inventory in contrast to the principles if they could get the silicon. Sales, demand planning and configuring pricing quoting products turned leads into opportunities and quotes that can forecast potential revenue before the actual sales orders come in. Demand forecasts gave the supply planner a buffer to estimate component purchases based on inventory catalog and category taxonomies. Agile businesses that could identify and adapt had high inventory levels yet reduced the time to convert the sale to cash when they could focus on the flow. The principles still applied even when we changed.

THE HUMAN FACTOR (PRELUDE TO RESOURCE MANAGEMENT)

Unlike the critical path method, critical chain scheduling considers the human side of project management. Our need to feel safe is an inherent behavior from birth designed to protect us from danger. The science of how the human mind behaves and functions permeates our every action. When epicureanism influences outcomes without consideration of the consequences, the devotion to personal comfort outweighs the benefits of the whole. Project management must consider the pleasure principal psychology related to people and how it significantly impacts the critical chain.

Critical Chain Scheduling: *A scheduling approach that incorporates resource constraints and project buffers to improve time management and prevent delays. This method prioritizes key activities while accounting for limited resources, ensuring a more realistic and achievable project timeline.*

The critical path method uses network diagrams to estimate project durations. Unfortunately, underlying assumptions in developing task estimates consciously or unconsciously tend to inflate the final estimates. There are hidden safeties built into each node derived from three different mechanisms. First, negative bias stimulated by our experiences pushes our need for safety toward pessimistic estimates. Second, projects with work breakdown structures have distinct task activities with multiple management levels, each estimating and adding safety buffers during each step. Thirdly, fear is a natural primitive human emotion that influences estimators to pad durations and efforts intentionally overstate in anticipation of executive management cuts. Finally, these psychological characteristics and attitudes control project manager scheduling decisions.

Critical chain scheduling goes a step further, introducing the scarcity of human resources and unique buffer strategies to the theory of constraints. Buffer efficiencies captured at each step of the project act as a sarcophagus trapping the value of early finishes in the body while the overall project never reaps the benefits. As a result, early deliveries are nonexistent when embodying safety within the project timeline. Ultimately consuming the buffer becomes a self-fulfilling prophecy as we are prebuilt for survival and success. Parkinson's law teaches us that work expands to fit the allotted time allocated for the task. Sensing that we have more time for a task, we naturally adjust the level of effort to meet the demand. The results are the inverse of our desire; the pressure to deliver on time overshadowed any incentive to complete early.

Network Diagram: *A graphical representation of project activities and their dependencies, used to visualize task relationships and optimize scheduling.*

Burst: *A point in a project network diagram where a single activity leads to multiple successor activities, creating* *parallel paths of execution. This phenomenon highlights the importance of resource planning and coordination, as multiple teams or functions may need to work simultaneously to maintain project efficiency.*

TIME: THE INDEFINITE CONTINUED PROGRESS OF EXISTENCE

Though the brilliance of past moments,
Once so vivid in our plans,
Has slipped beyond our grasp forever,
No force can reclaim the vanished hour.

Yet in the rhythm of each day,
We squander time with careless ease,
Letting precious moments drift away,
Unclaimed by purpose or by seize.

Time is the currency we hold,
Its value known in every choice.
In time, we could achieve so much more,
But wasted, it leaves no lasting voice.

These passages underscore time's irreversible nature and urges a passionate approach to daily living. As project leaders, we stand at the helm of time's flow, steering our teams through the relentless current of deadlines and deliverables. Once lost to distractions or poor prioritization, the "radiance" of a well-executed project plan cannot be restored. But unlike the irrevocable past, we *can* change how we manage the hours ahead. The frittered moments that consume away in indecision or low-value tasks can be reclaimed through disciplined time management. By embracing a Time Management Matrix,[67] we categorize tasks into to focus on what truly matters, ensuring that time, our most unforgiving resource, is spent with intention.

The Time Management Matrix: *Also known as the Eisenhower Matrix or the Urgent-Important Matrix, is a strategic tool used to prioritize tasks based on their urgency and importance, helping individuals and teams focus on what truly matters. Popularized by Stephen Covey in The 7 Habits of Highly Effective People, the matrix categorizes activities into four distinct quadrants:* [68]

- Quadrant I: Urgent and Important — Tasks that require immediate attention and are critical to success (e.g., crises, deadlines, problems).
- Quadrant II: Not Urgent but Important — Strategic activities that contribute to long-term goals, growth, and prevention (e.g., planning, relationship-building, skill development).
- Quadrant III: Urgent but Not Important — Activities that seem pressing but do not contribute meaningfully to goals (e.g., interruptions, some emails or meetings).
- Quadrant IV: Not Urgent and Not Important — Distractions or time-wasters (e.g., excessive social media, trivial busywork).

The power of the matrix lies not just in categorizing tasks, but in reshaping behavior. It encourages people to spend more time in Quadrant II, where proactive and meaningful work happens, rather than constantly reacting to urgent demands (Quadrants I and III). In doing so, it shifts focus from short-term firefighting to long-term effectiveness.

By using this matrix, individuals and leaders can reduce burnout, make more strategic decisions, and align their daily actions with their highest priorities, ultimately enhancing both productivity and purpose.

ECOTRACK BUILDOUT: A TIME-DRIVEN DELIVERY PLAN

As the project manager overseeing the development of EcoTrack, a mobile app designed to gamify sustainable living, I've learned that distinguishing between duration and effort is essential for keeping our ambitious nine-month timeline on track. Duration refers to the total time an activity takes from start to finish, including both active working periods and any elapsed time, like weekends or waiting for approvals. For example, coding the app's real-time carbon footprint calculator might have a duration of 10 days, factoring in not just the hours spent coding but also the time needed for code reviews and integration testing. This helps us build a realistic schedule, ensuring we account for the natural ebb and flow of project progress and avoid overly optimistic deadlines that could derail our launch.

In contrast, effort measures the actual work invested in an activity, typically in hours or workdays, and is critical for balancing our team's workload. Take that same coding task: while its duration spans 10 days, the effort might only be 40 hours if the lead developer is splitting time across multiple tasks or collaborating with a designer for half the day. Understanding this difference keeps us from confusing the calendar time (duration) with the human energy expended (effort). By calculating duration for scheduling and effort for resource allocation, I can ensure our team isn't overburdened, say, by assigning 80 hours of effort in a week when only 40 are available, while still mapping out a timeline that delivers EcoTrack to users on schedule. It's this clarity that keeps our project humming and our sustainability mission alive.

Baseline Dates: *The approved and planned schedule dates for project activities, serving as a benchmark for tracking progress. Baseline dates allow project managers to measure deviations, analyze project performance, and make informed decisions to address delays or inefficiencies.*

Duration: *The total time required to complete a specific activity, encompassing both the working time and any elapsed time. Duration estimates play a crucial role in project scheduling and must be carefully calculated to ensure realistic planning and resource allocation.*

Effort: *The total amount of work required to complete an activity, typically measured in work hours or workdays. Effort estimates are crucial for effective resource planning and ensuring that workloads are distributed efficiently across project team members.*

ECOTRACK SOFTWARE DEVELOPMENT PROJECT (PART 2)

In EcoTrack's development, buffers and feeding buffers are our safety nets, cushioning the project against the unpredictable. A buffer is extra time baked into the schedule to handle uncertainties, say, a third-party API integration for real-time environmental data takes longer than expected due to server downtime. For this critical task, I'd add a five-day buffer to its 10-day duration, pushing its completion from an optimistic Early Finish Date to a safer target, protecting our nine-month timeline. Meanwhile, feeding buffers come into play before tasks that feed into our critical chain, like designing the user onboarding flow, which must be ready before the gamified challenges can go live. If the design's 12-day duration risks slipping due to a designer's sudden illness, a three-day feeding buffer ensures that delay doesn't cascade into the critical coding phase, keeping our launch date intact. These buffers transform risk management from reactive firefighting to proactive planning, giving EcoTrack's team breathing room to deliver quality.

Then there's float and free slack, which offer flexibility to fine-tune our execution. Float (or slack) is the leeway an activity has before it jeopardizes the project's end date. For example, testing the app's push notification system might have 10 days of float, meaning it can slip from its Early Finish Date without derailing the final integration milestone. This lets me reallocate testers to a higher-priority task, like debugging the carbon calculator, if needed. Free slack, on the other hand, is more granular: it's the delay an activity can absorb without bumping the next task's start. Polishing the app's UI icons might have four days of free slack; I could push it back to prioritize database optimization, knowing the subsequent integration step won't shift. By leveraging float and free slack, I optimize resource use—say, shifting a developer's effort from 40 hours on icons to 40 hours on performance, while keeping EcoTrack's timeline lean and our sustainability vision on track for a timely, impactful launch.

Buffer: *Additional time factored into a schedule to account for uncertainties, potential risks, or resource constraints.*

Buffers help safeguard the project timeline against unforeseen circumstances and improve the likelihood of meeting critical deadlines. They are commonly used in risk management strategies to mitigate disruptions.

Feeding Buffers: *Additional time added before tasks that precede critical chain activities to absorb uncertainties and prevent delays from impacting the overall project schedule. Feeding buffers help maintain schedule integrity and reduce the likelihood of missed deadlines.*

Float (Slack): *The amount of time an activity can be delayed without impacting the project's completion date. Float is essential for project managers to identify scheduling flexibility and optimize resource utilization.*

Free Slack (Free Float): *The amount of time an activity can be delayed without affecting the start date of subsequent activities. Free slack provides scheduling flexibility and can be leveraged to optimize task execution.*

INNOVATIVE SCHEDULING SOLUTIONS: KEY TECHNIQUES

Effective project management requires a firm grasp of scheduling techniques to optimize timelines, allocate resources efficiently, and mitigate risks. In the context of a software development project, these techniques, Early Finish Date, Early Start Date, Late Finish Date, and Late Start Date play a crucial role in ensuring timely delivery. Below, we explore their application in a hypothetical software development project for an e-commerce platform.

> **Early Finish Date (EFD):** *The earliest possible date an activity can be completed based on the project's logical sequence and scheduling constraints. Understanding early finish dates allows project teams to optimize timelines and identify opportunities for accelerating project completion.*

Assume, an e-commerce platform project has a feature development phase that includes a "Shopping Cart Integration" task, which is estimated to take ten days. If this task begins on Day 5 of the project and follows an uninterrupted workflow, its EFD would be Day 15. By identifying this early completion possibility, the project team can optimize dependencies, potentially enabling earlier initiation of subsequent tasks such as "Payment Gateway Integration." If additional resources are allocated or parallel development is introduced, the EFD can be moved further ahead, accelerating project completion.

> **Early Start Date (ESD):** *The earliest possible date an activity can begin without affecting project dependencies. It helps in determining resource availability and optimizing task execution to prevent idle time.*

Consider a "User Authentication Module" development task that must precede all other application functionalities. Its ESD depends on when the project infrastructure is ready. If the project infrastructure setup is completed by Day 3, the ESD for "User Authentication Module" could be Day 4. By tracking ESDs, the project manager ensures that dependencies align optimally, avoiding unnecessary downtime while resources are efficiently utilized.

Late Finish Date (LFD): *The latest possible date an activity can be completed without delaying the project's overall timeline.*

Suppose the final testing phase, including "End-to-End Testing," must be completed by Day 50 to ensure timely deployment. If "Bug Fixing" is a prerequisite and takes a maximum of five days, then its LFD is Day 45. Any delay beyond this point would push the final testing phase and jeopardize the project's go-live date. Tracking the LFD ensures project managers proactively manage risks and maintain schedule integrity.

Late Start Date (LSD): *The latest possible date an activity can begin without affecting subsequent project tasks.*

Imagine, not the Beatles or Timothy Leary, but that our project task, "Database Optimization" must be completed by Day 30 to allow "Security Audits" to begin. If "Database Optimization" is a five-day task, its LSD would be Day 25. If it starts later than this date, "Security Audits" will be delayed, impacting final project delivery. By monitoring LSDs, project managers can prioritize critical activities and redistribute resources when necessary.

Football Metaphor for Scheduling Techniques in Project Management

Scheduling techniques such as the Backward Pass and Forward Pass are essential for establishing realistic timelines and identifying scheduling flexibility. To illustrate these concepts, we will use a football game as a metaphor for a software development project. Imagine our goal is to "win the championship" by delivering a high-quality software product on time.

Backward Pass*: A scheduling technique used to calculate the latest possible start and finish dates for each activity without affecting the overall project timeline. This method is instrumental in identifying scheduling flexibility and helps in resource leveling by allowing project teams to prioritize tasks strategically.*

Suppose the software development team is in the fourth quarter of the project, with the "Final Product Launch" representing the end of the game. The Backward Pass helps us work backward from this launch date to determine the latest possible deadlines for key tasks without jeopardizing the timeline.

For instance, if "User Acceptance Testing" (UAT) must be completed before launch, and it takes ten days, then the latest possible date to start UAT is ten days before launch. Similarly, "Bug Fixing" must be completed before UAT, so it has a latest start date based on the UAT deadline. Just as a football team ensures their prevent defensive plays do not allow last-minute scoring, project managers use the Backward Pass to ensure critical tasks do not delay the final goal.

Forward Pass: *A scheduling technique used to determine the earliest possible start and finish dates for project activities, helping establish a realistic project timeline.*

At the start of the game our team is starting from the kickoff (project initiation) and moving toward the goal line (project completion). Each phase of development, such as planning, coding, testing, and deployment represents a series of offensive plays. The Forward Pass helps establish the earliest feasible starting points for each phase, ensuring an aggressive but achievable project pace.

For example, if "Requirement Gathering" is the first play, and it takes five days, the earliest "UI/UX Design" can begin is Day 6. If UI/UX takes ten days, then "Backend Development" can start on Day 16. By using the Forward Pass, project managers ensure a smooth transition from one task to the next, just as a football team coordinates its plays to maintain momentum and avoid unnecessary delays.

Fast Tracking: *A schedule compression technique in which tasks that were originally planned in sequence are executed in parallel to reduce project duration. While fast tracking can accelerate project timelines, it may increase risks and require additional coordination to ensure quality standards are maintained.*

Fast tracking is like the no huddle offense, our project is behind schedule, and we need to make up for lost time. Instead of completing "Frontend Development" before "Backend Development" begins, we start both in parallel. This approach speeds up the process but requires careful coordination, just as a no-huddle offense demands players to be in sync to avoid penalties and mistakes. While fast tracking increases efficiency, it also raises risks, such as miscommunication or quality issues, similar to how an unprepared football team might fumble under pressure.

Crashing: *A schedule compression technique that shortens project duration by allocating additional resources or modifying task execution strategies. It involves making cost and scheduling trade-offs to accelerate critical activities while minimizing budget overruns. Crashing is typically applied when a project faces tight deadlines and requires expedited delivery.*

Crashing is like calling in our star players for critical drive. When our software project faces an urgent deadline, testing must be completed faster than originally planned. To crash the schedule, we allocate specialized or additional testers to speed up the process. This is similar to a football coach putting in top-tier players for a game-winning drive. However, crashing comes with trade-offs, such as increased costs or potential burnout, just as star players may face fatigue if overused.

Bringing It All Together: Winning the Championship

A successful football team must balance offense and defense, just as a well-managed project must use both Forward Pass and Backward Pass techniques. The Forward Pass ensures that activities begin as early as possible, keeping the project on an aggressive pace, while the Backward Pass prevents unnecessary delays by identifying the latest possible start times. Additionally, Fast Tracking helps accelerate progress like a no-huddle offense, and Crashing allows for strategic interventions when time is running out. Together, these techniques ensure that the software development project remains on track, just as a well-executed football strategy leads to a game-winning touchdown.

A BOLD APPROACH TO BUSY LIVES
AND HIDDEN CALENDARS

Scheduling meetings is a logistical puzzle that can feel like herding cats, aligning the client's availability with your team's, your own, and sometimes multiple organizations, all while wrestling with limited visibility into everyone's calendars. It's a dance of coordination, often complicated by the fact that tools like Microsoft Outlook only reveal schedules within your own organization, leaving external parties or busy executives as black boxes. Add an admin to the mix for C-suite involvement, and the process grows even thornier. Popular tools like Doodle or When2meet promise relief, send an email, list three time slots, let recipients vote, and voilà, the meeting's booked. Yet, too often, these solutions falter, responses trickle in slowly, or the "winner" still excludes key players, turning a simple task into a time-sucking ordeal. To cut through this chaos, the best approach is proactive, direct communication, propose a time upfront, rally quick consensus, and keep the momentum rolling without letting it stall on indecision.

The traditional method, pinging everyone for availability, waiting for replies, then cross-referencing calendars, wastes precious hours, especially when visibility is patchy. If I can't peek at a client's Outlook or an executive's assistant guards their schedule like a fortress, the back-and-forth becomes a slog. Automated tools sound appealing, but they lean on passive participation: you send a poll, hope folks respond, and pray the algorithm picks a slot that works. In reality, busy people procrastinate, forget, or ignore the email entirely, leaving you stuck chasing stragglers. I've seen teams burn half a day just nailing down a 30-minute sync, time better spent on the work itself. The inefficiency isn't just frustrating; it's a bottleneck that delays decisions and derails progress.

Here's a better way: take the reins with a proactive, streamlined strategy. Start by picking a single, well-reasoned time slot, say, Tuesday at 10 a.m., based on what you know about typical availability (e.g., avoiding Monday mornings or Friday afternoons). Send a crisp, clear request to all required attendees, team members, clients, admins, listing who's needed and why, and ask, "Does this work? If not, propose a new time by [deadline, like end of day]." Set the tone that silence means consent, barring objections, the meetings on. This flips the script from waiting passively for input to driving the process forward. If someone can't make it, they're empowered to counter with an alternative, like "No, but Wednesday at 2 p.m. works." The key? Never reject a meeting outright, always reply with a proposal. "Tuesday's out, how about Thursday at 11?" keeps the ball rolling, avoiding the dead-end of "no" without a next step.

This approach thrives on clarity and momentum. By proposing upfront, you sidestep the endless "When are you free?" loop, which bogs down when calendars are opaque, or schedules are packed. It's not about dictating; it's about setting a stake in the ground and inviting collaboration. For example, coordinating a client kickoff with my developers and their sales lead, I might suggest, "Let's meet Wednesday at 1 p.m. EST? If not, suggest another slot by tomorrow noon." If the client's admin flags a conflict, they might reply, "1 p.m.'s booked, how's 3 p.m.?" Done. No polling tool, no week-long email thread, just a quick exchange that locks it in. Pair this with a shared calendar view where possible (even if it's just your team's), and you've got a lean, effective system.

The beauty here is bold efficiency without rigidity. Busy schedules don't bend easily, and lack of visibility amplifies the challenge, but proactive communication, proposing, not just asking, slashes the time sink. It respects everyone's constraints while nudging them to act fast. Contrast this with the default: a vague "Let me know what works" that lingers unanswered, or a poll where half the group forgets to vote. By leading with a concrete option and a tight response window, you harness the power of momentum over inertia. And the "always propose" rule ensures no one's left hanging, every reply fuels progress. In a world of packed days and hidden calendars, this isn't just scheduling; it's a small triumph of clarity over chaos, getting us to the table faster so the real work can begin.

CHAPTER 9

Resources: The Helping Hands, The Merry Crew

ACQUIRING, DEVELOPING AND managing a project team is not simply writing job descriptions and filling recruiting requisitions. Each person comes with their own set of circumstances that perceive the world with unique perspectives. Every interaction, every communication has a deep and compelling psychological strategy to change behavior. Team building requires a deliberate approach to nurturing team development and synergy, grounded in understanding how teams function in practice. It involves enhancing group performance through targeted training, trust-building, skill enhancement, and cooperative efforts to boost efficiency and achieve project success.

Team Development: *The process of enhancing team performance through training, trust-building, collaboration, and skill development. Strong team development leads to improved efficiency and project success.*

Synergy, on the other hand, emerges when collective efforts yield outcomes greater than the sum of individual contributions, driving innovation, streamlined processes, and superior problem-solving. My approach emphasizes creating an environment where these principles thrive by first examining the practical dynamics of how teams operate. This involves empathetic listening to understand individual perspectives, acknowledging the unique circumstances and viewpoints each member brings, and strategically navigating interactions to align efforts toward shared goals. By blending structured team-building practices with the organic energy of synergy, we lay the foundation for cohesive and high-performing teams.

Synergy: *The concept that collaborative teamwork produces results greater than the sum of individual efforts. Effective synergy in projects leads to innovation, efficiency, and enhanced problem-solving.*

To explore how these concepts translate into effective team dynamics, we will first examine the structural frameworks that organizations and groups establish to guide collective efforts. These formal systems provide the scaffolding for teamwork, setting clear roles, responsibilities, and processes. However, the true strength of a team lies in the human element, how individuals interact, share ideas, and navigate challenges together. Following the structural discussion, we will shift focus to the behavioral and emotional aspects of teamwork, which are less rigid and more fluid, driven by human behaviors, motivations, and emotional connections. By understanding both the formal structures and the nuanced interplay of individual contributions, we can uncover how teams achieve synergy and drive meaningful outcomes.

TEAM WELLNESS AND PERFORMANCE LIFECYCLE

The Tuckman Model provides valuable insights for project managers and leaders by helping them anticipate team dynamics and apply the right interventions, such as coaching, conflict management, or team-building, at each stage to support high performance and team health.[69]

Tuckman Model: *The Tuckman Model, developed by psychologist Bruce Tuckman in 1965 and later expanded in 1977 with the addition of a fifth stage, is a widely recognized framework that describes the predictable stages of group development.[70] It outlines how teams evolve over time in terms of relationships, roles, and performance. The model identifies* **five key stages: Forming, Storming, Norming, Performing, and Adjourning,** *that teams typically progress through as they move from initial formation to disbandment.*

- *Forming: Team members get acquainted.*
- *Storming: Conflicts emerge as roles are established.*
- *Norming: Collaboration improves as norms develop.*
- *Performing: The team functions efficiently to achieve goals.*
- *Adjourning: The project concludes, and the team disbands.*

This process ALWAYS Happens, be ready for it!

While the Tuckman model alerts managers to the behavioral dynamics and evolutionary lifecycle of teams, real-world applications require integrating these stages with tangible structures and resources that support team development. This behavioral growth trajectory aligns with genuine situational observations found in real world processes and practices.

BRIDGING ORGANIZATIONAL PROCESSES AND REAL-WORLD PRACTICES

Organizational documented processes and the way things are actually done in reality regularly differ, creating a tension that poses significant challenges for effective project management.[71] This disconnect often forces leaders to walk a tightrope between rigid formality, which can stifle creativity, and unchecked innovation, which risks descending into chaos. The goal is to harness creativity at every level of the organization by blending structured processes with the organic, often undocumented practices that emerge in daily work. Traditional top-down approaches, such as business process reengineering or knowledge management systems, aim to formalize and institutionalize new ideas, but they frequently fail to capture the dynamic, in-the-moment activities observable simply by walking the factory floor or engaging with teams.[72] This gap places immense pressure on management to address challenges and resolve discrepancies, yet it also offers an opportunity: tapping into these grassroots practices can unlock innovative solutions already crafted by employees who navigate real-world constraints through informal means.

To establish a solid foundation, project management relies on traditional organizational frameworks like the *organizational breakdown structure (OBS)*, which maps out the hierarchy of departments and roles, and the *resource breakdown structure (RBS)*, which categorizes the personnel, equipment, and materials needed for a project.

Organizational Breakdown Structure (OBS)*: A hierarchical representation of an organization's structure that assigns responsibilities for specific work tasks. It helps define accountability, improve resource allocation, and streamline project execution*

Resource Breakdown Structure (RBS)*: A hierarchical framework that categorizes project resources, including personnel, materials, and equipment, to facilitate better planning and management of project resources.*

Equally important is the *responsibility assignment matrix (RAM)*, often visualized as a RACI chart (Responsible, Accountable, Consulted, Informed), which clarifies who does what. These tools, alongside a *team charter*, defining the team's purpose, goals, and norms, and a *staffing plan* outlining recruitment and allocation, serve as the skeleton of project execution. They provide baseline clarity and alignment, ensuring that resources and responsibilities are systematically organized. However, while these frameworks are indispensable starting points, they are static representations that often fall short of capturing the fluid, adaptive nature of work as it unfolds. For project management, the real challenge, and opportunity, lies beyond these blueprints, in balancing formal structure with the lived reality of practice. As mentioned earlier, if you are going to put time in effort in creating these documents, make sure they are useful.

Responsibility Assignment Matrix (RAM)*: A tool that links project tasks (as defined in the Work Breakdown Structure) with assigned team members (as defined in the Organizational Breakdown Structure) to clarify responsibilities.*

RACI Charts: *Responsibility Assignment Matrices (RACI) outline the roles of project stakeholders by categorizing them as Responsible, Accountable, Consulted, or Informed. These charts help clarify task ownership and decision-making responsibilities.*

Staffing Management Plan: *A project document outlining how and when team members will be recruited, assigned tasks, and released from the project. It ensures efficient workforce planning and resource allocation.*

Executives often attempt to ease this tension by compartmentalizing management approaches, as Brown and Duguid notes. They grant highly skilled workers flexibility to innovate, while striving to make the work of others predictable and routine. Yet this compartmentalization clashes with how modern teams and businesses actually function. Employees at all levels improvise to bridge the gap between the idealized conditions their processes were designed for and the unpredictable realities they encounter. For instance, a factory worker might devise a workaround for a malfunctioning tool, or a project team might adjust timelines informally to meet a client's shifting demands. These improvisations embody *tacit knowledge*, practical know-how that's rarely documented and hard for workers to articulate. Managers must first uncover this local expertise, assess its value, and then share it across the organization. This process reveals a stark divide: the task as it appears in a manual versus its execution in practice, and even between what employees believe they do and what an observer sees. Storytelling becomes a vital conduit for sharing these insights, preserving the richness of improvisation that formal documentation overlooks.[73]

Traditional organizational types, such as *functional*, *matrix*, and *projectized* structures further complicate this balancing act. In a functional organization, where employees report to departmental heads (e.g., engineering, marketing), loyalty to silos can hinder cross-team collaboration, leaving project managers reliant on informal negotiations to align efforts. A matrix structure blends functional and project authority, offering flexibility but often breeding confusion over accountability, exacerbating the gap between documented roles and actual contributions. Projectized organizations, fully dedicated to projects, streamline authority but may neglect the long-term knowledge-sharing that informal practices foster. Regardless of structure, the baseline tools (OBS, RBS, RAM, team charters, staffing plans) provide a starting scaffold, yet they cannot fully account for the human element, the improvisations and creative detours that define real work. Brown and Duguid argue that these undocumented practices, rich with tacit knowledge, are where true innovation lies.[74] Project managers must go beyond the skeleton, engaging with teams to uncover these hidden solutions and weaving them into a cohesive strategy.

Ultimately, the art of project management lies in this balancing act: honoring the structure provided by traditional tools while embracing the messy, creative reality of practice. Leaders must foster an environment where intrinsic motivation thrives, instilling purpose by connecting tasks to meaning, while removing extrinsic barriers like unclear expectations or rigid protocols that erode pride in workmanship. By listening to the stories of how work gets done, observing the gaps between theory and action, and integrating local ingenuity, managers can transform tension into synergy. As Brown and Duguid suggest, it's not the documented process alone, nor the unbridled chaos of pure creativity, but the interplay between the two that drives successful projects forward, marrying the stability of the skeleton with the vitality of lived experience.[75]

NURTURING INDIVIDUAL BEHAVIOR

Having explored the tactical frameworks for team building and pinpointed gaps through real-world applications, we now focus on techniques to nurture desired individual behaviors within a group. Effective project management prioritizes people over tasks, as most tasks can be mastered through experience. Achieving the expected outcomes hinges on the project manager's emotional intelligence. Emotional intelligence (EI) is more important than the intelligence quotient. How smart you are, your scores, your grades are all less important to the success of your project, organization or in life, than your ability to master your emotional intelligence. The chief components of EI are **self-awareness, self-regulation, motivation, empathy, and social skill**. Evaluating dynamic intelligence capabilities can be grouped into three categories, technical skills like accounting and business, cognitive analytical abilities such as reasoning, and emotional intelligence competencies like working with others. Although there is a genetic component to emotional intelligence, these skills can be strengthened through persistent practice and feedback from colleagues and others. Neurotransmitters of the brain's limbic system govern feelings and impulses that drive emotional intelligence behaviors.[76] Building emotional intelligence requires sincere desire and a concerted effort. I keep this guide on my desk as a reminder when that brief moment between stimulus and response occurs.

Emotional Intelligence (EI): *The ability to recognize, understand, and regulate one's emotions while also being attuned to the emotions of others. High EI contributes to effective leadership, improved teamwork, and better decision-making in project environments.*

Empathic Listening: *A deep listening approach that prioritizes understanding the speaker's perspective, emotions, and intentions. It involves active engagement, paraphrasing, and responding thoughtfully to build trust and effective communication.*

Self-awareness: Know thyself

Self-awareness is the ability to recognize moods, emotions, and reasons for them as well as understand their effect on others. Hallmarks include self-confidence, realistic self-assessment, and self-deprecating sense of humor. Leaders with strong self-awareness are not overly critical nor unrealistically hopeful, having a deep understanding of one's strengths, weaknesses, needs, and drives. Being honest with themselves and others, they recognize how their feelings affect others. People with high levels of self-awareness can better regulate their emotions, communicate effectively, and develop meaningful relationships. They are more likely to recognize when they are experiencing negative emotions, such as anger or anxiety, and take steps to manage these emotions constructively. Self-aware people are self-confident, have a firm grasp of their capabilities, and less likely to set themselves up for failure.[77]

Self-regulation

Self-regulation is controlling disruptive impulses and moods, suspending judgment and thinking before acting.[78] Hallmarks include being open to change, trustworthiness and integrity, and comfort with ambiguity. Biological impulses drive our emotions, we cannot remove them, but we can manage them. Self-regulation is an ongoing inner conversation that liberates us from being subverted by our own feelings. They have feelings and impulses but find ways to control them and channel them in valuable ways. For example, a self-regulated leader would choose a different approach and pick his words carefully without rushing into hasty judgment. Instead, he would stick back and consider the reasons for the failure.

Motivation

Motivation is a passion to work for intrinsic rather than extrinsic reasons. A tendency to pursue goals with energy and persistence. Hallmarks include a strong drive to achieve, optimism even in the face of failure, and organizational commitment. They are motivated by a deeply embedded desire to achieve for the sake of achievement. The signs include a passion for the work itself, seeking creative challenges, a desire to learn, and taking pride in a job well done. They are persistent with questions about why things are done one way rather than another and eager to explore new perspectives on their work. Traits of people driven to achieve include forever raising the performance bar and keeping score. Leaders who combine self-awareness with internal motivation will recognize those limits but won't settle for objectives that seem too easy to fulfill. They are optimistic and want a way of tracking progress to keep score.[79]

Effective leadership hinges on fostering both intrinsic and extrinsic motivation to instill a deep sense of purpose while dismantling barriers that strip individuals of pride in their workmanship. For salaried managers, intrinsic motivation, driven by a sense of meaning and autonomy, can be undermined by rigid annual performance ratings that reduce their efforts to mere numbers, disconnecting them from the joy of guiding teams with purpose. Meanwhile, hourly workers, often treated as commodities, face extrinsic barriers that rob them of pride in their output, such as unclear standards for acceptable work, orders to produce flawed goods, or insufficient time to maintain tools properly. These conditions fuel frustration, eroding group cohesion as workers feel trapped in roles where excellence is neither defined nor attainable. Leadership's goal must be to ignite intrinsic motivation by aligning tasks with personal fulfillment while clearing extrinsic obstacles through active engagement, offering advice, acting on suggestions, and ensuring every worker, from the factory floor to the corner office, can take pride in a job well done.

Intrinsic Motivation: *The internal drive to engage in activities for personal satisfaction, curiosity, or enjoyment rather than for external rewards. It is associated with higher creativity, commitment, and long-term productivity.*

Extrinsic Motivation: *A motivational approach driven by external rewards such as financial incentives, promotions, or recognition, as well as the avoidance of penalties. It can be effective in goal achievement but may not foster long-term engagement.*

Empathy

Empathy is easily recognizable, the ability to understand the emotional conditions of other people. Empathetic behavior is the skill of treating people individually and according to their emotions. Hallmarks include building and retaining talent, cross-cultural sensitivity, and service to clients and customers. Empathy means thoughtfully considering people's feelings, along with other factors, in the process of making intelligent decisions. One must not be worried about his own fate as much as one considers the feelings and anxieties of his colleagues. Intuitively know what people are feeling and acknowledge their fears with words.[80] Empathy is essential for three primary reasons, teamwork, globalization, and talent retention.

Empathy isn't feeling sorry for someone, it is:

- Sensing other people's emotions
- Mirroring someone's feelings

Mirroring: *A communication technique in which an individual subtly imitates the gestures, speech patterns, or behaviors of another person. It is often used to build rapport, enhance trust, and improve social interactions.*

- *Imagining what someone is thinking*
- *Identifying how a person is feeling*
- *Feeling overwhelmed by others tragedy*
- *Really listening to what others have to say*
- *Understanding another person's feelings*
- *Imagining how someone is feeling*
- *Seeing things from another point of view*

Social skills

Social skill proficiency is managing relationships, building networks, finding common ground, and building rapport. Hallmarks include effectiveness and leading change, persuasiveness, and expertise in building and leading teams. Empathy and social skills concern a person's ability to manage relationships with others. It's not just a matter of friendliness; it's friendliness with the purpose of moving people in the direction you desire. Socially skilled people have a wide circle of acquaintances and the knack for finding common ground and building rapport under the assumption that nothing gets done alone.[81] Such people have a network in place when the time for action comes; they are very effective in managing relationships when they understand and control their own emotions and can empathize with the feelings of others. When people are upbeat, they glow, casting upon conversations and other social encounters. Socially skilled people are adept at managing teams; that's their empathy at work; likewise, they are expert persuaders, a manifestation of self-awareness, self-regulation, and empathy combined.[82]

To better help your personal self-inspection into to these four areas I suggest you take a personal assessment test to see where your strengths and weaknesses lie. This will help you determine where your gifts can be an asset, and your shortcomings can be addressed. Next, I would perform an internal analysis of each of my team members to see where they would be a best fit and where they will excel. One of the best personal assessments test you can take is the Myers-Briggs test.[83]

Myers-Briggs Type Indicator (MBTI): *A widely used personality assessment tool that categorizes individuals into 16 personality types based on preferences in perception and decision-making. It helps in team composition, communication strategies, and leadership development.*[84]

The Myers-Briggs Type Indicator (MBTI), rooted in Carl Jung's groundbreaking theory of psychological types, offers a powerful framework for assembling and leading a project team when its insights are accessible.[85] Developed by Katharine Cook Briggs and her daughter Isabel Briggs Myers in the mid-20th century, the MBTI categorizes personalities along four dichotomies: Extraversion/ Introversion (E/I), Sensing/Intuition (S/N), Thinking/Feeling (T/F), and Judging/Perceiving (J/P). These dimensions provide a nuanced lens through which leaders can understand how team members process information, make decisions, and interact with the world— key factors in optimizing resource management. For instance, an extraverted, sensing team member (e.g., an ESFJ) might thrive in collaborative, detail-oriented tasks like coordinating logistics, while an introverted, intuitive colleague (e.g., an INTP) might excel at solitary, big-picture problem-solving, such as designing innovative workflows. By aligning roles with these natural tendencies, leaders can influence behavior effectively, encouraging an introspective planner to step up in structured settings or motivating a spontaneous visionary to embrace deadlines, ultimately maximizing the team's collective output.

Adding depth to this approach, integrating Social Style Profiles, developed by industrial psychologists David Merrill and Roger Reid, enhances the MBTI's utility by focusing on observable behaviors rather than internal preferences alone.[86] Social Styles categorize individuals based on two key determinants: assertiveness (the degree to which someone expresses opinions or takes charge) and respon- siveness (how openly someone displays emotions or connects with others). This creates four styles, Analytical (low assertiveness, low responsiveness), Driver (high assertiveness, low responsiveness), Amiable (low assertiveness, high responsiveness), and Expressive (high assertiveness, high responsiveness), each offering clues about how team members approach work and relationships. Pairing this with MBTI provides a richer picture: an INTJ "Driver" might push for efficiency with a cool-headed, strategic focus, ideal for leading a high-stakes project phase, while an ESFP "Expressive" could inject enthusiasm into brainstorming sessions, rallying the team around creative goals. Together, these tools illuminate how to tailor communication and tasks—whether it's motivating an Analytical to complete a meticulous report by emphasizing precision or guiding an Amiable to meet deadlines through supportive check-ins, ensuring work is performed, tasks are completed, and motivation remains high across diverse personalities and situations.

Take the test yourself and use it to better understand yourself, and how to utilize your resource pool. https://personality.co/

THE DYNAMICS OF POWER IN ORGANIZATIONS: A DEMOCRATIC REIMAGINING

Power, in its many forms, lies at the heart of how organizations function, shaping relationships, decisions, and outcomes. Yet, too often, our understanding of power defaults to a narrow, hierarchical lens, one where it is wielded as "power-over," a force of domination where one individual or group exerts control over another.[87] This traditional view, steeped in coercion and authority, imagines power as a zero-sum game: a finite resource that, when granted, diminishes the giver and elevates the receiver. However, a deeper exploration reveals a more democratic and expansive possibility, one rooted in freedom rather than repression, collaboration rather than subjugation. Drawing from the visionary ideas of Mary Parker Follett, a pioneering management theorist of the early 20th century, we can reframe power not as a tool of oppression but as a shared, generative force: "power-with."[88] Follett's revolutionary conception of power, contrasts with conventional models, and argues for its transformative potential in modern organizations, where the capacity for power can grow rather than simply shift.

Power: *The ability to influence or control the actions and decisions of others. Power in project management can stem from authority, expertise, relationships, or access to critical resources.*

Follett's perspective begins with a rejection of the authoritarian norms that dominated industrial-era management. She saw society, and by extension, its workplaces, as fundamentally democratic, where the goal should be to liberate, not enforce compliance. To her, the common interpretation of power as "power-over," management dictating to workers, or workers rebelling against management, missed the mark. Instead, she proposed "power-with," a co-active dynamic where influence is jointly cultivated rather than imposed. In her own words, she challenged the notion that "one person should give commands to another one," advocating for a model where authority emerges through mutual effort rather than unilateral decree.[89] Imagine a self-organized team not as a battleground of bosses and laborers, but as a collaborative space where ideas flow freely, and decisions reflect collective input. This isn't a utopian fantasy; it's a practical shift toward harnessing the strengths of every contributor, aligning their energies toward a shared purpose.

Coercive Power: *The ability to influence others by instilling fear, using threats, punishment, or other negative reinforcement to ensure compliance. This form of power is often effective in the short term but can lead to resentment, resistance, and a toxic work environment if overused.*

Self-Organized Teams*: A self-organized team is a group of individuals who manage their own workload, roles, and decision-making processes without relying on traditional, top-down management. Instead of being directed by a supervisor, team members collaboratively determine how best to achieve their goals, distribute tasks, and adapt to challenges. This structure encourages autonomy, accountability, and continuous improvement, and is especially common in agile and project-based environments where flexibility and responsiveness are key.*

What sets Follett's vision apart is her insistence that power isn't a commodity, a fixed pie to be sliced and distributed, as in traditional delegation. When a manager delegates tasks in a conventional hierarchy, they might hand over a sliver of authority, but the total sum of power remains static; it merely moves from one hand to another. Managers should liken power to emotions, love, hate, or pride, capable of expansion rather than depletion. You can delegate power without losing it by sharing the power with self-organized teams, a radical departure from the scarcity mindset. The manager takes care of the team, and the team takes care of the tasks. Picture a team leader who empowers a junior engineer to lead a trouble-shooting effort: the leader doesn't lose their influence but amplifies it through the engineer's success, creating a ripple of confidence and capability. Follett termed this expansive quality "capacity," suggesting that power, when shared, grows in scope and depth, enriching the organization as a whole.[90] It's a generative process, where the act of empowering others multiplies the total reservoir of influence rather than redistributing a limited stock.

This reimagining carries profound implications for hierarchical organizations, where power is typically tethered to positions rather than people. In a traditional setup, say, a functional structure with its rigid silos of department heads and subordinates, authority resides in titles: the CEO, the supervisor, the line worker. Power flows downward, and individuals wield it only insofar as their role permits. Critical thinking exposes the rigidity of this model: it binds influence to a flowchart, not to human potential. A factory supervisor might have positional power to enforce quotas, but if they lack the capacity to inspire or collaborate, that power remains hollow, coercive rather than constructive. By contrast, "power-with" transcends the org chart, rooting itself in relationships and shared goals.[91] A worker with deep knowledge of a machine's quirks might hold no formal title, yet their insight, when invited into decision-making, can elevate the entire team's output. Here, power becomes a living, breathing force, distributed not by rank but by contribution.

To bring this to life, consider a real-world parallel: a software development team facing a tight deadline. In a "power-over"scenario, the project manager might bark orders, assigning tasks with little input, leaving coders feeling like cogs in a machine. Morale dips, creativity stalls, and the product suffers. Now, reframe it with our lens: the manager convenes the team, soliciting ideas on how to streamline the sprint. A quiet tester suggests a debugging shortcut, a senior developer refines it, and the group rallies around the plan. Power isn't hoarded at the top; it's co-created, expanding as each member's capacity is tapped. The result? A faster, smarter solution, and a team that feels ownership over the outcome. This isn't about abandoning structure but about enriching it with a democratic ethos, where influence flows laterally as much as vertically.[92]

These ideas challenge us to rethink not just how we manage, but how we coexist. In a world of matrixed teams and flatter organizations, our emphasis on "power-with" feels prescient, bridging the gap between rigid control and chaotic freedom. It demands that leaders relinquish the instinct to dominate and instead cultivate capacity, trusting that power shared is power multiplied. For workers, it offers agency, transforming them from passive recipients of orders into active architects of progress. The distinction between "power-over" and "power-with" isn't academic; it's a call to action. By embracing this shift, we can move beyond the repressive undertones of traditional authority and toward a workplace where freedom, collaboration, and shared purpose reign, proving that power, at its best, is not a weapon to wield but a garden to grow.[93]

Legitimate Power: *Authority derived from an individual's position within an organization. This power is based on formal roles, responsibilities, and organizational hierarchy, influencing compliance among team members.*

Expert Power: *Influence derived from possessing specialized knowledge, skills, or expertise in a particular area. Leaders with expert power are often respected and trusted for their ability to provide guidance, solve problems, and drive informed decision-making.*

Mary Parker Follett's management philosophy hinges on a deceptively simple yet profoundly transformative idea: "the law of the situation." This concept, woven through her writings with phrases like "to see what the situation demands" or "discover the order integral to a particular situation," positions the unique circumstances of each moment as the ultimate arbiter of action.[94] The situation itself holds an inherent logic, a natural order that, once uncovered, guides decisions and behaviors more effectively than any rigid rulebook or top-down directive. This approach stands in stark contrast to the prevailing management doctrines of her time, most notably

Frederick Taylor's scientific management, outlined in his 1911 work The Principles of Scientific Management.[95] Taylor's system prized universal principles, standardized procedures and precise instructions, designed to optimize efficiency regardless of context, reducing workers to mere executors of pre-set orders. Follett, however, flipped this paradigm on its head, arguing that the specific demands of the situation should take precedence over abstract principles, making her a visionary precursor to modern contextual and situational leadership theories.

This situational focus also reshapes power dynamics with radical clarity. Leadership should "depersonalize the matter, to unite those concerned in a study of the situation, to see what the situation demands, to discover the law of the situation and obey that."[96] Here we dismantle the traditional command-and-obey structure Taylor endorsed, where authority flows from one person to another in a linear chain. We argue that when orders arise organically from the situation, say, a team collectively recognizing that a looming deadline requires overtime, the question of "someone commanding and someone obeying" evaporates.[97] Both parties, whether manager or worker, align around a shared understanding of what's needed, acting as co-interpreters of the context rather than adversaries in a power struggle. In a sales team facing a sudden client demand, for instance, the manager doesn't bark orders; instead, the group huddles, assesses the client's needs, and agrees that reallocating tasks is the logical response. The directive feels less like a mandate and more like a mutual conclusion, driven by the situation's inherent "law."

Referent Power: *Influence gained through personal charisma, reputation, or relationships rather than through formal authority. Leaders with referent power inspire loyalty and commitment through trust and admiration.*

Reward Power: *The ability to influence behavior by offering incentives such as promotions, bonuses, or recognition. It is an effective motivational tool but must be used judiciously to avoid fostering dependency on rewards.*

CONFLICT RESOLUTION

Power doesn't always resolve conflict, too often it amplifies the stress. Conflict resolution is an inevitable and valuable part of every project; conflict should be accepted and harnessed constructively. Understanding each individual's unique needs and ensuring they feel heard can transform disputes into opportunities for growth and collaboration. To navigate these tensions effectively, we can draw on five emotion regulation strategies: relocating to align our surroundings with our emotional needs, modifying the situation to shift its emotional tone, suppressing or amplifying feelings to match the moment, shifting attention away from triggers, and reframing the conflict as a creative challenge.[98] Reflecting on personal experiences brings this to life, recall a time when you had to summon a serious demeanor for a heated team debate despite feeling lighthearted, or when you chose to amplify joy for a colleague's success even as your own setbacks dimmed your mood. By regulating emotions thoughtfully, we honor the vision of turning conflict into a catalyst for deeper connection and innovation. These five strategies, developed by psychologist James Gross, provide a structured framework for managing emotions, enhancing our ability to resolve conflicts in ways that align with our reimaging power insights.[99]

1. **Change the situation:** This is likely a widespread tactic where individuals relocate to a different environment that better suits their emotional needs or aspirations. For example, people might step away from their cluttered home office to regain a sense of calm and clarity. Some avoid crowded coffee shops where noisy patrons disrupt their peace of mind. Freelancers with the freedom to work remotely might opt for a cozy library nook to immerse themselves in deep thought. A key challenge with this approach lies in understanding which emotions the individual sought to shift. Were these feelings tied to the demands of their craft (an artist needing solitude to create), or were they personal desires—like seeking out a bustling park to counter the loneliness of working in isolation?

2. **Modify the situation**. The "situation" could refer to a specific project, a conversation's focus, or even the sensory elements of one's surroundings. The book highlights the first two (switching to a more inspiring project, steering a chat with friends toward lighter topics). Yet, the physical space can also transform a person's mood. This might mean adjusting the ambiance, swapping harsh fluorescent bulbs for a soft amber glow from a vintage lamp—or bringing in a lush fern or a cherished sketch from a loved one to the workspace. Individuals should reflect on what emotions they aimed to alter: Were these feelings essential to their role (like a performer summoning courage before a show), or did they believe a shift in mood would sharpen their focus or satisfy deeper personal cravings?

3. **Suppress or amplify emotions**. This involves a deliberate effort to dial up or tone down the strength of one's feelings. If you're irritated by a demanding neighbor, you might consciously push that annoyance aside to maintain harmony. Conversely, if you're feeling too lethargic to tackle a looming deadline, you could inwardly rally yourself to stoke a fiercer drive to finish. This tactic is often mistaken for "reframing," discussed later, but it's more immediate, think of it as mentally coaching yourself to power through or quietly reasoning away a nagging doubt (like anxiety over an upcoming decision).

4. **Shift attention**. This method centers on redirecting your focus. While it might intersect with other emotion-regulation techniques (like reframing), it's most distinct when someone intentionally diverts their mind from troubling circumstances. Take an artist who's stewing over a harsh critique from a gallery showing earlier that day, it might derail their ability to paint that night. To cope, they could start with a playful sketch that lifts their spirits, imagine the thrill of a future exhibition, or retreat to a sunlit studio corner that doesn't echo the sting of the day's judgment.

My conflict resolution approach is to shift attention toward win-win strategies. In software development projects each morning we start an Agile Project Management scrum meeting with the customer that encourages collaboration, transparency, and adaptability. There are times when customers trigger disruptive impulses that can create strained environments. Anticipating the upcoming tension, the emotional labor I perform includes shifting attention by deliberately distracting myself from these feelings. My morning routine consists of consuming positive nourishment through the eyes, ears, and body, ingesting only nutrients that are healing. Avoiding toxic communication, which includes the news and negative judgment, I read excerpts from books like The Secret and Scripture, review my daily e-mail positive affirmation notifications, play uplifting meditation, music, or lectures.[100] Recently the customer lied to cover their own ***, which may require some initial surface acting however I have a policy not to allow other people to change my weather. Through mindfulness and practice, I'm able to transform my initial excitements and consciously regulate my emotions to a more desirable state. No one has the right or ability to change my mood, wasting time and energy on unproductive goals. In the immortal words of Abraham Lincoln, "Most folks are as happy as they make up their minds to."

Reframe the Situation. *This approach is about seeing things from a fresh angle, like choosing to see a rainy day as cozy rather than dreary. An artist might describe how they handled a prickly buyer by chalking up the buyer's sharpness to stress, not a jab at their work. Or they could recast a rejected painting as a bold experiment that taught them something new, especially since it wasn't their only piece in the show.*

System integration testing commonly results in additional development and incomplete outcomes versus what is expected. Reframing the situation between the developer and the customer is part of my role as a project leader. An initial observation would declare the test a failure when in fact I would be more concerned if everything had run smoothly. Why do I say that. The intended purpose of system integration testing is to identify gaps prior to deployment as a risk mitigation strategy. The software development process includes multiple iterations of testing that includes collaboration and adaptation to changing customer requirements. It's designed to be a learning experience where those closest to the situation heuristically observe and evaluate the results. Last Friday we tested an inventory control management system integration with the SCM supply chain application that that's resulted in a logic change to the testing program. Now is not the time to panic. Cognitively reframing the negative belief that the program doesn't work and replacing it with a more positive and empowering message we were able to alter the perceived conclusion that the test had failed when in fact it was part of a problem-solving tool needed for quality migration control to production upon deployment. The logic changes are in place and will be unit tested on Monday, and the user acceptance test has been scheduled for the first week in June.

THE CIRCULAR RESPONSE

In the realm of conflict resolution, techniques such as smoothing, withdrawal, collaborating, compromising, and forcing often focus on addressing immediate disputes through negotiation or adjustment. However, a deeper perspective on relational dynamics, as articulated by Mary Parker Follett, introduces a circular response framework that transcends these methods by emphasizing the interwoven nature of interactions. This perspective posits that every reaction in a relationship is not merely a response to another individual but to the dynamic interplay of "you-plus-me." In this context, resource allocation, resource leveling, and resource forecasting emerge as practical tools that align with this philosophy, facilitating not just project efficiency but also harmonious collaboration by anticipating and shaping the relational "interweaving" within teams.[101]

Smoothing Mode: *A conflict resolution approach that minimizes differences and emphasizes commonalities to maintain harmony. While useful for reducing tension, it may not fully resolve underlying issues.*

Withdrawal Mode: *A conflict resolution strategy where one party avoids engaging in a dispute. While this approach may help de-escalate tension temporarily, it can leave conflicts unresolved, potentially leading to future issues.*

Resource allocation, leveling, and forecasting embody the circular response by proactively shaping the relational and operational dynamics of a project. Resource allocation involves assigning resources, people, time, or tools, to tasks in a way that reflects the collective needs and capacities of the team, fostering a shared commitment to project goals. Resource leveling takes this further by adjusting schedules to prevent overburdening individuals or creating resource conflicts, ensuring that the "I-plus-you" dynamic remains balanced and sustainable.[102] Resource forecasting anticipates future needs based on current interactions and project trajectories, preparing the team for evolving demands. Together, these techniques mirror the idea that we become "something different" through the process of meeting, as they require continuous dialogue, mutual adjustment, and foresight to align individual contributions with collective objectives.

Forcing Mode: *A conflict resolution approach where one party imposes its solution without considering alternative viewpoints. This win-lose strategy may resolve conflicts quickly but can lead to dissatisfaction and strained relationships.*

Collaborating Mode: *A conflict resolution strategy where multiple perspectives are considered to find mutually beneficial solutions. This approach fosters teamwork, promotes creativity, and strengthens commitment among stakeholders by integrating diverse insights to develop consensus-driven outcomes.*

Implementing these resource management strategies within the circular response framework involves a blend of practical tools and relational awareness. Project managers can use software like Microsoft Project or spreadsheets to map out resource demands and schedules, but the process begins with understanding the team's dynamics, anticipating how individuals and their interactions will evolve. By engaging in regular team discussions, analyzing workloads, and forecasting potential bottlenecks, managers create a responsive environment where the "interweaving-between-you-and-me"is respected and nurtured. This approach not only ensures efficient resource use but also transforms potential conflicts into opportunities for collaboration, embodying Follett's vision of relational transformation raised "to the nth power."[103]

Compromise Mode: *A negotiation-based conflict resolution method in which all parties make concessions to reach an acceptable solution. While this approach fosters cooperation, it may result in partial satisfaction rather than an optimal resolution, as parties may need to sacrifice certain interests. Mary Parker Follett's integration mode is preferred to compromise mode.*

Integration Mode: *Integration stands in contrast to compromise as a superior method for resolving conflict. Instead of both parties giving something up (as in compromise), integration seeks a solution in which both parties' underlying interests are fully met.*

Confrontation Mode: *A direct approach to resolving conflicts by addressing issues head-on. This problem-solving method encourages open communication and allows conflicting parties to work through disagreements constructively to reach a sustainable solution.*

IT'S ABOUT THE PEOPLE

Getting the right people and effectively managing resources for a project requires a strategic approach to ensure tasks are completed efficiently and on schedule. Begin by identifying all necessary resources, including personnel, tools, and budget, and align them with the project's tasks and timeline. Prioritize resource allocation based on task dependencies and critical path analysis to optimize productivity. Implement a resource management tool to track availability, prevent overallocation, and maintain clear communication with the team. Regularly assess progress and adjust resource distribution as needed to address bottlenecks or shifting priorities. By maintaining flexibility, and leveraging data-driven insights, you can tactically manage resources to keep the project on track and achieve successful outcomes.

Resource allocation helps get the most from available resources. Based on team members' skills and capacity, resource allocation is the process of tackling projects using the resources we have at our disposal in the most efficient manner possible. It hinges on understanding the limits and strengths of what's available, whether it's a developer's coding expertise, a machine's operational hours, or a finite budget, and matching those to project demands. For instance, assigning a highly skilled graphic designer to a branding campaign leverages their capacity, while over-allocating them to multiple overlapping tasks risks burnout and delays.

Resource Allocation: *Resource allocation refers to the strategic process of distributing and assigning an organization's available resources, such as personnel, time, budget, equipment, materials, to specific tasks, projects, or operational needs in a way that optimizes efficiency, productivity, and goal achievement.*

Over-Allocation: *A scenario in which resources (such as personnel, equipment, or budget) are assigned to multiple tasks beyond their capacity, leading to scheduling conflicts, inefficiencies, and potential project delays.*

We need to get a clear view of allocation; these insights can give anywhere from a high-level view to a detailed rundown of resource availability, helping avoid schedule delays and going over budget. Tools like resource management software or detailed capacity reports can reveal whether a team is overstretched or underutilized, offering a snapshot of who's available, what's in use, and where bottlenecks might emerge. The better the reporting capabilities at our disposal, the more transparency and efficiency we will have in our projects. Transparent allocation prevents the chaos of double-booking a key team member or overspending on unnecessary rentals, ensuring every resource is deployed purposefully and every project stays on track.

Resource leveling is a sophisticated project management technique employed when limits on the availability of resources, be it personnel, equipment, or budget, take center stage as critical constraints. Unlike allocation or forecasting, which focus on distribution and prediction, resource leveling dives into the gritty reality of finite capacity, seeking to smooth out peaks and valleys in resource demand to maintain a steady, sustainable workflow. Its core mission is to identify underutilized or inefficiently deployed resources within an organization and strategically reposition them to maximize their impact, ensuring no asset sits idle while others are overstretched. This approach requires a deep understanding of both the project's needs and the organization's broader ecosystem, balancing immediate demands with long-term operational health.

Resource Leveling: *A scheduling technique used to resolve resource conflicts by adjusting task timelines. It helps in balancing workloads, preventing burnout, and optimizing resource utilization without exceeding project constraints.*

Resource Loading: *The measure of how project resources are allocated over a given period. Understanding resource loading helps managers prevent overwork, ensure efficient scheduling, and maintain team productivity.*

Consider a practical scenario: a mid-sized tech firm faces a bottleneck during a product launch, with its design team overwhelmed by a surge of content updates while a seasoned application designer from another department has downtime. Through resource leveling, this designer, already skilled in visual aesthetics, could step in to tackle smaller design-related content tasks, alleviating pressure on the core team. This isn't just about plugging gaps; it's about cross-training and workload balancing as strategic levers. By equipping the designer with basic content tools or pairing them with a mentor, the organization not only addresses the immediate crunch but also builds versatility across its workforce. Such moves prevent burnout, reduce overtime costs, and cultivate a culture of adaptability, turning a constraint into a catalyst for resilience.

Resource leveling often intersects with advanced scheduling techniques, adding layers of precision and realism to its execution. The Critical Chain Method (CCM), an evolution of the traditional Critical Path Method (CPM), enhances this process by scheduling projects with a sharper eye on resource dependencies and buffers.[104] Unlike CPM's focus on task duration alone, CCM prioritizes resource availability, identifying the longest sequence of resource-constrained tasks, the "critical chain", and building in time buffers to absorb delays without derailing the project. For instance, if that application designer's availability hinges on completing a prior app update, CCM ensures their schedule aligns with the design team's peak need, factoring in a buffer for unexpected hiccups like software bugs. This method grounds project timelines in the reality of resource limits, offering a more robust framework than traditional approaches.

Complementing this, fast-tracking injects agility into resource leveling by resequencing tasks to accelerate delivery. Traditionally chronological activities, like finalizing a design mockup before coding begins, can be shifted into parallel streams, allowing overlap where resources permit. Imagine the design team sketching wireframes while coders build foundational architecture simultaneously; fast-tracking compresses the timeline but demands careful coordination to avoid rework if designs shift midstream. It's a high-stakes trade-off, speed versus stability, that leans heavily on resource leveling to ensure no team is overburdened or left waiting. Together, these techniques transform resource limits from a liability into a disciplined challenge, driving efficiency through ingenuity and foresight. By leveling workloads, leveraging cross-functional talent, and syncing schedules with realistic methods, organizations can turn scarcity into a proving ground for smarter project execution.

Resource Forecasting: *Resource forecasting is the proactive process of predicting and estimating the resources, such as personnel, budget, equipment, and materials required to successfully complete a project or meet organizational objectives over a specific timeframe.*

Forecasting involves analyzing historical data, current resource capacity, project scope, and future demands to anticipate what will be needed, when, and in what quantities, allowing for informed planning and allocation. For example, a project manager might forecast the need for additional developers during a software rollout's peak phase or predict equipment downtime based on past maintenance trends. This forward-looking approach helps identify potential shortages or surpluses, enabling adjustments before issues arise, such as hiring temporary staff or reallocating funds. By aligning resource availability with project timelines and goals, resource forecasting minimizes risks like delays or cost overruns, ensuring a smooth execution while optimizing efficiency and preparedness in dynamic environments.

A resource management forecast is critical to optimizing people, materials, and budget efficiency. During the planning stages of a project, we should consider the project's scope, possible constraints, unforeseen costs, and potential risks. This means looking beyond the immediate task list to account for variables like seasonal staffing shortages, unexpected equipment repairs, or market-driven material price spikes. A thorough forecast ensures that the team isn't caught off guard, preserving both productivity and profitability.

To make these predictions, project managers must collaborate. Familiarity with the project lifecycle and objectives, coupled with an overview of available resources within the organization, provides this level of visibility, as well as easy access to our projects and resources, all in one place. Collaboration might involve consulting with department leads to gauge team availability, reviewing past project data with analysts for accuracy, or using centralized software to track real-time resource status. This integrated approach empowers managers to anticipate needs, whether it's securing extra hands for a tight deadline or reserving budget for a contingency, turning foresight into a strategic advantage that keeps projects on track and teams aligned.

Resource Histogram*: A graphical representation (usually a bar chart) that illustrates the distribution of project resources over time. It helps in identifying resource shortages, workload imbalances, and potential scheduling issues.*

CHAPTER 10

Communication: Talking Strings That Tie Us Tight

THE ART OF EFFECTIVE COMMUNICATION: HARNESSING INTUITION AND CLARITY

C OMMUNICATION, AT ITS essence, is about connecting, bridging the gap between one mind and another with precision and purpose. Yet, as Nobel laureate Daniel Kahneman illuminates in his seminal work *Thinking, Fast and Slow*, the human mind processes information through two distinct systems, each with profound implications for how we craft and deliver messages.[105] System 1 operates automatically, swiftly, and effortlessly, like a reflex, think of recognizing a friend's face in a crowd or catching a familiar tune. It requires no deliberate control, humming along beneath our conscious awareness. System 2, by contrast, is the slow, deliberate engine of effortful thought, engaged when we wrestle with complex math, weigh tough decisions, or focus intently on a task.[106] It's tied to agency, choice, and concentration, demanding mental bandwidth. Understanding these systems offers a roadmap for effective communication: we must aim for System 1's intuitive ease, quick, clear, and seamless, while minimizing the heavy lift of System 2, lest our messages drown in complexity and noise.

What does this mean in practice? People are wired to favor the path of least resistance. System 1 thrives on familiarity, snapping up messages that align with what we already know or expect, short, punchy sentences that land like a well-timed punchline. A call to action like "Sign up now!" cuts through the clutter because it's instantly recognizable, requiring no pause for deciphering. Long, detailed, labyrinthine communications, however, trigger System 2's gears, demanding focus and effort that most simply won't spare. Picture an overstuffed email crammed with jargon and caveats, readers skim, tune out, or bypass it entirely, their attention hijacked by the mental labor it demands. Our brains evolved to perceive the world efficiently, spotting patterns, orienting to threats, recognizing objects, not to slog through dense prose or untangle convoluted ideas. When we ask others to generate complex insights or sustain intense focus, we risk adding static to the signal, diluting the message we intend.

This tension mirrors a busy train station, lights flashing, horns blaring, bodies weaving in every direction. Amid the chaos, a shouted "Train leaves in five minutes!" cuts through, while a rambling announcement about platform changes and ticket policies fades into the din. The lesson is clear: communicate in short, crisp bursts that pierce the noise. Clarity and concision are king, especially for directives or calls to action, "Submit by Friday" beats "Please ensure submission of all required documents by the end of the business day on Friday." Why? Because System 1 thrives on automaticity, and any conflict between that instinctual snap and System 2's deliberate control, like pausing to parse a tangled sentence, creates friction. That friction taxes working memory, the mental scratchpad we use to analyze, process, and understand. The more we demand of it, the less likely our message sticks.

The goal of all communication should be to meld Kahneman's "thinking fast and slow" into a unified strategy: leverage System 1's speed while sidestepping System 2's slog.[107] Start with the receiver in mind, what's intuitive to them? A seasoned coder might grasp "Debug this module" instantly, but a novice needs "Check the code for errors." Context shapes the lens, and our job is to match it, stripping away excess so the message flows seamlessly into their mental map. Avoid overloading with details, say "Meet at 10 a.m." not "We're convening at 10 a.m. in Conference Room B unless it's booked, then it's Room C, bring your notes." Each added layer forces System 2 to kick in, sapping attention and muddying intent. Even when complexity is unavoidable, explaining a new process, break it into bite-sized chunks: "Step 1: Log in. Step 2: Click 'Settings.' Step 3: Save." This scaffolds understanding, easing the load on working memory and keeping System 1 engaged.

The stakes are high. A misstep, overcomplicating, assuming clarity, ignoring the receiver's lens, turns communication into a missed opportunity. A manager might think "Increase output" is straightforward, but a team juggling priorities hears ambiguity, not urgency, and effort stalls. The map we draw isn't the territory they navigate. Effective communication, then, is an act of empathy and restraint: distill the essence, anticipate the intuitive leap, and deliver it with razor-sharp simplicity. By reducing cognitive noise and honoring System 1's primacy, we don't just inform, motivate, or instruct, we connect. In a world of distraction, where attention is a scarce commodity, the communicator who masters this balance doesn't just speak, they resonate.

The Purpose of Communications: Bridging the Gap Between Message and Meaning

Communication is the lifeblood of any organization, team, or relationship, yet its success hinges not on the clarity of the sender's intent but on the receiver's understanding. We often assume that a well-crafted message, be it an email, a briefing, or a casual directive, carries its meaning intact, like a parcel delivered unblemished to its destination. But this assumption overlooks a fundamental truth: the lens through which the receiver interprets the message may differ vastly from our own. As the saying goes, "the map is not the territory," the words we use, the frameworks we rely on, are mere representations of reality, not reality itself.[108] What we perceive as a clear instruction might unravel into confusion, misalignment, or even resistance if the recipient's perspective skews the meaning. This section explores why communication's effectiveness lies in ensuring the receiver grasps the intended purpose, whether to inform, gather input, motivate, instruct, coach, counsel, mentor, or build teams and how failing to bridge this perceptual gap undermines every goal we set out to achieve.

1. **To Inform**: Share clear, accurate, and relevant information to enhance understanding and ensure all parties are aligned. This may include status updates, reports, or policy announcements.
2. **To Gather Information**: Collect data, feedback, or insights from others to aid decision-making, identify issues, or develop solutions. This often involves surveys, interviews, or brainstorming sessions.
3. **To Motivate**: Influence or inspire individuals or teams to adopt specific behaviors, increase productivity, or take desired actions. This may involve recognition programs, motivational speeches, or goal-setting discussions.
4. **To Instruct and/or Train**: Provide clear guidance or educational content to equip individuals with the

skills and knowledge needed to perform tasks, follow procedures, or use new tools effectively.

5. **To Coach and/or Discipline**: Support professional development and corrective actions by offering feedback, guidance, and encouragement. Coaching fosters growth and performance improvement, while discipline addresses behavioral or performance issues.

6. **To Counsel**: Assist individuals in managing personal challenges that impact their productivity or morale. This involves listening, providing support, and offering appropriate resources.

7. **To Mentor**: Guide and support less-experienced individuals by sharing knowledge, insights, and advice to help them navigate organizational practices, enhance skills, and achieve career growth.

8. **To Build Teams**: Strengthen collaboration, trust, and cohesion within work groups by fostering interpersonal relationships, promoting shared goals, and encouraging open communication.

At its core, communication serves distinct yet interconnected purposes, each demanding that understanding, not just transmission, takes center stage. When we aim *to inform*, the goal isn't merely to relay facts, a project deadline or a policy update, but to ensure the recipient comprehends both the information and its implications. A manager might announce, "The report is due Friday," feeling the message is crystal clear, yet a team member juggling multiple tasks might hear it as a vague priority, not a firm mandate, leading to delays. Similarly, *gathering information*, soliciting feedback to solve problems or make decisions, falters if the receiver misinterprets the request. Asking "What do you think about this timeline?" might yield surface-level nods from someone who sees it as rhetorical, not a genuine call for critique, because their lens filters out the invitation to challenge. The sender's map, precise, intentional, doesn't match the territory of the receiver's assumptions, and critical insights slip through the cracks.

This disconnect grows more pronounced when communication seeks *to motivate*. Here, the aim is to shift behavior or spark action, perhaps rallying a sales team to hit a target. A leader might deliver an impassioned pep talk, "Let's crush it this quarter!" only to find half the team unmoved, their lens clouded by burnout or skepticism about the goal's feasibility. Motivation hinges on the receiver internalizing the why, not just the what, and a message that feels clear to the sender can land as hollow noise if it doesn't resonate through the recipient's worldview. Likewise, when we *instruct or train*, enabling someone to execute tasks correctly, think of teaching a new hire to use software, the stakes rise. A trainer might say, "Click here to save," assuming clarity, but if the learner's mental map lacks context (say, they've never used a similar tool), the instruction dissolves into confusion, and the task falters.

The complexity deepens with purposes like *coaching or disciplining*. These interactions aim to accelerate growth, curb poor performance, or refine skills, perhaps guiding an employee to manage time better. A supervisor might offer, "You need to prioritize your workload," believing it's constructive, yet the employee might hear it as criticism through a lens of insecurity, missing the intent to uplift. Similarly, *counseling*, addressing personal issues affecting work, like stress impacting morale, requires the recipient to feel supported, not judged. A well-meaning "Let's talk about what's going on" could be perceived as intrusive if the employee's territory is one of guarded privacy, derailing the effort to help. In each case, the sender's clarity is irrelevant if the receiver's understanding doesn't align.

Mentoring and team-building push this principle further. To *mentor*, imparting wisdom about organizational nuances, like navigating office politics, relies on the mentee grasping not just the advice but its relevance to their path. A mentor might say, "Build alliances with marketing," feeling it's sage counsel, yet a junior staffer might dismiss it as abstract if their lens prioritizes immediate tasks over long-term networking. *Building teams*, meanwhile, seeks to forge rapport and cohesion, imagine a retreat to boost esprit de corps. A facilitator's icebreaker might land as forced fun to a reserved introvert, whose map of connection differs from the extroverted planner's, fracturing rather than uniting the group. The purpose collapses unless the message pierces each unique perspective.

The lesson is stark: communication's power lies not in how eloquently we send a message, but in how fully it's received. We craft our words through our own maps, our experiences, assumptions, and goals, yet the territory of the listener is a foreign landscape, shaped by their history, emotions, and context. A directive that feels unambiguous to us might twist into ambiguity, resistance, or apathy through their lens. This is why active effort, checking for understanding, adapting to cues, asking "What did you hear?", is non-negotiable. The receiver's grasp is the true measure of success, not our confidence in delivery. Every purpose, informing, motivating, coaching, demands we bridge this gap, recognizing that what we say is only half the equation. In a world of diverse minds, communication isn't a monologue; it's a dialogue, a negotiation of meaning where the map meets the territory, and understanding, not just intent, reigns supreme.

HOW TO BUILD AN EFFECTIVE COMMUNICATION PLAN

Having established the importance of intuition and clarity in aligning message with meaning, the focus now shifts to implementing a communication plan that strengthens team dynamics. This plan is crafted to inform council members and mentor team leaders, encouraging unity through targeted instruction, training, coaching, and discipline. By bridging the gap between intent and understanding, it lays the foundation for effective communication that empowers individuals and builds a resilient, collaborative team.

Communications Management Plan: *A formal document that outlines how project-related information will be shared among stakeholders. It specifies communication methods, frequency, audience, and responsible parties to ensure effective information flow and minimize misunderstandings.*

So where do we start? Building a killer communication plan is about crafting crystal-clear messages that hit the mark, rally your team, and drive results with precision. Here's a step-by-step guide to crafting the formal document:

1. **Identify Stakeholders**
   - List everyone involved or impacted—team, clients, execs, vendors, users.
   - Assess their influence and interest (e.g., a power-interest grid) to prioritize communication needs.
   - *Example*: A client with high influence gets weekly updates; a low-stakes vendor gets as-needed pings.
2. **Define Objectives**
   - Clarify what each channel aims to achieve: inform (status), gather input (feedback), motivate (milestone wins), or resolve (conflict).

- *Example*: Daily stand-ups inform and align the team; monthly exec briefs motivate and assure.

3. **Map Communication Channels**
   - Specify *who* talks to *whom* and *how*.
   - Team to PM: daily Slack updates; PM to client: weekly emails; execs to PM: monthly reviews.
   - Calculate channels ($n(n-1)/2$) to gauge complexity— 10 stakeholders = 45 potential links, so streamline ruthlessly.

4. **Set Frequency and Timing**
   - Match cadence to stakeholder roles (as above).
   - Schedule proactively, e.g., "Team stand-ups: M-F, 10 a.m.; Client sync: Tuesdays, 2 p.m."
   - Build in flexibility for escalations, e.g., "Ad-hoc calls if risks spike."

5. **Choose Tools and Methods**
   - Pick channels that fit the message and audience:
     - *Face-to-face/Zoom*: High-stakes (client demos, exec briefs).
     - *Email*: Formal, documented (weekly reports).
     - *Chat*: Quick, informal (team queries).
     - *Docs/Boards*: Ongoing reference (plans, trackers).
   - *Example*: Jira for task visibility, email for client recaps.

6. **Assign Responsibilities**
   - Designate owners, e.g., PM sends client updates, team leads run stand-ups.
   - Clarify escalation paths: "Blockers to PM within 24 hours."

7. **Document and Share the Plan**
   - Compile it into a table or matrix:

Stakeholder	Purpose	Channel	Frequency	Owner
Team	Task updates	Stand-up	Daily, 10 a.m.	Lead
Client	Progress	Email/Call	Weekly, Tue 2 p.m.	PM
Execs	Strategy	Slides	Monthly	PM

- Distribute it, email it, post it in a shared drive, so everyone knows the rhythm.
8. **Monitor and Adapt**
   - Solicit feedback: "Is this cadence working?"
   - Adjust as the project evolves, e.g., shift client calls to biweekly post-milestone.
   - Watch for overload (too many emails) or gaps (unheard stakeholders).

Putting the Plan in Context

For a website redesign project, the PM might set daily Slack check-ins for designers and coders, weekly Zoom recaps for the client, and monthly exec briefs on ROI. If a vendor's delivering hosting, biweekly emails suffice, until integration, when calls ramp up. Using the channels mathematical formal, $(n(n-1)/2)$ to gauge complexity, the plan warrants the 12 stakeholders have 66 channels, however, don't spiral into chaos, keep communication lean and purposeful. By mapping channels, setting frequencies, and choosing tools with intent, the PM turns a tangle of voices into a symphony of progress, proving that a solid communication plan isn't just logistics, it's the backbone of project success.

UNDERSTANDING COMMUNICATION CHANNELS

A **project communication channel** refers to the pathways or methods through which information flows between stakeholders in a project, team members, clients, executives, vendors, and others, to ensure alignment, transparency, and progress. These channels aren't just about picking tools (like email, meetings, or reports);

they're about defining *who* communicates with *whom*, *how*, and *when* to keep everyone informed, engaged, and accountable. In project management, communication channels are the arteries of collaboration, carrying critical updates, decisions, and feedback. The number of potential channels can be calculated using the formula $n(n-1)/2$, where n is the number of stakeholders, five people yield 10 channels, ten yield 45, highlighting how complexity skyrockets as teams grow, making structured channels essential.

Communications Channel: *A communication channel refers to the medium or method used to convey information between individuals or groups. It is the pathway through which messages are transmitted, received, and interpreted. Communication channels can be formal or informal, synchronous or asynchronous, and vary based on the mode of interaction.*

You might be wondering, "Now that I understand a communication channel is a medium or method for transmitting messages, how do I actually apply that?" The answer lies in using clear, tangible tools that support effective communication. Below is a list of standard **options** for communication channels you can use in your project.

- **Project Dashboard:** A project dashboard is a visual representation of key project metrics, data, and performance indicators displayed in real time. It provides a centralized overview of project status, allowing stakeholders to monitor progress, identify risks, and make informed decisions. Dashboards typically include charts, graphs, and data visualizations that highlight critical information such as milestones, budget status, resource allocation, and task completion rates.

- **Blogs:** Web-based journals or online platforms where users can write and share personal or professional insights. These entries can include text, images, videos, and hyperlinks, while readers can engage by posting comments. Blogs are widely used in knowledge-sharing, corporate communications, and project documentation.
- **Google Docs:** A cloud-based suite of online applications provided by Google that allows users to create, edit, and collaborate on documents, spreadsheets, and presentations in real time. Google Docs enhances team productivity by enabling simultaneous editing and version control.
- **Wiki:** A collaborative website that allows multiple users to create, edit, and update content dynamically. Wikis are commonly used for knowledge management, documentation, and team collaboration, enabling users to contribute and refine information collectively.
- **Project Archives:** A comprehensive repository of all project-related records, including documents, reports, communications, and deliverables. Project archives serve as a historical reference for future projects, audits, and organizational learning.
- **SharePoint Portal:** A web-based collaboration tool developed by Microsoft that enables users to create, manage, and share documents, applications, and information across teams. SharePoint enhances workflow automation, document versioning, and centralized access to project resources.

ELABORATING WITH STAKEHOLDER FREQUENCY

In project communication, frequency matters as much as content. Just as advertisers understand that a consumer must see a message multiple times before taking action,—often referred to as the *Rule of 7*—project managers must recognize that stakeholder engagement thrives on consistent, repeated communication.[109] The "Rule of 7" suggests that a person needs to hear or see a message at least seven times before it resonates or prompts a decision.[110] Applied to stakeholder management, this principle reminds us that a single update is rarely sufficient. Frequent touchpoints, tailored to stakeholder roles, interests, and influence, reinforce clarity, alignment, and trust. For example, high-influence stakeholders like executives may benefit from weekly strategy-focused updates, while frontline contributors may require more frequent operational check-ins. Just like in advertising, repetition, delivered in the right context and tone, drives engagement and action.

The frequency of communication varies by stakeholder, tied to their role, influence, and need for information. Here's how it might break down:

1. **Project Team Members (Core Contributors)**
   - *Frequency*: Daily or near-daily
   - *Why*: Developers, designers, or engineers need real-time updates, task assignments, blockers, progress, to stay synced.
   - *Channels*: Daily stand-ups (15-minute meetings), Slack/Teams chats, task boards (e.g., Jira).
   - *Example*: A software team gets a 10 a.m. huddle to flag delays, plus instant messages for urgent pivots.

2. **Project Manager**
    - *Frequency*: Daily internally, weekly externally
    - *Why*: The PM bridges the team and stakeholders, needing constant internal pulse-checks and regular outward reporting.
    - *Channels*: Team check-ins, weekly status emails, one-on-one syncs with leads.
    - *Example*: Daily team debriefs, plus a Friday summary to the client.

3. **Client or Sponsor**
    - *Frequency*: Weekly or biweekly
    - *Why*: They require high-level updates, milestones, risks, budget, without drowning in minutiae.
    - *Channels*: Formal reports, Zoom reviews, milestone emails.
    - *Example*: A biweekly dashboard with a 30-minute call to discuss.

4. **Executives or Senior Leadership**
    - *Frequency*: Monthly or at key milestones
    - *Why*: They focus on strategic alignment and ROI, not operational details, unless escalation is needed.
    - *Channels*: Executive summaries, quarterly briefings, ad-hoc alerts.
    - *Example*: A monthly slide deck with cost and timeline highlights.

5. **External Vendors or Partners**
    - *Frequency*: As-needed or biweekly
    - *Why*: Coordination depends on deliverables, frequent during integration, sparse otherwise.
    - *Channels*: Email threads, scheduled syncs, shared docs (e.g., Google Drive).
    - *Example*: Biweekly calls during a hardware delivery phase.

6. **End Users or Public (if applicable)**
    - *Frequency*: Periodic (e.g., launch updates)
    - *Why*: They need outcome-focused info, not process details.
    - *Channels*: Newsletters, social posts, webinars.
    - *Example*: A pre-launch email blast to beta testers.

Frequency adjusts dynamically, escalating during crises (daily client calls if a deadline slips) or tapering off in stable phases. The key is tailoring cadence to stakeholder needs, avoiding overload while ensuring no one's left in the dark.

VISUAL MODEL: STAKEHOLDER COMMUNICATION FREQUENCY AS STIMULUS CONTROL

- **Model Title:** Reinforcement-Based Communication Strategy for Stakeholders
- **Conceptual Foundation:** Based on Cooper, Heron, and Heward's principles of Applied Behavior Analysis (ABA), particularly stimulus control and reinforcement, this model frames stakeholder communication as a behavioral intervention.[III] Repeated and context-appropriate communication increases the likelihood of stakeholder engagement and decision-making, analogous to increasing stimulus salience in ABA.

1. Stakeholder Category Breakdown

Stakeholder Role	Influence Level	Info Need	Suggested Frequency	Communication Type	Behavioral Objective
Executive Sponsors	High	Strategic	Weekly	Briefings, dashboards	Maintain decision readiness and alignment
Project Managers	High	Tactical	2-3x/week	Status updates, meetings	Reinforce leadership behaviors and planning
Functional Leads	Medium-High	Tactical	2x/week	Reports, coordination calls	Sustain operational focus and accountability
Project Team Members	Medium	Operational	Daily or As Needed	Stand-ups, task lists	Drive task execution and behavioral momentum
External Stakeholders	Variable	Strategic	Monthly or Milestone	Newsletters, presentations	Maintain transparency and reinforce trust

2. ABA Alignment Table

Communication Element	ABA Principle	Effect on Behavior
Frequency	Stimulus Control	Repetition increases recognition and response
Relevance of Message	Discriminative Stimuli	Enhances clarity of expected action
Positive Feedback	Reinforcement	Increases likelihood of desired participation
Timely Delivery	Contingency	Aligns message with current behavior needs

3. Application Notes:

- *Stimulus control* is strongest when communication is consistent, relevant, and reinforced.
- Communication acts as a discriminative stimulus when it signals a clear opportunity or need for action.
- Reinforcement (e.g., recognition or action taken based on input) strengthens the behavior of staying engaged.

STANDARD COMMUNICATION OUTPUTS

After the plan is set, the meeting is held, and the communication medium is defined, we must produce **standard outputs,** the tangible results or deliverables that confirm progress, capture decisions, and drive the next steps in the project. Below is a list of standard outputs, perform some independent research on preferred formats, test what works for your projects and make adjustments.

Kick-Off Meeting: *The initial formal gathering of all key stakeholders at the start of a project. Its primary purpose is to establish alignment, clarity, and momentum. During this meeting, project sponsors, team members, and other participants are introduced, and the project's objectives, scope, high-level timeline, roles, and expectations are reviewed in detail. It sets the tone for collaboration and communication, helping to ensure everyone starts on the same page. The kick-off also often includes,* **Project Management Knowledge Areas**, *a review of key risks, success criteria, and how progress will be tracked, making it a crucial moment to create a shared vision and commitment to success.*

DNA: Date, Name, Action (Meeting Minutes):
Meeting minutes are the official written record of what occurred during a meeting. They summarize key discussions, decisions made, and actions to be taken. Each action item is typically documented with the date of the meeting, the name of the person responsible, and the specific action they are assigned to complete. This format ensures accountability and provides a clear reference for follow-up.

Progress Reports: *Periodic reports that provide an overview of a project's achievements within a specified time-frame. They highlight completed tasks, ongoing activities, potential risks, and upcoming milestones to keep stakeholders informed and aligned.*

Status Reports: *Detailed reports that provide a snapshot of a project's current state at a given point in time. These reports typically include key performance indicators (KPIs), budget updates, schedule status, and identified risks to support informed decision-making.*

Gate Review: *A gate review is a formal checkpoint or decision-making meeting held at specific milestones during a project's lifecycle. It serves as a go/no-go evaluation, where stakeholders assess the project's progress, performance, and alignment with objectives before approving its continuation to the next phase. Gate reviews are essential for ensuring quality, managing risks, and verifying that deliverables meet predefined criteria.*

Retrospectives: *A retrospective is a structured review meeting held at the end of a project phase or iteration to reflect on the team's performance, processes, and outcomes. The goal is to identify strengths, uncover challenges, and implement continuous improvements. Retrospectives are commonly used in Agile project management, but they are also valuable in traditional methodologies for enhancing future project phases.*

Lessons-Learned Report — *A reflective document created by project managers and team members to capture valuable insights, best practices, and mistakes encountered during a project. These reports help organizations improve future project planning, execution, and decision-making.*

MESSAGE FRAMING: APPLYING CIALDINI'S *INFLUENCE* PRINCIPLES

Robert Cialdini's *Influence: The Psychology of Persuasion* outlines six key principles, reciprocity, commitment and consistency, social proof, liking, authority, and scarcity, that shape how people respond to persuasion.[112] In project management, these principles offer a powerful tool for framing messages to align teams, secure buy-in, and drive action. Effective framing leverages these psychological triggers to make requests compelling and intuitive, ensuring stakeholders, whether team members, clients, or executives, act decisively.[113]

Message Framing: *Message framing is a communication strategy that involves presenting information in a way that influences how it is perceived by the audience. The same information can be framed positively or negatively, affecting how recipients interpret and respond to it. Positive framing highlights gains or benefits, while negative framing emphasizes losses or risks.*

Below is an example of how a project manager might frame a message using Cialdini's principles to mobilize a team for a critical project milestone, demonstrating how influence can transform communication into a catalyst for success.

Imagine a construction project where the team must complete a foundation pour by next Friday to stay on schedule for a high-profile client. Delays loom due to weather risks and a stretched crew, and the project manager needs everyone to commit extra hours this week. A straightforward ask might be, "We need overtime this week to hit the pour deadline." It's clear but lacks punch, some might shrug it off, citing personal plans or fatigue. Now, let's reframe it using Cialdini's principles for maximum impact.

The manager gathers the team and says: "Last month, you all pulled off that roof framing ahead of schedule, and I made sure the client knew it was thanks to your grit; they're raving about us now (social proof). I've already lined up coffee and lunches on me through Friday to fuel this push (reciprocity), because hitting this pour is our chance to lock in their trust for the next phase, they're watching us closely (scarcity). I'm in too, I'll be here late with you, and our site lead, Mike, who's done 20 pours like this, says it's doable if we sync up (authority).[14] We've crushed it before; let's do it again and own this milestone (commitment and consistency, liking). Who's with me?"

Here's how it breaks down. *Social proof* kicks off with a nod to past success, "you all pulled off that roof framing", reminding the team they're capable and respected, tapping into the human drive to align with proven winners. *Reciprocity* follows with the manager's gesture, "coffee and lunches on me", a small gift that triggers an urge to give back through effort, subtle but effective. *Scarcity* amps up stakes, "our chance to lock in their trust", framing the deadline as a rare opportunity, not just a chore, making action feel urgent. *Authority* leans on Mike's expertise, "20 pours like this", lending credibility that reassures doubters it's feasible. *Commitment and consistency* ties it to their track record, "we've crushed it before", nudging them to stay true to their reputation, while *liking* weaves in camaraderie, "I'm in too, let's own this", building rapport with a leader who's relatable, not aloof. The close, "Who's with me?" invites a public yes, sealing the deal.

Contrast this with the bland original. The unframed version risks indifference, team members might nod but not feel the pull to act. Cialdini's framing flips it into a story: you're part of a winning crew, rewarded for stepping up, chasing a rare shot at glory, guided by expertise, and led by someone in the trenches with you. It's not a demand; it's a call to join a shared mission. In project management, where deadlines hinge on collective will, this approach turns a logistical ask into a psychological win. The team doesn't just agree, they commit, fueled by influence that hits all the right notes. Cialdini's principles prove that how you frame the message doesn't just deliver information, it shapes behavior, turning a task into a triumph.

Let's simplify, in another demonstration, how framing significantly influences decision-making. In this experiment, participants were split into 2 groups, each receiving one output of testing results for a hypothetical systems integration project expected to test 600 use case scenarios:

- Positive Frame: "400 use case tests were successful."
- Negative Frame: "200 use case tests failed."

Although the outcomes were mathematically identical, more participants **chose the positively framed option.** This experiment illustrates how people are more likely to **choose risk-averse solutions** when the message is framed positively and are more inclined to **take risks** when facing a negatively framed message.

FRAMING USING THE ANCHORING AFFECT

Another method of framing is based on our psychological theory of anchoring whereas we can influence the preferred outcome by planting seeds that help guide our decisions.[115]

Anchoring Affect: *The anchoring effect is a cognitive bias where an initial piece of information, known as the anchor, disproportionately influences subsequent judgments or decisions, even if the anchor is irrelevant or arbitrary.*

In the high-stakes arena of project contract pricing and negotiations, the anchoring effect, often tied to the broader concept of framing, wields remarkable influence over how costs, budgets, and agreements take shape. When bidding on a project, communicating change orders, or hashing out financial terms, the first number tossed into the ring acts as an anchor, subtly steering all that follows. This isn't just about numbers on a page; it's about how human minds, wired for quick judgments, latch onto that initial figure and let it color every subsequent decision. Drawing from Kahneman's insights, the anchoring effect bridges System 1's snap intuition and System 2's slower reasoning, often tilting the scales in negotiations before the real haggling even begins.[116] For project managers and negotiators, mastering this bias isn't just a tactic, it's a game-changer.

Consider a scenario in contract pricing: you're pitching a software development project to a client, and your team's cost estimate lands at $80,000. In the negotiation, you open with, "We're looking at $100,000 to deliver this on time and exceed expectations." That $100,000 becomes the anchor, etched in the client's mind via System 1's automatic uptake. When they counter with $85,000, they've adjusted from your starting point, not the unstated $80,000 baseline. Without that anchor, they might've lowballed at $60,000, pegging their offer to their own budget constraints. Research backs this: in one study, visitors asked if they'd pay $5 to enter a museum later, averaged $20 donations when prompted for a contribution, far less than the $64 average from those unprimed by the low anchor. The initial $5 skewed their frame, pulling their willingness down. In contracts, setting a high anchor, like a premium list price, plants a seed that makes your actual target seem reasonable by comparison.

This dynamic thrives in the murky waters of project negotiations because plans are often best-case scenarios, not hard truths. Anchoring on an optimistic timeline or budget, like "We'll finish in 12 weeks for $90,000", can lock everyone into an unrealistic frame, blinding them to risks like scope creep or delays. System 1 grabs the shiny number, while System 2 skimps on adjusting for what could go wrong. A smarter play? Set the anchor deliberately and favorably. In a change order discussion, instead of saying, "This fix adds $5,000," frame it as, "To keep us on track, this enhancement's value is $10,000, can we settle at $7,000?" The $10,000 anchor makes $7,000 feel like a win, not a concession, leveraging System 1's love for quick wins over System 2's plodding math. The aim isn't to mislead but to steer perception toward your goal.

Anchoring's power shines in unsettling ways too. Random numbers can sway seasoned pros, executives approving a $1 million budget might balk if you'd first floated $500,000, even if both were ballparks. Why? System 1 doesn't care about logic; it clings to the first cue. This explains why arbitrary rationing—think "limited-time offer" in marketing, works so well; it sets a frame that feels urgent and exclusive. In contract talks, the same ploy applies: "Our standard rate's $150/hour, but for you, we'll do $120" anchors high, making the discount pop, even if $120 was your target all along. Clients, vendors, and teams use anchors to decide how much to bid, concede, or fight for, often without realizing how that first number warps their lens.

The takeaway for project managers is clear: own the anchor. In negotiations, don't wait for the other side to drop a lowball figure, get your number out first. Propose $120,000 confidently, and their $100,000 counter feels like progress, not a loss. When forecasting costs or timelines, avoid anchoring on rosy plans, build in buffers and frame them as prudent, not pessimistic: "We're targeting $110,000 to cover unknowns, aiming to come in under." This nudges System 1 toward acceptance while giving System 2 room to rationalize. Communication here is king—crisp, intentional framing sets the stage, ensuring your anchor sticks. In a world where money and time are judged through biased minds, anchoring isn't just a quirk—it's your edge in turning proposals into profits and plans into reality.

NONVERBAL COMMUNICATION IN ACTION: LIOR SUCHARD'S MENTALIST MASTERY

Nonverbal communication is the art of conveying messages without words, relying on a rich tapestry of body language, facial expressions, gestures, posture, tone of voice, eye contact, and physical space. It's a silent yet potent force that reveals emotions, attitudes, and intentions, sometimes amplifying spoken words, other times betraying them. In the realm of project management or everyday interaction, nonverbal cues can make or break understanding. Now, imagine this power wielded with precision by Lior Suchard, a world-renowned mentalist whose performances hinge on reading and manipulating these unspoken signals to create jaw-dropping illusions of mind-reading. Let's explore an example of how Suchard might use nonverbal communication to captivate an audience, drawing from his signature style.[117]

Nonverbal Communication: *Nonverbal communication refers to the transmission of messages and information without the use of words, relying instead on body language, facial expressions, gestures, posture, tone of voice, eye contact, and physical space. It plays a crucial role in conveying emotions, attitudes, and intentions, often enhancing or contradicting spoken messages.*

Picture a live show: Suchard stands on stage, facing a volunteer, let's call her Sarah, tasked with thinking of her childhood pet's name. He begins, "Focus on that name, see it in your mind." His voice is calm, almost hypnotic, but it's his nonverbal cues that do the heavy lifting. He locks eyes with Sarah, his gaze steady and piercing, signaling confidence and control, classic eye contact that builds trust and primes her to follow his lead. As she concentrates, Suchard tilts his head slightly, mirroring her subtle shift in posture, a gesture rooted in rapport-building, making her feel unconsciously connected. His hands, open and relaxed, gesture toward her gently, a nonverbal invitation to share her thoughts without pressure, subtly encouraging her System 1 (intuitive) response over System 2 (analytical) resistance, as Daniel Kahneman might describe.[18]

Sarah hesitates, her lips parting as if to speak, then closing, a microexpression of uncertainty. Suchard catches it instantly. He narrows his eyes briefly, a flicker of focus, then softens his face into a warm smile, projecting reassurance that lowers her guard. "It's a short name, isn't it?" he ventures, his tone rising playfully at the end, paired with a raised eyebrow. The question isn't random; it's informed by her quick blink and the faint twitch of her mouth, cues suggesting a simple, familiar word. She nods, almost involuntarily, her shoulders relaxing as his read lands. Suchard steps closer, shrinking the physical space between them, amplifying the intimacy of the moment—proxemics at work. "I'm seeing… B… then an 'ee' sound— maybe Beebee?" Sarah gasps, her eyes widening, hands flying to her cheeks in shock.

Here's the breakdown: Suchard's "mind-reading" isn't telepathy—it's a masterclass in nonverbal decoding. Her initial hesitation signaled a mental search, the blink hinted at brevity, and her relaxed nod confirmed his guess aligned with her memory. His smile and tone softened the exchange, leveraging Cialdini's liking principle to keep her engaged, while his proximity dialed up scarcity—this moment feels rare, personal. He might've used a cold-reading technique, starting broad ("short name") and narrowing based on her reactions, but it's his nonverbal finesse, reading her posture, mirroring her energy, steering her with gestures that sells the illusion. To the audience, it's magic; to Suchard, it's the silent language of the body, speaking louder than words.

In project management, this translates to reading a team's unspoken signals, slumped shoulders signaling burnout, averted eyes hinting at doubt, and adjusting your approach. Suchard's example shows nonverbal communication isn't just garnish; it's the main course, conveying what words alone can't, and when wielded with intent, it turns a message into an experience. Sarah didn't just hear him guess Beebee; she felt seen, understood, proof that the real power of communication often lies beyond the spoken.

Rapport: *A relationship built on mutual trust, respect, and understanding. Establishing rapport among project stakeholders enhances collaboration, communication, and team cohesion.*

ESCALATION & SUPPORT COMMUNICATION

The escalation tree ensures that issues are addressed by the appropriate level of authority or expertise when they exceed the capabilities or decision-making power of the current handler. This structured process prevents delays, improves problem resolution efficiency, and ensures that critical incidents receive the necessary attention.

Escalation Tree: *An escalation tree is a structured framework used in project management, service delivery, and incident response to define the communication and resolution pathways for handling issues or risks. It establishes a hierarchical chain of command that outlines how problems are escalated based on their severity, complexity, and impact.*

ISIL Support Tree (Information Systems Infrastructure Library): *ISIL is a hierarchical framework that defines the structure of support roles, communication* *flows, and escalation paths within an IT service management (ITSM) environment. It outlines how incidents, requests, and issues are managed, escalated, and resolved, ensuring efficient and consistent service delivery.*

The ISIL support tree typically includes:

- **Frontline Support (Tier 1):** The first point of contact, responsible for handling basic incidents and service requests, such as password resets or troubleshooting common issues.
- **Specialized Support (Tier 2):** Escalation point for more complex issues requiring subject matter expertise, such as configuration errors or software bugs.
- **Advanced/Expert Support (Tier 3):** Handles critical and complex incidents, including system failures or performance issues, often involving senior engineers or vendor support.
- **Management and Oversight:** Senior leadership or service managers oversee the support process, ensuring adherence to SLAs (Service Level Agreements) and initiating major incident reviews.

COMMUNICATION FLOW EXAMPLE IN A CLOUD IAAS ENVIRONMENT:

Imagine a **cloud service provider** managing **IaaS infrastructure** (e.g., virtual machines, storage, and networking). When **a customer reports a latency issue,** the ISIL support tree manages the incident as follows:

1.   **Tier 1 (Helpdesk):**
   - **Receives the ticket** and verifies the issue by review-
     ing basic metrics (e.g., CPU usage, memory load).
   - Attempts basic troubleshooting, such as **restarting
     the virtual machine** or clearing temporary logs.
   - If unresolved, **escalates the incident** to Tier 2.
   - **Communication:**

     - Email confirmation to the customer with the
       ticket number.
     - Updates the ticket with **diagnostic actions
       performed**.

Tier 1: Helpdesk

   - Analyzes infrastructure
   - First point of contact
   - Handles basic issues
   - Creates & categorizes tickets
   - Escalates complex issues

Escalation │ Resolution Updates

2.   **Tier 2 (Cloud Infrastructure Team):**
   - Analyzes logs and metrics, identifying the **underly-
     ing cause**, such as a network configuration error.
   - Implements a **configuration fix** or patch.
   - If the issue persists, escalates to Tier 3.
   - **Communication:**

     - Provides **technical updates to Tier 1.**
     - Documents the resolution process in the ITSM tool.

Tier 2: Infrastructure Team

- Analyzes infrastructure
- logs & metrics
- Implements fixes & patches
- Provides updates to Tier 1

Escalation | Resolution Updates

3. **Tier 3 (Cloud Architecture Team or Vendor):**
   - Investigates **deep-level infrastructure issues**, such as hardware faults or vendor-related failures.
   - Collaborates with the **cloud service provider** (e.g., AWS, Azure) if necessary.
   - Resolves the incident and **closes the ticket**.
   - **Communication:**
     - Provides a **detailed incident report** to management.
     - Communicates resolution details to Tier 2 and Tier 1.

Tier 3: Cloud Architecture

- Handles deep-level issues
- Hardware/vendor issues
- Works with cloud provider
- Provides technical reports

Escalation | Resolution Updates

4. **Management and Oversight:**
   - Reviews the incident to **identify root causes and prevention strategies**.

- Adjusts **SLA agreements or support protocols** if needed.
- **Communication:**

    - Sends a **post-incident report** to stakeholders.
    - Conducts a **retrospective meeting** to discuss improvements.

Management & Oversight
(Service Managers, CTO)

- Reviews incidents
- Ensures SLA compliance
- Conducts post-incident
- reviews and retrospectives
- Communicates with execs

Key Takeaway:

This ISIL support tree structure ensures efficient and organized incident management in a cloud IaaS environment. The clear escalation paths, communication flows, and tiered support levels help reduce downtime, improve service quality, and enhance customer satisfaction.

CHAPTER 11

Cost: The Treasure Chest of Coins and Gold

E VERYBODY WANTS TO know one thing when a grand idea hits the table: How much is this going to cost me? It's the universal icebreaker, the first question off everyone's lips, whether they're funding a software implementation, a new business venture, or, in this case, a new opportunity, a treasure chest brimming with coins and gold. Picture this: a room full of eager planners, solution architects, and executives, all leaning in, eyes wide, waiting for the magic number. It's like a pirate crew eyeing a freshly unearthed chest, except instead of "Argh, matey!" it's "So, what's the damage?" She counts her coins, both big and small, to build her dream without a fall, and trust me, everyone's holding their breath to hear the tally.

That is the sound of the customer procurement manager when they see the original estimate. By integrating techniques such as Project Cost Management, Cash Flow Analysis, and Budgetary Estimation techniques, organizations can smooth this conversation by methodically planning, estimating, and controlling costs while maintaining financial viability. The procedures explored in detail herein, if followed, will enable precise budgeting for informed decision-making, proactive financial oversight, and ultimately drive project success through robust financial planning.

Project Cost Management: *Project Cost Management: The discipline of planning, estimating, budgeting, and controlling project costs to ensure completion within the approved budget. Effective cost management is critical for project viability and success.*

Cash Flow Analysis: *A financial assessment method used to evaluate the estimated inflows (revenues) and outflows (expenses) of a project over time. This analysis helps determine financial feasibility, investment returns, and liquidity management.*

Budgetary Estimate: *A preliminary cost estimation used during the early stages of project approval and financial planning. It helps organizations allocate funds, assess feasibility, and make informed decisions regarding project funding and resource distribution.*

BALLPARKING

A ballpark estimate refers to a rough, preliminary cost or time estimate made with limited information, typically during the early stages of a project. It provides a broad range of expected costs or durations to help stakeholders assess feasibility and make initial decisions. In project cost management we refer to these as Rough Order or Magnitude Estimates.

Rough Order of Magnitude (ROM) Estimate: *A ROM estimate provides a very preliminary cost approximation, often expressed as a range (e.g., -25% to +75% of the actual cost). It's typically based on limited information, sometimes just a project concept or scope without detailed historical comparisons or breakdowns. ROM estimates are used when little is known about the project, such as during initial feasibility discussions, high uncertainty.*

ROM estimates are a far less precise estimation method than the detailed approaches discussed in the next section, with accuracy ranges often spanning -50% to +100%. They're ballpark figures, relying on rough assumptions or expert judgment rather than detailed historical comparisons. For example, a ROM might estimate a new hotel build at $5M–$10M based solely on square footage and market norms, without specifics. They occur at the very outset, often during the conceptual or pre-initiation phase. They're used to assess whether a project is worth pursuing (e.g., "Can we build this resort for under $10M?") before investing in detailed planning. ROM relies on minimal data, sometimes just expert intuition, industry averages, or high-level metrics (e.g., cost per square foot). It doesn't necessitate detailed records, making it feasible when specifics are unavailable. The following section broadens the discussion into detail estimation methods.

Top-Down and Analogous Estimating Techniques: Applications and Value

In the realm of budgeting and cost estimation, organizations often face the challenge of balancing speed, cost, and accuracy. Two techniques, top-down estimates and analogous estimates, offer practical solutions by leveraging historical data to streamline the process. While these methods may sacrifice some precision compared to detailed bottom-up approaches, their efficiency and adaptability make them invaluable in specific situations. This section explores how these techniques can be applied and the value they bring, particularly in scenarios involving standardized products, tight timelines, or limited resources.

The strength of these techniques lies in their reliance on codified, repeatable processes. For organizations offering relatively standard products or services—such as a chain of hotels, a software firm with modular solutions, or a manufacturer producing consistent goods—historical data provides a reliable foundation. Through experience and execution, these entities build economic models that can be reused, enabling faster and more dependable cost estimates.

Top-Down Estimates: *Top-down estimating is a high-level cost-estimating method that uses historical data from similar projects to establish a budget. Rather than breaking a project into individual components, it applies a broad perspective, often relying on past experiences or industry benchmarks.*

Analogous Estimates: *Analogous estimating, a subset of the top-down approach, refines this concept by drawing specific parallels between a current project and a previous one with comparable characteristics. Both methods prioritize speed and cost-effectiveness over granular detail, making them ideal for early-stage planning or when precision is less critical than a quick financial overview.*

Applications in Real-World Situations

Top-down and analogous estimating shine in situations where time is of the essence or resources for detailed analysis are scarce. For instance, consider a health and leisure company like Hotel Resorts launching a new property with amenities similar to existing locations. Using top-down estimates, the corporate team could quickly project the budget by referencing the costs of a recently opened resort of comparable size and scope. This approach bypasses the need for exhaustive departmental breakdowns, allowing leadership to allocate funds and secure approvals swiftly.

Similarly, analogous estimating proves valuable when bidding on contracts or responding to market opportunities. A catering company, for example, might use data from a past event, say, a 200-guest wedding to estimate costs for a similar upcoming event. By adjusting for variables like inflation or venue-specific fees, the company can generate a proposal in hours rather than days, gaining a competitive edge. The repeatability of their service model (e.g., standard menus, staffing ratios) ensures that these estimates remain reliable despite their simplicity.

These techniques also excel in preliminary planning phases. When a tech startup needs to pitch a new app to investors, it might lack the time or data to perform a bottom-up analysis of development costs. Instead, it could use analogous estimates based on a prior app with similar features, providing a ballpark figure that informs negotiations without delaying the process. In such cases, speed eclipses precision, as stakeholders often seek a general sense of feasibility rather than a line-item budget.

VALUE DELIVERY TOOLS

The primary value of top-down and analogous estimating lies in their efficiency and cost-effectiveness. By leveraging historical data, organizations avoid the labor-intensive process of building estimates from scratch, saving time and reducing planning overhead. This is particularly beneficial for resource-constrained teams or projects with tight deadlines, where a rapid response can mean the difference between securing a deal and losing it to a competitor.

Another key advantage is their scalability. For businesses with standardized offerings, the codification of past projects into reusable economic models enhances consistency and predictability. A retail chain opening its 50th store, for example, can confidently apply costs from its 49th location, adjusted for regional differences, knowing that the model has been refined through repetition. This repeatability minimizes guesswork and fosters trust in the budgeting process.

Moreover, these methods provide strategic flexibility. In dynamic industries like hospitality or technology, where market conditions shift rapidly, top-down estimates offer a quick baseline that can be refined later as more data emerges. This adaptability allows decision-makers to act decisively, whether launching a project, responding to a client, or reallocating funds without being bogged down by exhaustive analysis.

The Bottom-Up Approach used in the Travel and Leisure Industry: A Case Study:

In the dynamic and competitive landscape of the travel and leisure industry, effective budgeting and workforce planning are critical to ensuring operational efficiency, profitability, and guest satisfaction. Great Escape Resorts, a prominent player in this sector with over

32 property locations, has adopted a bottom-up approach to its budgeting process. This method, driven by general managers (GMs) at each property, empowers local leadership to craft detailed departmental budgets that are eventually consolidated at the corporate level. By starting with granular estimates at the property level, encompassing departments such as Housekeeping, Front Desk, and Laundry, including the integration of workforce planning, Great Escape Resorts exemplifies a meticulous and labor-intensive process. Currently reliant on Excel-based templates, the company was poised to transition to a more sophisticated system, an Enterprise Planning and Budgeting Cloud Service, to enable monthly forecasting and streamline operations. This segment elaborates on the bottom-up budgeting approach, its implementation at Great Escape Resort, and the implications of this shift in planning methodology.

Bottom-Up Estimates: *A detailed cost-estimating technique where individual work items are estimated separately and aggregated to derive the total project cost. This method provides high accuracy but requires significant time and effort.*

The current budgeting process at Great Escape Resorts begins with the distribution of Excel-based templates to the GMs of its 32+ properties. These templates serve as standardized tools for capturing detailed expense plans across various departments, such as Housekeeping, Front Desk, and Laundry, which are pivotal to resort operations. Each GM collaborates with department heads to estimate costs, incorporating factors like supplies, maintenance, utilities, and, critically, workforce planning. Workforce planning is a cornerstone of this process, given the labor-intensive nature of the leisure industry. GMs assess staffing needs based on historical occupancy rates, seasonal fluctuations, and anticipated guest volumes, ensuring that labor costs, often the largest expense category, are both realistic and optimized.

For instance, in Housekeeping, a GM might estimate the number of housekeepers required per shift, factoring in room turnovers and deep-cleaning schedules, while the Front Desk budget might account for additional staff during peak check-in periods. Similarly, Laundry operations require projections for detergent, water usage, and personnel to handle linens for a fluctuating number of guests. These granular estimates are compiled into the Expense Plan for each property, forming the foundation of the bottom-up approach.

Revenue planning, however, diverges from this decentralized model. It is managed centrally by the (Room) Inventory Department's Revenue Management team, which leverages data on occupancy trends, pricing strategies, and market conditions to forecast income. This division of labor, expenses from GMs and revenue from a specialized team, ensures a balanced approach, though it introduces complexity when consolidating the two streams at the corporate level.

Once GMs complete their templates, the data is submitted to corporate finance teams, who aggregate the property-level budgets into a cohesive organizational plan. This consolidation phase requires reconciling discrepancies, aligning departmental estimates with revenue projections, and ensuring compliance with strategic goals. The Excel-driven process, while effective in capturing detail, is labor-intensive and prone to errors, such as formula inconsistencies or manual data entry mistakes, prompting Great Escape Resorts interest in a more automated solution.

GUESS LESS, WIN MORE: MASTERING THE ART OF ESTIMATION

Alright, let's debug the myth of "ballpark figures" and craft some solid estimates! In the fast-paced world of software development, where deadlines loom like server crashes and budgets can vanish faster than a poorly timed *"git push"*, knowing the difference between an estimate and a guess is your ticket to staying sane. An estimate is a calculated, data-driven prediction grounded in models, metrics, or historical data, think Parametric Estimating, Function Point Analysis (FPA), or Three-Point Estimates, all sharpened by the wisdom of the learning curve lifecycle. A guess, on the other hand, is what happens when your PM asks for a delivery date during a coffee-fueled standup with zero context, it's a wild stab in the dark, as reliable as a flaky API. In this section, Guess Less, Win More: Mastering the Art of Estimation, we'll dive into battle-tested techniques to transform your gut feelings into precise, defensible forecasts that keep your projects, and your sanity, on track.

Parametric Estimating*: Parametric Estimating: A quantitative cost-estimating technique that applies statistical relationships between project characteristics (parameters) and costs to predict future expenditures. This approach enhances accuracy by leveraging historical data and mathematical modeling.*

A construction company may use parametric estimating to determine the cost of building a new office complex. Based on historical data, they know that constructing one square foot of office space typically costs $200. To estimate the total project cost, they multiply the planned 10,000 square feet by the $200 per square foot rate, resulting in a projected cost of $2,000,000. Whereas a project software company would list out the skill sets and locations of the developers and team members, use bill rates and cost rates to determine estimates and margins.

Function Points (FPA): *A method of measuring software size by assessing functionalities meaningful to end users. This technique is used for estimating software development costs and effort.*

Agile projects are best suited for the function points analysis method because we lean on value as primary constraint. A notable application of FPA is detailed in the study "Measuring the Function Points for Migration Project: A Case Study."[119] This research focuses on assessing the functional size of a source code migration project using FPA, particularly when migration tools are employed. The study highlights that while FPA is effective for measuring software size based on user functionality, its application in source code migration projects requires careful consideration, especially when automated tools are involved. Key insights from the case study include:

- **Objective Measurement:** FPA offers an objective and structured technique to measure software size by quantifying the functionality provided to the user, based on value and logical design.
- **Application to Migration Projects:** The study extends the use of FPA to measure source code-based migra-

tion projects, addressing the challenges and considerations unique to such contexts.

- **Comparison with Re-engineering Projects:** The results obtained from applying FPA to the migration project were compared with those from re-engineering projects, providing insights into the effectiveness and adaptability of FPA in different project scenarios.

This case study underscores the adaptability of Function Point Analysis in various project contexts, including migration projects, and emphasizes the importance of tailoring the FPA methodology to specific project characteristics to achieve accurate measurements.

Three-Point Estimate*: A technique that incorporates three cost estimates, optimistic, most likely, and pessimistic to improve accuracy and account for uncertainties. This method enhances risk assessment in budgeting.*

The three-point estimating technique becomes especially valuable when applied to real-world scenarios involving technical integrations. For example, consider a use case where multiple system components must interface using different protocols and skill sets. With limited information and a shortened delivery timeline we instructed the technical team to craft a topology map outlining all necessary integrations. Alongside this, we've documented integrations, conversions, enhancements, and other development elements, excluding reports for now, in a CEMLI playbook, Conversions, Enhancements, Modifications, Localizations and Integrations. This playbook employs a matrix similar to the MoSCoW method, where we apply a three-point estimate technique, categorizing tasks as low, medium, or complex during our preliminary analysis. At this early stage, detailed data is often lacking, making precise cost calculations impractical and time-intensive. Instead, the three-point estimate provides a practical workaround, allowing us to assess effort and duration without exhaustive breakdowns.

For this approach, we form a resource lists, detailing the skilled unnamed personnel needed for coding, building, and development of the object. Next, we assign a placeholder to each difficulty level: low, medium, or complex. By applying the three-point estimate formula, averaging optimistic, most likely, and pessimistic scenarios, we estimate timelines ranging from $2 - 4$ weeks for low-complexity tasks to 8, 12, or even 16 weeks for more intricate ones, from initiation to deployment. Our estimates draw on the project's broad scope, the number of available resources, their associated costs, and the complexity labels tied to effort and duration. While critical chain constraints and resource availability introduce some variability, this method delivers a reliable delivery period estimate, balancing accuracy with efficiency until more granular details emerge.

To apply this, we pair each complexity label with skilled resource lists and their associated costs, then calculate a weighted average: (Optimistic + 4 × Most Likely + Pessimistic) ÷ 6. For example, a medium-complexity integration might have an optimistic timeline of 2 weeks, a most likely of 8 weeks, and a pessimistic of 12 weeks, yielding an expected duration of 7.3 weeks [(2 + 4 × 8 + 12) ÷ 6]. Factoring in resource costs, say, $1,000 per week per developer, and assuming two developers, the cost estimate becomes approximately $14,600, adjusted for critical chain dependencies and resource availability. This method scales across the project: low tasks might span 2-8 weeks, medium 8-12 weeks, and complex 12-16 weeks, providing a reasonable delivery window, give or take constraints, until detailed data refines our figures further. During the later stages of the project, provided we included scalability and adaptability into the SOW, we can provide a more definite estimate.

Definitive Estimate: *A highly accurate cost estimate that is typically developed later in a project when more information is available. This estimate enables precise budgeting and financial control.*

Having explored the application of Three Point Estimates and Definitive Estimation techniques, we now close this section discussing two related estimation concepts, learning curve theory and life cycle costing, that offer valuable insights into optimizing efficiency through repetitive application of tasks and understanding the long-term financial implications of such projects.

Learning Curve Theory: *A principle stating that repetitive production of items leads to efficiency improvements, reducing per-unit costs over time. This concept is relevant in manufacturing, construction, and software development projects.*

Life Cycle Costing: *A comprehensive cost assessment approach that considers both the initial investment and the long-term operational and maintenance costs of a project or product. This method aids in making cost-effective decisions over the entire lifespan of an asset.*

THE GOAL & THE OBSTACLES: COSTS

As a project manager, my primary goal is to drive profitability and ensure our projects deliver strong financial returns. Making money is not just about completing work, it's about strategic execution that maximizes revenue while minimizing waste. Our focus is on achieving robust profits, the financial gain when revenues surpass expenses, as this is a critical indicator of success in our commercial projects. We aim for a high profit margin, the ratio of net profit to total revenue, which reflects our ability to manage costs efficiently and create value. By keeping cost overruns, the excess of actual costs over estimates, whether in dollars or percentages, in check, we avoid setbacks from poor planning, scope creep, or unexpected expenses. In the following sections, we dive into the cost baseline, and other obstacles for controlling expenses and safeguarding our profitability, ensuring every dollar spent aligns with our goal of financial success.

Cost Baseline: *A time-phased budget used to track and manage project costs. The cost baseline is a crucial tool for measuring cost performance and identifying budget variances.*

Direct Costs: *Expenses directly attributable to a project's activities, such as labor, materials, and equipment costs. These costs are specific to the production of project deliverables.*
- *Wages and salaries of employees working specifically on the project.*
- *Raw materials used exclusively for the project.*
- *Software licenses purchased solely for the project.*

Indirect Costs: *Expenses that are not directly tied to specific project deliverables but are essential for overall project execution. Examples include utilities, administrative salaries, rent, and general facility maintenance.*
- *Office rent and utilities.*
- *Administrative staff salaries.*
- *Insurance and security expenses.*
- *General office supplies.*

Intangible Costs or Benefits: *Non-financial factors that are difficult to measure in monetary terms but can influence project outcomes. Examples include brand reputation, employee morale, and customer loyalty. Though hard to quantify, they can have a significant impact on long-term success.*
- *Improved customer satisfaction from better service.*
- *Enhanced employee morale due to a positive work environment.*
- *Strengthened brand reputation from a successful marketing campaign.*
- *Loss of customer trust due to a product recall.*

Sunk Cost: *Funds that have already been spent and cannot be recovered. Recognizing sunk costs is important for making rational financial decisions, as it helps prevent further investments driven by past expenditures.*
- *Money spent on initial research and development that cannot be recovered.*
- *Non-refundable deposits on equipment or services.*
- *Investments in outdated technology that is no longer usable.*
- *Marketing expenses for a canceled product launch.*

Tangible Costs or Benefits: *Measurable financial factors associated with a project, such as labor wages, material expenses, and revenue increases. These quantifiable elements are critical for accurate budgeting and financial planning.*

- *Material costs for project construction (e.g., steel, concrete).*
- *Employee wages and contractor fees.*
- *Revenue generated from product sales.*
- *Equipment rental fees.*

RESERVES: BETWEEN AMBITION AND REALITY

Having established the importance of profitability and disciplined cost management to achieve our financial goals, we must now address the inherent uncertainties that threaten project success. While a solid cost baseline keeps us on track, it's not enough to ensure resilience against unforeseen challenges. This brings us to the critical role of reserves, strategic buffers designed to absorb risks and maintain project stability. Through tools like contingency allocation, strategic risk absorption capacity, and a mitigative cushioning framework, we proactively manage cost uncertainties. By leveraging data-driven approaches such as the embedded uncertainty allowance, project flexibility margin, predictive variance reserve, and risk-tolerant buffering mechanism, we empower our team to adapt swiftly without sacrificing deliverables or profitability. In the following section, we'll delve into how these reserves are carefully planned and applied to safeguard our project's financial and operational objectives.

Reserves: *Financial allocations included in a project's cost estimate to provide flexibility in managing cost uncertainties. These reserves serve as a safety net, allowing the project team to address potential financial variances caused by unexpected changes, price fluctuations, or minor scope adjustments. By incorporating reserves, organizations can maintain budget stability and reduce the likelihood of financial shortfalls.*

Management Reserves: *A portion of the project budget specifically set aside to cover unforeseen and unpredictable risks, also known as "unknown unknowns." Unlike contingency reserves, management reserves are not tied to identified risks but are instead allocated for completely unexpected challenges or events. These reserves act as a strategic financial buffer, giving management the flexibility to respond to surprises without derailing the overall budget or schedule.*

Contingency Reserves: *Funds deliberately included in the project budget to address known risks, often referred to as "known unknowns." These reserves are based on risk assessments and are designed to cover potential cost overruns or delays resulting from identified uncertainties, such as material price increases or supplier delays. By accounting for these anticipated risks, contingency reserves help prevent budget overruns and enhance financial predictability.*

HARNESSING EARNED VALUE

"So, how are we doing?" To maintain clarity and control throughout the project, every manager must conduct Earned Value Management

(EVM) calculations to assess profitability, monitor costs, and ensure sufficient reserves are in place to handle unexpected challenges. These measurements offer a transparent view of whether our progress tracking and adaptive adjustments are delivering sustainable value, keeping projects on track and securing long-term financial success. In the next section, we will explore a practical use case to demonstrate how EVM, combined with learning curve theory and life cycle costing, is applied in a real-world software development project to drive effective decision-making and measurable outcomes.

Earned Value Management (EVM): *A comprehensive project performance measurement framework that integrates scope, schedule, and cost data to evaluate project health and forecast outcomes. By comparing planned progress with actual performance, EVM enables proactive decision-making, helping project managers identify variances early and implement corrective actions to maintain efficiency.*

ECOTRACK'S SUCCESS: USE CASE

To deliver the EcoTrack project, a mobile app designed to gamify sustainable living, I relied heavily on Earned Value Management (EVM) to keep our nine-month development timeline and budget on track. EVM integrates scope, schedule, and cost into a cohesive framework, giving me a clear snapshot of project health at any moment, like now, four months into development. For instance, building the app's real-time carbon footprint calculator is a critical task. The Planned Value (PV), the budgeted cost of work scheduled might be set at \$20,000 by this point, based on our timeline and resource allocation. Meanwhile, the Earned Value (EV), the value of work actually completed stands at $18,000, reflecting 90% completion of the feature. Comparing this to the Actual Cost (AC) of $22,000 spent on developer hours and testing tools reveals our performance. This data fuels proactive decisions: a Cost Variance (CV) of -$4,000 (EV - AC) signals we're over budget, while a Schedule Variance (SV) of -$2,000 (EV - PV) shows we're slightly behind. With EVM, I can spot these variances early and adjust, perhaps reallocating effort to catch up without inflating costs further.

Digging deeper, EVM's efficiency metrics sharpen my oversight. The Cost Performance Index (CPI), EV divided by AC, yields 0.82 ($18,000 / $22,000), confirming we're less efficient than planned; every dollar spent delivers only 82 cents of value. The Schedule Performance Index (SPI), EV over PV sits at 0.9 ($18,000 / $20,000), indicating a modest lag. These ratios guide our next steps: a CPI below 1 prompts me to negotiate overtime with developers or trim non-essential features, while an SPI under 1 suggests accelerating testing to hit our Early Finish Date. Looking ahead, the Estimate at Completion (EAC) projects our total cost based on current trends. If our Budget at Completion (BAC) is $200,000, and we continue at this CPI, the EAC might climb to $243,000 ($200,000 / 0.82), flagging a need for cost controls. The Estimate to Complete (ETC), EAC minus AC tells me we'll need $221,000 more to finish, refining our financial strategy as we push toward launch.

EVM's predictive power shines with the To-Complete Performance Index (TCPI), showing the efficiency we must hit to meet our goals. To stay within the $200,000 BAC, with $182,000 left to spend (BAC - AC) and $182,000 of value remaining (BAC - EV), our TCPI is 1.0 meaning we can maintain current efficiency if we eliminate variances. But if we accept the EAC as our new target, the TCPI adjusts to 0.82, aligning with our current pace. For EcoTrack, this means tightening resource use, like cutting unnecessary debug cycles, or leveraging float elsewhere, such as delaying UI polish with free slack, to focus effort where it counts. By weaving PV, EV, and AC into actionable insights, and balancing CPI, SPI, and EAC forecasts, EVM transforms raw data into a roadmap. It's how we'll deliver EcoTrack on time and within budget, ensuring our sustainability mission doesn't just launch, it thrives.

Planned Value (PV): *The estimated cost of work planned to be completed by a specific point in time, based on the project schedule and budget allocation. PV serves as a critical reference for assessing whether work is progressing as expected and ensuring that financial resources are aligned with the planned execution.*

Actual Cost (AC): *The total financial expenditure incurred for project activities within a given period, encompassing labor, materials, equipment, and indirect costs. AC is a vital metric for budget tracking, ensuring that project spending remains within the approved financial limits and identifying cost overruns before they escalate.*

Earned Value (EV): *The monetary worth of work actually completed at a given point in time, expressed in terms of the budgeted cost for that work. EV helps gauge real progress against planned objectives, providing insight into whether the project is keeping pace with expectations or experiencing delays.*

Cost Variance (CV): *A key financial performance indicator calculated as the difference between earned value (EV) and actual cost (AC). A positive CV indicates that work is* *being completed under budget, reflecting cost efficiency, whereas a negative CV signifies overspending, signaling the need for cost-control measures.*

Schedule Variance (SV): *A critical schedule performance metric that measures the difference between earned value (EV) and planned value (PV). A positive SV suggests the project is ahead of schedule, allowing potential resource reallocation, while a negative SV indicates delays, requiring mitigation strategies to prevent further timeline slippage.*

Cost Performance Index (CPI): *A fundamental efficiency ratio that compares earned value (EV) to actual cost (AC). A CPI above 1 indicates the project is utilizing resources efficiently, staying within budget, whereas a CPI below 1 signals cost overruns, necessitating budget reassessment and corrective actions.*

Schedule Performance Index (SPI): *A project schedule efficiency indicator calculated as the ratio of earned value (EV) to planned value (PV). An SPI greater than 1 reflects accelerated progress, potentially allowing for early completion, while an SPI below 1 highlights schedule delays, requiring adjustments to maintain project timelines.*

Estimate at Completion (EAC): *A forward-looking projection of the total cost required to complete the project based on actual performance trends. EAC accounts for current variances and anticipated future conditions, helping project managers refine financial strategies and ensure adequate funding for successful project completion.*

Estimate to Complete (ETC): *The projected cost required to finish the remaining work, determined by subtracting actual costs (AC) from the estimate at completion (EAC). ETC enables teams to assess remaining financial needs and optimize resource allocation to stay within budget constraints.*

To-Complete Performance Index (TCPI): *A predictive metric that calculates the efficiency rate needed to complete the project within a specific financial target, whether the original budget (BAC) or the revised estimate (EAC). TCPI provides insight into whether the current cost performance must improve or be maintained to achieve financial goals.*

Budget at Completion (BAC): *The total approved budget assigned to the project from initiation to completion. BAC serves as a foundational financial benchmark, allowing project teams to compare actual performance against planned expenditures and forecast final costs with greater accuracy.*

To wrap up the EcoTrack project overview using Earned Value Management (EVM), we've defined the key elements, such as, Planned Value (PV), Earned Value (EV), Actual Cost (AC), and the related performance indices that form the foundation for financial benchmarking. These metrics offer a structured lens through which to measure project performance and forecast future outcomes. Now, with a clear understanding of these classifications, let's take on a transformation project and dig deeper into the calculations that bring these concepts to life, supported by real data and practical application.

PREVIEW: EARNED VALUE MANAGEMENT IN THE TRANSFORMATION PROJECT

Imagine overseeing a Transformation Project, a bold initiative to revamp a company's digital infrastructure, with a *Budget at Completion (BAC)* of $764,700. Over 12 months in, the *Earned Value Management (EVM)* metrics paint a vivid picture of progress and pitfalls. The *Planned Value (PV)* matches the BAC at $764,700, reflecting the full scope of work scheduled, while the *Earned Value (EV)* of $344,115 shows we've completed about 45% of the project's value. Yet, the *Actual Cost (AC)* of $341,155 reveals a lean operation, yielding a *Cost Variance (CV)* of $2,960, proof we're slightly under budget. The *Cost Performance Index (CPI)* at 101% confirms this efficiency, delivering $1.01 of value per dollar spent. With an *Estimate at Completion (EAC)* of $758,122 and *Estimate to Complete (ETC)* of $416,967, we're on track to finish below budget, and a *To-Complete Performance Index (TCPI)* of 99% suggests we can maintain this pace to hit our financial target.

But the schedule tells a different story. A glaring *Schedule Variance (SV)* of -$420,585 signals we're far behind, with the *Schedule Performance Index (SPI)* at 45% underscoring that we've earned less than half the value planned by now. This lag, perhaps from delayed identification on a rogue inventory management system, threatens our timeline, even as costs stay in check. In the next section, we'll dive into how these metrics shape our strategy for the Transformation Project, balancing fiscal wins with schedule recovery to deliver a modernized system that's worth the wait.

Earned value Management

1. **Planned Value (PV)**: Authorized budget

2. **Actual Cost (AC)**: costs incurred

3. **Earned value (EV)**: Estimate of physical value

4. **Cost Variance (CV): EV (3) -AC (2)** negative is bad

5. **Schedule Variance (SV): EV (3) – PV (1)** negative is bad

6. **Cost Performance Index (CPI)**: used to estimate COST to complete EV (3) / AC (2)

7. **Schedule Performance Index (SPI)**: used to estimate TIME to complete EV (3) / PV (1)

8. **Estimate at Completion (EAC): BAC/CPI (6)**

9. **Estimated to Complete (ETC): EAC (8) /CPI (6)**

10. **To complete Performance Index (TCPI) 2 ways for EAC or BAC**
    - **TCPI (BAC-EV/BAC-AC**
    - **TCPI (BAC-EV)/EAC-AC)**

11. **Budget at Completion (BAC) same as planned value**

Transformation Project	EVM Metrics	Analysis
Total Budget at Completion	**$ 764,700**	
1. Planned Value (PV):	$ 764,700	**Authorized budget**
2. Actual Cost (AC):	$ 341,155	**Costs Incurred**
3. Earned value (EV):	$ 344,115	**Estimate of Physical Value (Project Plan % completion)**
4. Cost Variance (CV):	$ 2,960	**Earned value minus actual costs (Positive)**

Transformation Project	EVM Metrics	Analysis
5. Schedule Variance (SV)	(-420,585)	**Not a dollar metric, a schedule metric. Took longer than plan**
6. Cost Performance Index (CPI)	101%	**On Budget earned value to actual costs near 1, As budgeted**
7. Schedule Performance Index (SPI):	45%	**Behind Schedule earned value to planned value (*) See timeline**
8. Estimate at Completion (EAC):	$ 758,122	**On Budget**
9. Estimated to Complete (ETC):	$ 416,967	**On Budget**
10. To complete Performance Index (TCPI)	99%	**Cost Performance On Target**

Rate of Performance (RP): *A metric used in EVM to compare actual work completed against planned progress. This ratio aids in assessing productivity and forecasting completion timelines.*

CHAPTER 12

Risk: The Sneaky Shadows, The Twisty Turns

G RAPPLING WITH RISK isn't just about spreadsheets and contingency plans, it's a wrestling match with the human mind. Our brains, as Daniel Kahneman outlines in Thinking, Fast and Slow, juggle two systems when judging risk: System 1, the quick, intuitive gut-check, and System 2, the slower, analytical deep-dive.[120] These systems shape how I assess threats, whether it's a tight deadline or a flaky vendor, and they're both a blessing and a curse. System 1 churns out snap judgments with ease, but it's riddled with biases that cloud my view, while System 2 demands effort I don't always have time for. In the chaos of managing a project, or launching a mobile app, these mental quirks make risk a slippery beast, amplifying challenges like spotting real threats, weighing their impact, and convincing my team to act. Here's how this plays out and how I navigate managing risk.

Risk: *Any uncertainty that can positively or negatively influence a project's objectives. Risks can arise from various* *sources, including technical, financial, environmental, and organizational factors.*

Risk Events: *Specific uncertain occurrences that can affect a project positively or negatively. Identifying and assessing risk events is a key aspect of risk management.*

IT'S ALL IN OUR HEAD: HOW OUR MINDS JUDGE RISK

Risk evaluation starts with questions, endless ones. What could delay coding? Could the client balk at costs? I ask myself these, my team peppers me with more, and there's no cap on what I can evaluate: timelines, budgets, tech glitches. System 1 kicks in first, scanning memory and the environment with zero effort, think of it as my internal radar. It flags "Server crash" because we had one last year, or "Team burnout" since I've seen the late-night Slack pings. These gut calls are fast and feel right, but they're heuristics, shortcuts swapping tough questions ("What's the crash probability?") for easy ones ("Does this feel familiar?"). System 2, though, is the heavy lifter, crunching numbers, dissecting causes, but it's not automatic; I have to force it online, and often I don't.

The catch? System 1's impressions, like "This API's solid" after a smooth demo, carry bias. Paul Slovic's affect heuristic nails it: if I like the API (it's sleek, trendy), I downplay its risks; if I dread testing (it's tedious), I overestimate its pitfalls.[121] Emotions steer me, and intensity matching piles on, my brain scales risk by how loud it feels, not how likely it is. A red-flashing bug report screams "crisis" even if it's minor, while a quiet vendor delay slips under the radar. System 1 loves coherence too, stitching a story, "We're on track!", from scraps, ignoring gaps. It's biased toward losses (a missed deadline stings more than a win feels good) and frames risks narrowly, isolating them from the big picture. Without System 2's pushback, I'm half-blind.

A PROJECT MANAGER'S REALITY: THE APP LAUNCH

Take my current gig: launching a retail app by Q3. My risk register lists "Payment integration fails" (20% chance, high impact) and "User testing flops" (30%, medium impact). System 1 kicks off, last project's payment glitch flashes, so I think, "We've got this; it's familiar." I like the payment vendor (their rep's charming), so the affect heuristic whispers, "They're fine," despite spotty uptime stats. Meanwhile, testing feels like a slog, so I inflate its risk, imagining a user revolt. Intensity matching skews it further, a tester's loud "This sucks!" outweighs quiet data saying it's fixable. My coherence-seeking brain ties it up: "We're good, just tweak testing," sidelining a deeper look.

Then testing hits: the payment system lags under 1,000 users, an unforeseen scale issue. System 1 didn't ask, "What's the max load?", it assumed "It worked before." Now, my contingency reserve ($10,000 for known risks) won't cover a full fix, and no management reserve was set for this "unknown unknown." My risk-averse lead dev panics, pushing a rewrite, while my risk-seeking designer shrugs, "Ship it, users won't care." My risk appetite, normally risk-neutral, wavers under emotion; I dread the lag's fallout more than data justifies. Without System 2, I'd greenlight a hasty patch, birthing secondary risks like "Support tickets spike."

The Cognitive Challenges

These quirks make risk a beast: Understand the concept from the example discussed, then study the differences between the thought and how our brain perceives it.

Heuristics: *Mental shortcuts or rules of thumb that simplify decision-making by allowing individuals to make quick judgments without exhaustive analysis. These cognitive strategies help people solve problems efficiently by relying on past experiences, patterns, and intuition rather than extensive logical reasoning. While heuristics can be beneficial in speeding up decision-making, they can also lead to biases and errors, as they often involve simplifications and generalizations.*

- **Heuristics:** *System 1 swaps "What's the crash cost?" for "Does it feel bad?"—skewing priorities.*

Affect: *The emotional experience or feeling state that influences an individual's mood, behavior, and decision-making. It encompasses both short-term emotional reactions (such as joy, anger, or fear) and longer-term mood states (such as contentment or anxiety). In psychology, affect is typically categorized into positive affect (characterized by emotions like happiness, enthusiasm, and satisfaction) and negative affect (marked by emotions such as sadness, frustration, or stress).*

- **Affect:** *Liking the vendor blinds me to red flags; disliking testing bloats its threat.*

Coherence: *The quality of being logical, consistent, and well-organized, making ideas, processes, or systems clear and easy to understand. It reflects how effectively different components fit together in a unified and meaningful way, creating a sense of clarity, continuity, and stability.*

- **Coherence:** *I cling to "We're fine" narratives, missing risk events like scale limits.*

Loss Bias: *Loss bias refers to the cognitive tendency to focus more on avoiding losses than on acquiring equivalent gains, even when the outcomes have the same value. This bias is rooted in loss aversion, which suggests that people perceive the pain of losses as more intense than the pleasure of equivalent gains.*

- **Loss Bias:** *A delay looms larger than a win, narrowing my frame, ignoring benefits of a fix.*

System 2 isn't immune, it's effort-heavy and still bends to System 1's nudge. If I learn the lag risk is low, I'll see benefits rosier too, but only if it fits my beliefs. Challenging that takes grit.

TAMING THE BEAST: SYSTEM 1 AND 2 IN SYNC

I've learned to lean on both systems. System 1's radar flags risks fast, "Payment's shaky", and I log them in the risk register. But I don't trust the vibe. I force System 2 with a risk breakdown structure (RBS): technical (lag), operational (testing), external (vendor). I assign risk owners, the dev lead owns payment, and demand data: "What's the lag threshold?" We calculate: 20% chance × $20,000 impact = $4,000 expected loss, so I pad a contingency plan (test at scale, $5,000). For surprises, a $15,000 management reserve waits. I list pros/cons, vendor's charm versus uptime, to bust affect bias, and brainstorm secondary risks, "If we fix lag, does QA suffer?"

Weekly, I review the top ten risks, not my gut. Testing's lag jumps the list; we pivot, not panic. It's not easy, System 1 fights for control, but pairing its speed with System 2's depth keeps us real. In app-land, this meant a pre-launch scale test, a funded fix, and a launch that didn't flop. Risk isn't just out there, it's in our heads, and winning means mastering both.[122]

TYPES OF RISKS

Former U.S. Secretary of Defense Donald Rumsfeld famously articulated a useful framework for understanding risk:

> *"There are known knowns; there are things we know we know. We also know there are known unknowns; that is to say, we know there are some things we do not know. But there are also unknown unknowns, the ones we don't know we don't know."*

Love him or hate him, it is profoundly true.

Known Risks: *Risks that have been identified, analyzed, and can be managed proactively through mitigation, contingency planning, or other risk response strategies. These risks are accounted for within the project planning process.*

Unknown Risks: *Unforeseen risks that cannot be proactively managed because they have not been identified or anticipated in project planning. These risks require adaptive problem-solving when they emerge.*

Unknown Unknowable Risks: *Unknown Unknowable Risks are risks that are completely unforeseeable and beyond the scope of prediction or preparation. These risks arise from unprecedented events, extreme randomness, or factors so far* *outside existing knowledge and experience that they cannot be anticipated. Unlike unknown risks, which may become apparent with deeper analysis, unknown unknowable risks remain hidden until they occur, requiring organizations to rely on resilience, adaptability, and rapid response strategies when they emerge.*

Nassim Nicholas Taleb, the author of *The Black Swan* introduced the concept of highly improbable, high-impact events that are difficult to predict but have extreme consequences.[123] While **Black Swan events** are rare and largely unforeseeable, most project risks do not fall into this category. Instead, they belong to what Don Rumsfeld described as **"known unknowns"**, risks that, while not explicitly acknowledged, have underlying patterns and early warning signs that could have been recognized with better awareness and analysis. To proactively prepare for risk there are several strategies to consider before they endanger a project.

EXPECT THE BEST PLAN FOR THE WORST: THE ROLE OF RESERVES

In the intricate world of software development, where unpredictability is as common as code commits, reserves are the unsung heroes of project stability. These financial and strategic safeguards, contingency allowances, contingency reserves, management reserves, contingency plans, and fallback plans, equip teams to navigate the inevitable twists of building complex systems. Far from being mere afterthoughts, reserves are proactive tools, woven into the fabric of the project from the outset, ideally within the Statement of Work (SOW). They address both the "known unknowns", risks we can name but not fully predict, and the "unknown unknowns", surprises no one saw coming. Using a software development project as a lens, we explores the purpose of reserves, how they're applied with practical examples like custom reporting needs and technical gaps uncovered late in testing and why embedding them in the SOW is critical for success.

The purpose of reserves is to armor a project against disruption. Software development is a minefield of variables, shifting client needs, technical hurdles, regulatory demands, that can balloon costs or derail schedules. Contingency allowances, set by sponsors, act as financial or resource cushions to absorb these shocks, ensuring the project doesn't grind to a halt when the unexpected strikes. Contingency reserves, meanwhile, are budgetary buckets carved out for specific, identified risks, the "known unknowns", like the certainty that out-of-the-box reporting tools won't fully meet a client's operational, statutory, or regulatory needs. Management reserves go further, guarding against the "unknown unknowns", wildcards no one anticipated, like a sudden third-party API failure. Together, these reserves maintain flexibility, keeping the project on track without constant renegotiation or panic.

Take a software project to build a customer relationship management (CRM) system. In drafting the SOW, the team knows standard reports (e.g., sales by region) won't cut it, clients always demand tailored views, like compliance reports for regulators or operational dashboards for daily use. Here, contingency reserves shine. The SOW might allocate $20,000 and 100 hours for "custom report development," a buffer for the inevitable request to track unique metrics, say, customer churn by support ticket type. This isn't guesswork; it's a calculated provision for a known risk: off-the-shelf tools never suffice. Without this reserve, mid-project demands would force scope creep, budget overruns, or rushed hacks. By baking it into the

SOW, the team signals foresight, clients see it as value, not padding, and secures the funds upfront, avoiding later haggling.

Now, picture a scenario where development hums along, iterations roll out, and testing reveals a gap: the system's search function can't handle complex queries (e.g., "Find customers with over 50 purchases who've contacted support twice"). This wasn't flagged earlier, requirements focused on basic searches, but user testing exposes the shortfall. This is where management reserves step in. The SOW might include a $15,000 pot for "unforeseen technical enhancements," a safety net for such "unknown unknowns." The team taps this to build a robust search engine, averting a late-stage crisis. A gap analysis during testing, comparing "what we built" to "what's needed", caught this, proving reserves aren't reactive; they're proactive when planned early. Including this in the SOW signals preparedness, not uncertainty, and ensures resources are ready when surprises emerge.

For known risks with teeth, contingency plans and fallback plans add muscle. Suppose the CRM's third-party payment integration is flaky; a 40% chance it'll fail certification. The contingency plan, detailed in the SOW, might be: "If certification fails by Week 8, switch to Vendor B, budgeted at $10,000 from contingency reserves." If Vendor B flops too, the fallback plan kicks in: "Pivot to an in-house payment module, funded by $25,000 from management reserves." These pre-set strategies, tied to specific triggers, minimize chaos if the risk hits. The SOW lays this out: "Payment integration risks are mitigated with Vendor B ($10K contingency) or in-house build ($25K management reserve)," giving clients confidence and the team a roadmap. Without this upfront clarity, a failure would spark frantic scrambles, not calm execution.

Why anchor these in the SOW? It's the project's contract, its North Star, aligning expectations, budgets, and plans from day one. Embedding contingency allowances (e.g., 10% of the $200,000 total for overruns) signals realism to sponsors: "We've got buffers for the unpredictable." Listing contingency reserves for custom reports or integration risks ties funds to specific "known unknowns," justifying costs with purpose. A management reserve line, say, 5% or $10,000, covers the rest, a catch-all for surprises like that search gap. Spelling out contingency and fallback plans in the SOW's risk section, "If X fails, we do Y with Z dollars", turns vague worries into actionable steps, baked into the baseline. This upfront transparency builds trust, secures approval, and avoids mid-flight renegotiations that erode momentum.

In this CRM project, reserves aren't luxuries, they're necessities. The $20,000 report cushion delivers client-specific value, the $15,000 tech enhancement saves the search function, and the $35,000 payment plans dodges a integration disaster. Without them, the team's juggling change orders or cutting corners, both poison to success. By weaving reserves into the SOW, the project starts resilient, not rigid, ready for the real world of software development where surprises aren't if, but when. Tracking risks fuels this machine, but reserves, planned, funded, and documented, turn foresight into action, proving that in projects, the best offense is a well-funded defense.

Contingency Plans: *Predefined strategies or actions developed by project teams to respond effectively to known risks should they materialize. These plans help mitigate disruptions, minimize delays, and maintain project continuity.*

Contingency Allowances: *Financial or resource-based provisions set aside by project sponsors or organizations to mitigate the impact of unforeseen cost or schedule overruns. These allowances, also known as contingency reserves, act* as buffers to maintain project stability and ensure smooth execution.

Contingency Reserves: *Budgetary allocations included in project cost estimates to address potential risks that have been identified but whose exact occurrence or impact remains uncertain. Often referred to as "known unknowns," these reserves ensure financial flexibility within the project scope.*

Management Reserves: *Funds or resources set aside to address unforeseen project challenges, often referred to as "unknown unknowns." Unlike contingency reserves, management reserves are not allocated to specific risks but serve as a general safety net.*

Fallback Plans: *Alternative strategies prepared for high-impact risks when initial mitigation efforts prove ineffective. These plans act as secondary measures to safeguard project objectives and maintain continuity in the face of adverse events.*

Risk Appetite: *The level of risk an organization or individual is willing to accept in pursuit of project goals or potential rewards. A higher risk appetite suggests a greater tolerance for uncertainty.*

Risk-Averse: *A cautious approach to risk management in which individuals or organizations prioritize stability and actively seek to minimize uncertainty, even at the cost of potential opportunities.*

Risk-Neutral: *A balanced approach to risk management in which decisions are based on a rational analysis of potential risks and rewards, rather than a strong preference for risk avoidance or seeking.*

Risk-Seeking: *A preference for taking on higher levels of risk in pursuit of greater rewards, often seen in organizations or individuals with an aggressive growth strategy.*

Risk Enhancement*: A proactive strategy aimed at increasing the probability or impact of a positive risk (opportunity) by optimizing key contributing factors.*

Risk Exploitation: *A strategy used to ensure that an identified opportunity occurs by taking deliberate steps to maximize its benefits, such as allocating additional resources to a high-reward task.*

Risk Utility: *The perceived value or benefit of a potential outcome, which varies depending on an individual's or organization's attitude toward risk-taking.*

THE PURPOSE AND PRACTICE OF TRACKING RISKS

In the unpredictable terrain of project management, tracking risks is not just a precaution, it's a strategic imperative. Risks, those potential events or conditions that could derail timelines, inflate costs, or compromise quality, lurk in every endeavor, from software launches to construction builds. The purpose of tracking them is twofold: to shine a spotlight on threats before they strike and to orchestrate a response that keeps the project on course. By identifying, categorizing, and monitoring risks systematically, teams transform uncertainty into a manageable variable, ensuring resources are focused where they're needed most. This section explores why tracking risks matters, how it's executed using tools like a risk register, and the practical steps to capture and manage them effectively, drawing on key concepts like risk owners, RAID logs, risk breakdown structures, top ten risk item tracking, and watch lists.

The primary purpose of tracking risks is to preempt disruption. A missed deadline or a budget overrun isn't just a hiccup, it can cascade into lost trust, strained teams, or a failed deliverable. By keeping a finger on the pulse of potential issues, say, a vendor delay or a software bug, project managers can shift from reactive fire-fighting to proactive stewardship. Tracking isn't about eliminating uncertainty (an impossible feat) but about understanding it: gauging likelihood, assessing impact, and preparing responses. It's a lifeline for decision-making, letting teams allocate time, money, and talent where risks loom largest. Beyond prevention, it raises accountability and clarity, everyone knows who's watching what and what's at stake, turning a nebulous worry into a concrete plan.

How do we track risks? The cornerstone is the risk register, often called a RAID log (Risks, Assumptions, Issues, Dependencies), a centralized hub where all identified risks are documented. Think of it as the project's risk diary: it logs each threat's description, likelihood, impact, response strategy, and status. For a website redesign, the register might list "Server downtime during launch" with a 30% chance, high impact, and a mitigation plan of "Pre-test backup servers." The risk owner, the person or group tasked with monitoring and managing that risk, owns this entry. If the server risk materializes, the IT lead (the risk owner) activates the backup plan, ensuring swift action. The register isn't static; it's a living document, updated as risks evolve, new threats emerge, old ones fade, keeping the team aligned.

To capture risks comprehensively, we start with a risk breakdown structure (RBS), a hierarchical tool that sorts risks by source: technical (e.g., coding errors), financial (e.g., cost overruns), operational (e.g., staff shortages). In a construction project, the RBS might branch into "Weather delays" under operational risks or "Material cost spikes" under financial. This framework forces systematic thinking, teams brainstorm across categories, uncovering blind spots like "What if the supplier flakes?" rather than fixating on obvious tech hiccups. Capturing risks begins early—during planning, via workshops or interviews with stakeholders—and continues throughout, as scope shifts or surprises pop up. Each risk gets logged in the register with details: who spotted it, its RBS category, and the risk owner assigned.

Not all risks warrant equal attention, which is where top ten risk item tracking shines. This tool zeroes in on the project's ten most critical risks, those with the highest likelihood-impact combo, keeping them front and center. In a software rollout, the top ten might include "Data migration failure" or "Key developer quits," ranked by severity. The project manager reviews this list weekly, ensuring mitigation stays on track, say, extra testing for migration or a retention chat with the developer. Meanwhile, lesser threats, like "Minor UI glitch" with low impact, land on the watch list, a roster of low-priority risks monitored passively. If that glitch's likelihood spikes (say, user feedback flags it), it escalates to the register for active management. This tiered approach balances vigilance with efficiency, avoiding paralysis by over-analysis.

Putting it together, imagine a bridge-building project. The risk register captures "Steel delivery delay" (financial RBS, 40% chance, high impact), owned by the procurement lead, with a response of "Source a backup supplier." It's in the top ten, reviewed biweekly, while "Rain slows concrete pour" (operational, 20% chance, low impact) sits on the watch list, checked monthly. Capturing starts with a kickoff session, engineers flag steel risks, planners note weather, and updates roll in via team check-ins. The register lives in a shared spreadsheet, color-coded for status (red = active, green = mitigated), while top ten risks headline the weekly status report. Frequency varies: daily team huddles catch new risks, monthly client briefs share the top ten, and the watch list gets a quarterly glance.

Tracking risks this way isn't busywork; it's the project's early warning system. The register centralizes knowledge, the RBS structures it, risk owners own it, and top ten/watch list tools prioritize it. Together, they turn chaos into control, ensuring that when the steel's late or the rain pours, the team's not scrambling, they're ready. In project management, where stakes are high and margins thin, this disciplined dance with uncertainty isn't just smart, it's survival.

Risk Owner: *The individual or group assigned responsibility for monitoring and managing a specific risk, including implementing response strategies if the risk materializes.*

Risk Register (RAID Log): *A centralized document or database that records all identified risks, along with their attributes, response strategies, and monitoring status.*

Issue Log: (RAID Log) *— An issue log is a structured document used to **record, track, and manage project-related issues** that require resolution. It provides a central location for logging issues, assigning ownership, prioritizing their resolution, and tracking progress. Keeping an up-to-date issue log enhances transparency and accountability while helping project teams address obstacles before they escalate.*

Risk Breakdown Structure (RBS): *A hierarchical framework that categorizes risks into different levels based on their source, such as technical, financial, or operational risks, helping teams systematically analyze and address potential threats.*

Top Ten Risk Item Tracking: *A risk management tool that continuously monitors and prioritizes the ten most significant risks throughout the project lifecycle, ensuring heightened awareness and proactive management.*

Watch List: *A compilation of low-priority risks that do not require immediate action but are monitored over time in case their likelihood or impact increases.*

RAID LOG - RISKS, ACTION ITEMS, ISSUES AND DECISIONS

The process to create a risk register or RAID Log starts using a centralized medium that the team can all access like SharePoint or global document repository.

Risks:

Project risks are defined as uncertain events or conditions that, if occurs, has a negative effect on a project's objectives. Any known mitigation plan must be associated with the risk so that the team is prepared for the risk. The risk can be evaluated and given a rating depending on the severity. This rating helps on monitoring the risk regularly.

Action Items

An action item is a documented event, task, activity, or action that needs to take place.

Issues:

An issue is a problem encountered during the project execution. Issues are roadblocks that can delay the project delivery, they have an impact on the project activities. The issue will be resolved immediately or in a specified period. If it cannot be resolved it may become a risk. The issues are documented in the Issues Log.

Decisions:

A conclusion or resolution reached after consideration. Add decisions as the arise to the decision log, according to the level of detail required for project/program, with justification on why the decision was made.

Typical RAID Log Entry Items:

1.	Title	Single line of text
2.	Description	Multiple lines of text
3.	Track Name	Choice
4.	RAID Type	Choice
5.	Assigned To	Person or Group
6.	RAID Status	Choice
7.	Priority	Choice
8.	Due Date	Date and Time

9.	Related Issues	Lookup
10.	Progress Updates	Multiple lines of text
11.	Modified	Date and Time
12.	Created	Date and Time
13.	Created By	Person or Group
14.	Modified By	Person or Group

HAVE A PLAN

In this section, we'll walk you through how to create and apply two essential tools in effective risk management: the Risk Management Plan (RMP) and the Risk Assessment. By following a structured approach that begins with a clear problem statement and proceeds through a thorough assessment process, you'll learn how to build a comprehensive RMP that outlines the strategies and methodologies for managing risk across the project lifecycle. We'll also show you how to conduct a risk assessment that systematically identifies, analyzes, and evaluates potential risks, enabling you to prioritize threats based on their likelihood and impact. Together, these tools provide a proactive framework for navigating uncertainty and safeguarding project success. Follow through the problem statement and the assessment process.

Risk Management Plan (RMP): *A comprehensive, strategic document that outlines the processes, strategies, and methodologies for identifying, assessing, mitigating, and monitoring risks throughout a project's lifecycle. It serves as a blueprint for proactively managing uncertainties that could* *impact project objectives, ensuring that potential threats are systematically addressed.*

Risk Assessment*: Risk assessment is a systematic process of identifying, analyzing, and evaluating potential risks that could impact a project, organization, or operation. It involves examining both internal and external factors that may introduce uncertainty, such as technical failures, financial instability, regulatory changes, or operational inefficiencies. During the assessment, risks are categorized based on their likelihood and potential impact, allowing organizations to prioritize and develop proactive mitigation strategies.*

Triggers: *Early warning signs or indicators that signal the potential occurrence of a risk event, allowing teams to take preemptive action before the risk escalates.*

Secondary Risks*: New risks that arise as a direct consequence of implementing a risk response plan. These risks require separate assessment and potential mitigation.*

PROBLEM STATEMENT: HCM BUSINESS UNITS IN SOFTWARE DEVELOPMENT

The Human Capital Management (HCM) application we were delivering encompassed 30+ business units (BUs), each of which impacts critical areas such as approvals, intercompany transactions, supply chain orchestration (SFO), distribution, inventory management, and payroll for Phases 1 and 2 of implementation. The major risks and their impacts remain largely unknown, posing significant challenges to the project timeline and overall success.

Each of the business units (BUs) play a vital role in approvals, intercompany transactions, supply chain orchestration (SFO), distribution, inventory management, and payroll throughout Phases 1 and 2 of the implementation. However, the project faced significant challenges due to the lack of comprehensive risk visibility, with major risks remaining largely unidentified and unquantified. This created uncertainty around potential failure points, making the project vulnerable to timeline delays, budget overruns, and operational inefficiencies. The interconnected nature of the BUs further amplified these risks, as issues in one unit, such as delayed intercompany approvals, could create bottlenecks in downstream processes, like supply chain operations or payroll execution. Additionally, the complexity of SFO and distribution heightened the risk of data inaccuracies, system integration failures, and distribution delays, which could lead to inventory shortages and customer dissatisfaction. On the financial side, payroll processing risks, such as miscalculations, data corruption, or compliance failures, could result in payment delays, legal penalties, and reputational damage. The absence of a robust risk management framework made it difficult to accurately forecast timelines, allocate resources, or develop effective contingency plans. Without proactive risk identification and mitigation, the project faced increased exposure to operational disruptions and financial instability, which could compromise the overall success and reliability of the HCM implementation. To safeguard against these threats, the project required a structured and iterative risk assessment strategy, including collaborative risk workshops, quantitative and qualitative analysis, and real-time monitoring through automated dashboards. This approach provided the necessary visibility, control, and adaptability to mitigate risks and ensure the long-term stability and success of the HCM program.

ASSESSMENT PROCESS: STEP BY STEP

Step 1: Identify Potential Risks

Risk Factors: *Quantifiable indicators that determine the overall risk level of an event by analyzing both its probability and potential consequences.*

The complexity of HCM's structure creates a wide range of potential risks. Employees are loaded into most or all business units, and each BU is associated with legal entities and multiple balancing segments. Key risk areas include:

1. **Approvals:** Approval workflows for Accounts Payable (AP) and requisitions are heavily dependent on the BU configuration. Any misalignment could delay operational efficiency.

2. **Intercompany Transactions:** The current structure increases processing complexity and reconciliation efforts, potentially leading to inefficiencies and errors.

3. **Supply Chain Financial Orchestration (SFO):** Dependencies between HCM configurations and financial flows could disrupt transaction handling.

4. **Order Fulfillment and Distribution:** Misconfigured inventory management flows within 30 inventory organizations (1 per distribution center) could lead to delays or bottlenecks.

5. **Payroll:** Dependencies on HCM employee data across BUs, along with absent or incorrect configurations, may affect accurate payroll processing.

6. **Dependency on Non-Cloned Environment Plans:** Risks associated with incomplete and incorrect data in lower environments must be addressed to ensure data integrity during testing and go-live phases.

Step 2: Determine the Probability of Each Risk

The management team has decided to evaluate these risks following the completion of Iteration 1 (CRP1) and HCM SIT testing. Key milestones include:

1. **HCM SIT Testing:** Completed by 9/18, providing insights into current configuration issues.
2. **Finance Iteration 1 (CRP1):** Scheduled for 9/25, offering additional data on integration dependencies.

While the exact probabilities remain uncertain, the initial analysis suggests a high likelihood of significant issues, particularly in areas such as approval workflows, intercompany processes, and inventory flows.

Step 3: Determine the Impact of Each Risk

Initial qualitative assessments suggest that the impact of these risks is almost certain to materialize if not addressed. For example:

1. **Approval Risk:** If workflows are misaligned, operational bottlenecks may occur, significantly affecting processing timelines.
2. **Intercompany Risk:** Inaccurate reconciliations could lead to financial discrepancies, regulatory non-compliance, and strained stakeholder relationships.

3. **Inventory Management Risk:** Inefficient flows and poorly maintained inventory structures could disrupt supply chain fulfillment, impacting customer satisfaction.

The plan is to re-evaluate these risks post-Iteration 1 (CRP1) and HCM SIT, leveraging quantitative assessments to validate initial findings.

Step 4: Determine the Risk Score of Each Event

Using current observations, risk scores range from moderate to severe:

1. **Severe Risks:**
   - Legal entity and balancing segment assignments to BUs.
   - Subledger build-out for all BUs.
   - Security and user access configurations.
2. **Moderate Risks:**
   - Employee cross-referencing for approvals.
   - HCM data loads and configurations (e.g., cost flex, supervisor assignments).
   - Use of common sets for jobs, grades, and other shared configurations.

Moderate workarounds have been brainstormed, including using common sets and revising configurations post-CRP1 evaluation.

Workarounds: *Unplanned and often improvised responses to unexpected risk events that were not accounted for in contingency plans, requiring quick decision-making and adaptability.*

Brainstorming: *A collaborative technique used to generate creative solutions or ideas by encouraging free-flowing, spontaneous contributions from participants. The process focuses on quantity over quality, with judgment and criticism deferred to a later stage, allowing for innovative and unconventional thinking.*

Step 5: Understand Your Risk Tolerance

Risk Tolerance: *The maximum level of risk an organization or stakeholder is willing to accept while pursuing project objectives, influencing decision-making and strategy formulation.*

Management recognizes the downstream complications of maintaining 30 BUs in HCM. While only two BUs are currently needed for Finance and SCM, HCM's configuration impacts absences, benefits, and other administrative workflows. The principle that "the second consequence is always worse than the first" drives a cautious approach, emphasizing long-term sustainability over short-term fixes.

The CEO highlighted this point, stating, "I do not want to complicate things further." This sentiment underscores the need to justify the necessity of maintaining 30 BUs and assess the trade-offs comprehensively.

Step 6: Decide How to Prioritize Risks

Management has deferred final risk prioritization until after Iteration 1 (CRP1). However, irreversible configurations should take precedence, as they are more challenging to amend later. Specific focus areas include:

1. Legal entity and BU alignment.
2. Inventory organization structure.
3. Approval workflows for critical transactions.

Step 7: Develop Risk Response Strategies

Mitigate:

Risk Mitigation: *Actions taken to reduce the probability or impact of a risk event, such as implementing safeguards, diversifying suppliers, or improving quality control.*

Residual Risks: *Risks that persist even after mitigation strategies have been applied. These risks are monitored continuously to ensure they do not escalate beyond acceptable thresholds.*

---

1. Rebuild BUs and HCM configurations to simplify processes and reduce long-term maintenance.
2. Rebuild PeopleSoft integrations with improved mapping and alignment.
3. Use common sets for shared configurations, reducing redundancies and inconsistencies.

Avoid:

Risk Avoidance – *A strategy that seeks to eliminate a risk entirely, usually by altering the project scope, processes, or objectives to remove the risk's root cause.*

I. Delay the HCM go-live if risks are deemed unacceptably high after CRP1 evaluation.

Transfer:

Risk Transference – *A strategy that shifts the financial or operational impact of a risk to a third party, such as outsourcing high-risk activities or purchasing insurance.*

I. Shift certain HCM responsibilities to Finance and SCM teams to streamline configurations and processes.

Share:

Risk Sharing – *Distributing risk exposure among multiple parties, such as through partnerships, joint ventures, or insurance arrangements, to minimize individual liability.*

I. Conduct a deep dive post-Iteration 1 with stake-holders, including Finance, SCM, and HCM leads, to distribute risk ownership and collaborate on solutions.

Accept:

Risk Acceptance — *A strategy where a project team acknowledges a risk but chooses not to take proactive action, typically because the risk's impact is minimal, or the cost of mitigation outweighs potential consequences.*

---

1. Proceed with the current configuration, acknowledging risks but prioritizing the benefits of a timely go-live. Any issues would be addressed through phased post-go-live improvements.

Next Steps and Proposed Actions

1. **Post-Iteration 1 Retrospective:**
   Convene a meeting to compile findings from the finance team and allow HCM stakeholders to justify the need for 30 BUs.
2. **Gap Evaluation:**
   Evaluate gaps identified during CRP1 and HCM SIT to reassess risk impacts and refine mitigation strategies.
3. **Stakeholder Engagement:**
   Engage cross-functional teams, including executive management, to ensure alignment on priorities and develop a unified approach to risk management.

By addressing these risks methodically and incorporating feedback from critical milestones, the project team can navigate the complexities of HCM implementation and ensure long-term success.

TOOLS & USE CASES

The closing section reviews additional tools with associated use cases one could apply to their own specific projects.

INFLUENCE DIAGRAM USE CASE EXAMPLE (IAAS – CLOUD INFRASTRUCTURE MIGRATION)

Influence Diagram: *A graphical tool that illustrates key elements of decision-making, including uncertainties, decisions, and their interrelationships. These diagrams help project teams visualize dependencies and optimize decision outcomes.*

A company migrating its on-premises infrastructure to an IaaS cloud provider (e.g., AWS, Azure, or Google Cloud) uses an influence diagram to assess the interdependencies between key decisions, uncertainties, and outcomes.

Decisions*: Choosing between cloud providers, migration strategy (lift-and-shift vs. re-architecting).*

Uncertainties*: Potential downtime, data integrity risks, or performance degradation.*

Outcomes*: Improved scalability, potential cost savings, or performance bottlenecks.*

The influence diagram helps the project team visualize the impact of different choices and identify which variables have the greatest influence on project success.

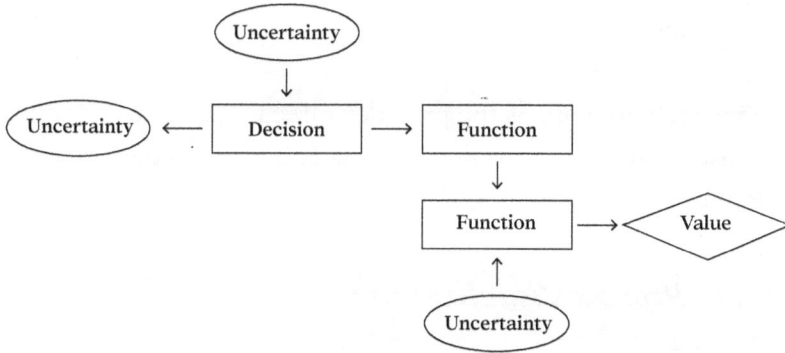

DELPHI USE CASE EXAMPLE (PAAS – NEW CLOUD SERVICE DEPLOYMENT)

Delphi Technique: *A structured forecasting method that gathers insights from a panel of experts to reach a consensus on future developments. By using multiple rounds of anonymous input, this technique minimizes bias and enhances the accuracy of predictions.*

A cloud PaaS provider (e.g., Microsoft Azure App Service) wants to predict adoption rates for a new serverless platform offering. The company uses the Delphi technique to:

- Assemble a panel of industry experts, cloud architects, and analysts.

- Collect anonymous forecasts on customer adoption rates and potential technical issues.
- Refine and aggregate responses over multiple rounds to minimize individual biases and reach a reliable consensus.

This technique helps the provider forecast demand and identify risks before full-scale deployment, enhancing product launch planning.

Delphi Process Visualization:

Round 1: Experts provide anonymous predictions →
Round 2: Responses are summarized →
Round 3: Experts adjust predictions based on group insights →
Final Consensus: Refined and aggregated forecast data.

EXPECTED MONETARY VALUE USE CASE EXAMPLE (SAAS – SUBSCRIPTION PRICING RISKS)

Expected Monetary Value (EMV): *A quantitative risk assessment metric that calculates the financial impact of a risk by multiplying its probability of occurrence by the projected monetary loss or gain. EMV helps organizations prioritize risks based on potential financial implications.*

A SaaS company offering a customer relationship management (CRM) platform uses EMV to evaluate pricing risks associated with customer churn.

> **Risk 1:** High churn rate due to service outages.
> Probability: 15%
> Financial Impact: -$100,000
> EMV = 0.15 × (-$100,000) = -$15,000

> **Risk 2:** Price increase leads to increased revenue.
> Probability: 10%
> Financial Impact: +$200,000
> EMV = 0.10 × $200,000 = +$20,000

The total EMV helps the company balance financial risks with potential gains, guiding pricing and risk-mitigation strategies.

EMV Formula:

$$EMV = \sum (\text{Probability} \times \text{Impact})$$

DECISION TREE USE CASE EXAMPLE (IAAS – MULTI-CLOUD DEPLOYMENT STRATEGY)

Decision Tree*: A structured diagram that maps out different decision paths and possible outcomes, helping project*

managers evaluate options in uncertain situations. By
visualizing risks, costs, and benefits, decision trees facilitate
informed decision-making.

A company using multi-cloud infrastructure (e.g., AWS and Google Cloud) uses a decision tree to determine:

- Whether to standardize on one provider or maintain a multi-cloud approach.
- Path 1: Standardize → Lower complexity → Vendor lock-in risk.
- Path 2: Multi-cloud → Increased flexibility → Higher management costs.

By assigning probabilities and financial impacts to each branch, the decision tree helps the team evaluate the best course of action.

Visualization Decision Tree:

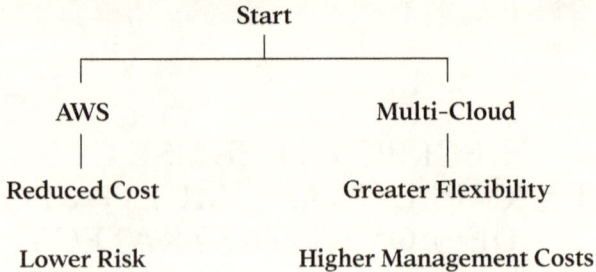

```
                        Start
                          |
       ┌──────────────────┴──────────────────┐
       |                                      |
      AWS                                 Multi-Cloud
       |                                      |
   Reduced Cost                        Greater Flexibility

   Lower Risk                        Higher Management Costs
```

SENSITIVITY ANALYSIS USE CASE EXAMPLE (PAAS – PERFORMANCE SCALING)

Sensitivity Analysis: *A technique used to determine how changes in one or more variables affect a project's overall outcome, helping managers understand which factors have the greatest influence on success.*

A PaaS application running on Azure Kubernetes Service (AKS) performs sensitivity analysis to determine how CPU and memory allocation impact system performance.

- Variables: CPU cores, memory, and storage.
- Outcome: Application response time and stability.

The analysis reveals that memory allocation has the greatest influence on performance, guiding the team to prioritize memory optimization.

PROBABILITY/IMPACT USE CASE EXAMPLE (SAAS – SERVICE OUTAGE RISKS)

Probability/Impact Matrix – *A tool that visually represents the likelihood and potential impact of identified risks. By categorizing risks based on severity and probability, project managers can prioritize response efforts accordingly.*

A SaaS provider uses a matrix to evaluate risks related to service outages.

- **Risk 1:** Database failure → High probability, high impact.
- **Risk 2:** Minor bug → Low probability, low impact.
- **Risk 3:** DDOS attack → Medium probability, high impact.

By plotting risks on the matrix, the company prioritizes mitigation strategies for high-probability, high-impact risks.

	Impact		
	Low	*Medium*	*High*
Minor Bug	X	-	-
DDOS attack	-	X	-
DB Failure	-	-	X

Use a python code tool to run simulations for Monte Carlo Analysis.

Monte Carlo Analysis: *A simulation technique that models the probability of different project outcomes by running thousands of potential scenarios. This method helps quantify uncertainty and assess overall project risk exposure.*

CHAPTER 13

Quality: The Shiny Stamp of "Job Well Done"

A T ITS CORE, the knowledge of variation is about distinguishing signal from noise. In a factory, for instance, the hum of machines, the output of a production line, or the quality of a finished product all fluctuate, not randomly, but in ways that whisper truths about the process. A part might measure 0.01 millimeters off-spec one day and 0.02 the next; a batch might yield 98% perfection while another dips to 95%. To the untrained eye, these shifts seem erratic, a frustrating departure from the ideal. But to those who study variation, they are data points in a story, clues to stability, capability, and opportunity. This is where the intellectual leap begins: variation is not merely a problem to solve but a teacher to heed.

Yet the knowledge of variation transcends technical application; it is a mindset. It demands humility, an acceptance that perfection is a myth and that systems thrive not on uniformity but on resilience. It requires curiosity, a willingness to ask why one bolt bends while another holds, why one shift outperforms another. And it calls for discipline, the rigor to measure, analyze, and act on what the data reveals rather than what intuition assumes. In a world obsessed with averages and absolutes, the knowledge of variation pulls us back to the edges, where the outliers live, where the real lessons hide.

Variation: *Measurable differences, inconsistencies, or deviations from expected behavior, outputs, standards, or specifications within an IT system, process, or service. In the context of IT quality, variation is a key indicator of instability or lack of control and can impact everything from system performance and user experience to security and compliance.*

Variation is not always a defect, but it is always an indicator, an alert that something in the system may be behaving differently than intended. For example, an application that processes a transaction in 1 second for one user and 5 seconds for another is exhibiting performance variation. A build that occasionally fails due to environment-specific conditions is showing environmental or process variation.

Types of variation in IT environments can include:

Process Variation: *When standard operating procedures (SOPs) are executed inconsistently across teams or locations.*

Performance Variation: *Differences in system response times, resource usage, or throughput under similar conditions.*

Configuration Variation: *Inconsistencies in infrastructure, application, or environment settings across development, test, and production.*

Behavioral Variation: *When features or functionalities behave differently across user sessions or platforms.*

Code Variation: *Divergences between environments due to branching, incomplete merges, or inconsistent deployments.*

Understanding and controlling variation is central to any effective IT quality strategy because it enables teams to:

- Detect emerging problems before they cause failure.
- Ensure consistent and predictable system behavior.
- Drive standardization and automation across environments.
- Identify process weaknesses and opportunities for improvement.
- Build trust in the stability, reliability, and repeatability of services.

Left unmanaged, variation introduces risk , not just to system outcomes, but to timelines, costs, compliance, and customer satisfaction. High-performing IT organizations treat variation as a leading indicator of quality erosion and invest in tools, metrics, and governance to detect and reduce it.

In short, variation is the **early warning system** of IT quality , not always a problem in itself, but often a sign that one is developing.

Project Quality Management: *A structured and systematic approach to ensuring that a project meets its defined objectives and satisfies customer expectations by applying* *quality* planning, assurance, and control techniques. This process involves identifying quality requirements, implementing processes to achieve them, and continuously monitoring deliverables for compliance. Project quality management minimizes defects, reduces rework, and enhances stakeholder satisfaction by emphasizing proactive quality measures and ongoing improvements. It also ensures that the final product or service adheres to industry standards and organizational policies, ultimately contributing to the project's success.

Quality: *The degree to which a product, service, or process meets customer expectations, industry standards, and predefined requirements, directly influencing overall satisfaction and business success. High-quality outputs are characterized by reliability, durability, and consistency, while poor quality can result in customer dissatisfaction, increased costs, and reputational damage. Quality is not only about defect-free deliverables but also about ensuring that the product or service is fit for its intended purpose and consistently performs as expected. Organizations prioritize quality to enhance customer loyalty, reduce waste, and maintain a competitive edge.*

Metric: *A standard of measurement used to evaluate performance, efficiency, or quality.*

Reliability: *The probability that a product, system, or service will perform as expected over a specified period under normal conditions.*

Maintainability: *The ease with which a product, system, or process can be maintained, repaired, or updated to ensure long-term functionality and reliability.*

Process Adjustments: *Modifications made to improve quality and address deviations in a process based on data-driven analysis.*

Acceptance Decisions: *Formal evaluations that determine whether project deliverables meet the predefined criteria for approval. These decisions influence whether a product or service is accepted for implementation or requires further refinement.*

BEST PRACTICES FOR ZERO-DEFECT CONFIGURATION MIGRATION

Achieving zero defect variations in the migration of configurations from a lower environment, such as a user acceptance testing (UAT) instance, to production is a non-negotiable requirement for ensuring quality in IT projects. Configurations that have been rigorously tested, approved, and signed off in the non-production environment must be replicated in production with 100% fidelity. Any deviation risks undermining user trust and project success, as customers frequently report discrepancies between what they approved in UAT and what is deployed in production. To maintain this zero-defect standard, organizations must adopt robust processes, leveraging best practices such as gold core environments, automated migration tools, and portable extracts. These methods, combined with meticulous documentation and audit trails, minimize errors and ensure that the production environment mirrors the approved configurations exactly, eliminating the "this isn't what we signed off on" complaints that stem from poor-quality migrations.[124]

LEVERAGING GOLD CORE ENVIRONMENTS AND AUTOMATED TOOLS

One of the most effective strategies for achieving zero-defect configuration migration is the use of a gold core preconfigured environment. This approach involves maintaining a standardized, pre-tested configuration template that serves as a baseline for all environments. Once validated in UAT, the gold core environment can be cloned directly into production, ensuring consistency and reducing manual intervention. Alternatively, automated migration tools provide a reliable mechanism to transport configurations from non-production to production environments. These tools, such as a Configuration Migration Assistant or custom-developed scripts, systematically transfer setups like Setup #1 and Setup #2, preserving their integrity. Portable extracts, configuration data exported from the UAT environment in a standardized format (e.g., XML or CSV) and imported into production, offer another layer of precision. These extracts are particularly useful for complex configurations, ensuring that every parameter is replicated without alteration. By prioritizing these methods, organizations can significantly reduce the risk of configuration drift and maintain quality standards.

IMPLEMENTING RIGOROUS VALIDATION AND COMPARISON PROCESSES

To ensure configurations are migrated without defects, rigorous validation and comparison processes must be embedded in the migration workflow. Before migration, a comprehensive validation checklist should confirm that all configurations in the UAT environment match the signed-off requirements, including record counts, field values, and system behaviors. Post-migration, a side-by-side comparison of the non-production and production environments is essential. This involves generating configuration reports from both environments, such as a Configuration Summary Report or custom database queries and analyzing them for discrepancies. Automated comparison tools can streamline this process, flagging any variances for immediate resolution. Additionally, random spot checks further assurance of quality. These validation steps, documented in a master migration log, create a transparent audit trail that supports accountability and compliance.

MAINTAINING AUDIT TRAILS AND CONTINUOUS IMPROVEMENT

A robust audit trail for zero-defect configuration migration enables organizations to track every step of the process and address customer concerns about quality. The audit trail should include detailed documentation of the UAT sign-off, migration method used (e.g., gold core cloning, automated tool, or portable extract), validation results, and pre- and post-migration comparison reports. For instance, screenshots of configuration settings in both environments, along with logs from tools like the Configuration Playbook, provide verifiable evidence of fidelity. To further enhance quality, organizations should establish a feedback loop for continuous improvement. Post-migration reviews should analyze any reported issues, to refine processes. Training teams on best practices, regularly updating gold core templates, and enhancing automated tools based on lessons learned can prevent recurrence of errors. By combining meticulous audit trails with a commitment to iterative improvement, organizations can deliver flawless configuration migrations, ensuring production environments align perfectly with approved UAT configurations and maintaining customer satisfaction.

CONFORMANCE, PERFORMANCE, AND OPERATIONAL DEFINITIONS

Conformance: *The practice of ensuring that a project, product, or process consistently meets predefined requirements, industry standards, and customer expectations. Conformance involves strict adherence to quality specifications, regulatory guidelines, and contractual obligations. By maintaining conformance, organizations minimize defects, enhance product reliability, and boost customer satisfaction. It also promotes consistency in performance, reduces rework, and strengthens the overall credibility of the deliverables.*

Performance*: A quantitative and qualitative measure of how effectively a product, service, or system fulfills its intended function under real-world conditions. Performance evaluation considers factors such as **speed, reliability, accuracy, and efficiency** in delivering expected outcomes. For instance, in cloud services, performance might be assessed by measuring **latency, uptime, and throughput** to ensure the system handles user requests promptly and reliably. High performance indicates that the solution consistently meets or exceeds user expectations, while poor performance may result in inefficiencies, customer dissatisfaction, and potential financial losses. Organizations continuously monitor and optimize performance through **testing, benchmarking, and performance tuning** to maintain service quality and competitiveness.*

Operational Definition: *A clear, precise, and measurable description of a concept, process, or variable used to ensure consistency and accuracy in data collection and evaluation. Operational definitions eliminate ambiguity by specifying how to observe, measure, or test a particular characteristic. For example, defining "customer satisfaction" operationally might involve measuring the percentage of positive survey responses. This approach enables teams to achieve uniformity in interpreting and analyzing results, fostering clearer communication and more reliable decision-making.*[125]

Meaning starts with a concept, which is in somebody's mind and only there; it is too indescribable to be expressed in words. An operational definition refers to a clear and concise description of a concept, term, or variable in terms of the specific procedures or operations used to measure or manipulate it. An operational definition specifies the observable, measurable, and quantifiable characteristics that define a concept or term, enabling researchers or practitioners to apply the concept consistently and systematically. For any word, prescription, specification, measure, or attribute to have meaning is to record what happens in a specified operation or test. An operational definition puts transmissible meaning into a concept. Adjectives like good, reliable, round, and safe have communicable meaning once they are expressed in operational terms of sampling, test, and criterion.[126]

In a cloud services company, the term "latency performance" is defined operationally to ensure consistent measurement and evaluation of service quality. Rather than relying on subjective interpretations, the company establishes a precise operational definition: "Latency performance is measured as the time taken (in milliseconds) for a data packet to travel from the client request to the cloud server and back, with an acceptable threshold of ≤100 ms for 95% of requests over a 24-hour period." During performance monitoring, automated systems track and log the round-trip time (RTT) for each request. If more than 5% of the requests exceed the 100 ms threshold within the specified time frame, the service is flagged as underperforming. This operational definition ensures that latency claims are objectively measured using consistent, quantifiable criteria. It also allows the company to provide transparent and verifiable service-level agreement (SLA) reports to customers, reducing disputes and building trust. Furthermore, by defining clear latency metrics, the company can accurately identify quality performance and mitigation strategies of its infrastructure offering.

Conformance to Requirements: *A core quality management principle that ensures project deliverables strictly adhere to documented specifications, industry standards, and customer expectations. By maintaining conformance, organizations reduce the likelihood of defects, minimize the need for rework, and enhance overall product reliability. This principle involves rigorous quality control processes, thorough testing, and consistent monitoring to verify that each deliverable meets the defined criteria. Ensuring conformance not only improves customer satisfaction but also reduces project risks, such as schedule delays and cost overruns, resulting from noncompliance.*

Defect: *A defect refers to any deviation or shortcoming in a product or service that fails to meet predefined customer specifications, quality standards, or functional requirements. It represents an instance where the delivered output does not* *align with expected performance or design criteria. Defects can range from minor cosmetic flaws to critical functional issues that impact usability, reliability, or safety.*

Cost of Nonconformance: *The total financial burden incurred when a project or product fails to meet established quality standards. This includes direct costs, such as rework, scrap, and warranty claims, as well as indirect costs like loss of customer trust, reputational damage, and potential legal penalties. For example, a software company releasing a flawed product may face customer refunds, support expenses, and harm to its brand image. To mitigate these costs, companies invest in proactive quality assurance practices, such as regular testing, inspections, and employee training, which ultimately reduce the likelihood of defects and associated financial losses.*

Fitness for Use: *The extent to which a product or service effectively fulfills its intended purpose and meets customer expectations. Fitness for use goes beyond simply meeting technical specifications, it considers whether the product delivers the expected value and functionality in real-world conditions. For example, a cloud storage service may meet technical performance standards but would lack fitness for use if it frequently crashes or has slow access speeds. Ensuring fitness for use involves aligning product features with customer needs, conducting usability testing, and continuously improving based on user feedback to enhance satisfaction and reliability.*

Benchmarking: *A strategic process of comparing an organization's practices, processes, or performance metrics* *against industry standards, best practices, or competitors. It serves as a tool for identifying areas for improvement and driving innovation. Organizations use benchmarking to enhance performance and innovation.*

Yield: *A key performance metric that represents the percentage of products or services that meet quality standards without requiring rework or correction. It is calculated by dividing the number of defect-free units by the total units produced. For example, if a cloud service provider processes 1,000 customer requests and 980 are successfully completed without errors, the yield is 98%. High yield rates indicate efficient processes and strong quality control, while low yield rates signal frequent defects and the need for process improvements. By consistently monitoring and optimizing yield, organizations can reduce waste, lower production costs, and enhance overall efficiency.*

QUALITY IS FREE, THE TRUE COST OF QUALITY

Quality is indeed free; it is nonconformance that wastes assets, make it right the first time, and there is no such thing as a quality problem.[127] What costs money is the "unquality" of things and the inefficient actions involved in not doing the job right the first time. When products or services fail to meet established standards, the resulting rework, delays, and corrective actions incur unnecessary expenses. This section is about the art of making quality certain, making quality certain means getting people to do better all of the worthwhile things they ought to be doing anyway.[128] People, from top management to lower-level employees, care about prevention fighting, defects that could have prevented an incident in the first place. It's a cultural shift, transforming routine duties into opportunities, drawing on Fayol's Esprit de Corps to unite teams in a shared purpose.[129]

Cost of Quality (COQ): *The Cost of Quality refers to the total financial investment required to ensure that project deliverables meet quality expectations. It encompasses all expenses associated with preventing, detecting, and addressing defects, making it a comprehensive measure of the true cost of delivering quality products or services. COQ is divided into four primary categories: Prevention Costs, Appraisal Costs, Internal & Externals Costs.*[130]

In traditional management environments, all quality costs are measured, evaluated calmly, and dispositioned all that is except quality which is merely falling off, the costs of poor quality. The lack of obvious measurement methods forces others to cling to concepts of inadequacy. Quality professionals cling to sacred cow concepts that allow them to remain nonconforming, so the cost of quality measurements are never really implemented. Bringing together costs like rework, scrap, warranty inspection, and testing show the accumulation of expenses that make management listen, quantitative financial facts. It is an opportunity to increase profit by not doing rework, including clerical processing and handling, returns, after-service warranty, inspection, and testing, increasing the cost of errors and cost of quality (COQ).

Prevention costs are all the activities undertaken to prevent defects, design reviews, product qualifications, drawings, and engineering, quality make-certain programs, supplier evaluations, tool control, operation training, acceptance planning, and zero-defect programs. Appraisal costs are incurred when conducting inspections, tests, and planned evaluations are used to determine if they conform to requirements. Requirements include specs from marketing and customer as well as engineering documents. Failure costs are associated with things that have not been found to conform to the requirements as well as evaluation, disposition, and consumer affairs aspects of failures. Consumer affairs redesign engineering, change orders, purchase change orders, corrective action, rework, scrap, warranty, and the largest insurance cost, product liability. Economics of quality does not exist; it is less expensive to do the job right the first time; the only performance measurement is the cost of quality, and the only performance standard is Zero Defects.[131]

Prevention Cost: *Prevention cost refers to the financial investment made in proactive measures aimed at avoiding defects before they occur. It encompasses all activities, processes, and resources dedicated to preventing quality issues, thereby reducing the likelihood of costly rework, delays, or customer dissatisfaction.*

Appraisal Cost: *Appraisal cost refers to the expenses associated with evaluating and monitoring processes, products, or services to ensure they meet quality standards. These costs are preventive in nature, aimed at detecting defects before they reach the customer.*

Internal Failure Cost: *Internal failure cost represents the expenses incurred when defects are identified and corrected before reaching the customer. These costs arise from flaws detected during internal testing, inspections, or production processes, allowing the organization to address issues early.*

External Failure Cost: *External failure cost refers to the financial losses and associated expenses that arise when defective products or services reach the customer. These costs reflect the consequences of delivering substandard quality, which can significantly impact customer satisfaction and business reputation.*

Measurement and Test Equipment Costs: *The capital expenditures required for acquiring tools and systems necessary for quality inspections and testing.*

Capability Maturity Model Integration (CMMI): *A structured process improvement framework that helps organizations refine their processes to achieve higher levels of efficiency and effectiveness. It provides a roadmap for continuous process enhancement across various industries.*

Design of Experiments (DOE): *A statistical method used to determine which variables impact a process or product outcome the most. It is widely applied in process optimization and quality control.*

DMAIC (Define, Measure, Analyze, Improve, Control): *A structured Six Sigma methodology for process improvement that follows a five-phase approach to identify problems, measure performance, analyze data, implement improvements, and sustain gains.*

ACHIEVING EXCEPTIONAL DATA QUALITY IS CLIENT RESPONSIBILITY

Data quality is the linchpin of successful IT projects, particularly those involving data migration or system integration, and it is fundamentally the client's responsibility to uphold. The principle of "bad data in equates to bad data out" highlights the critical need for clean, reliable data. Master data management (MDM) presents a universal challenge, as data quality degrades over time due to evolving nomenclature, inconsistent data entry, and organizational growth. These factors introduce errors, duplicates, and mismatches that disrupt conversion processes for both master and transactional data. Poor data quality delays reconciliation and validation, complicates integrated data mismatches, and risks project setbacks. To ensure exceptional data quality, clients must implement rigorous activities, data validation and reconciliation, defining and documenting the validation process, outlining the Extract, Transform, Load (ETL) conversion cycle, and updating the master conversion document, while focusing on three critical areas for audit and control: conversion cycle, data reconciliation, and validation assumptions and prerequisites.

CONVERSION CYCLE: ENSURING QUALITY THROUGH STRUCTURED STEPS

The conversion cycle, comprising Extract, Transform, Load (ETL), is meticulously designed to safeguard data quality, relying on assumptions such as environment capability, resource availability, configuration readiness, and test tool procurement. Prerequisites include completing configurations (Setup #1, Setup #2) and ensuring transactions or data requiring manual updates are prepared. The cycle unfolds in five quality-driven steps: **Step 1: Extract Data** uses extract programs, development code, and specific formats from source systems, leveraging designated tools. **Step 2: Preparation** consolidates sources through defined file prep and consolidation processes, ensuring file readiness. **Step 3: Systematic Transformation** applies quality-focused updates like unique IDs and links to existing Lists of Values (LOVs), incorporating black-box changes. **Step 4: Manual Updates** involves physical data manipulation and user-driven changes to refine data. **Step 5: File Ready for Load** ensures the data is templated, staged, and ready for loading. Concurrently, data reconciliation employs three methods, record counts, data quality validation, and data process checks, to verify quality at every stage, with results documented in the CEMLI Playbook and Master Conversion Document for audit purposes.

DATA VALIDATION AND RECONCILIATION: MEASURING QUALITY WITH PRECISION

Data reconciliation and validation are critical for assessing data quality during each mock conversion and final cutover, ensuring the quantity and quality of converted data meet expectations. Manual cross-checking of every record is impractical, so three methods are employed: **Record Counts**, **Data Quality Validation**, and **Data Process Checks**. **Record Counts** run concurrently with ETL, tallying rows for each business object and comparing them against expected counts. Discrepancies are investigated, accounted for, and communicated to validators and the technical team via email, with counts logged in the Master Sheet. **Data Quality Validation**, conducted by functional teams post-load, verifies field content using online checks, custom verification reports (e.g., Customers_Report.xdo vs.legacy source reports), and backend queries. Specific validation steps include selecting the top 10 or 10% of records, random spot checks (10 records per data type), and verifying totals, with screenshots saved for documentation. For example, an application customer data dump was compared to data extracts, validating 36,720 of 36,731 records, with 9 discrepancies due to errors and 2 minor address truncations deemed acceptable. These processes ensure high-quality outcomes and robust audit trails.

DATA CLEANING AND AUDIT: FORTIFYING QUALITY STANDARDS

Data cleaning is a proactive, quality-centric activity performed before conversion to eliminate duplicates, standardize formats, and resolve inconsistencies, ensuring the receiving system is ready. This includes manual updates to transactions or data and verifying that configurations (Setup #1, Setup #2) are complete. For audit and control, the project emphasizes three critical areas: the conversion cycle, data reconciliation, and validation processes, each supported by documented assumptions (e.g., environment stability) and pre-requisites (e.g., resource readiness). The conversion cycle is detailed in the master conversion document, outlining extract programs, transformation logic, and manual update procedures. Reconciliation results, including record counts and validation outcomes, are meticulously logged in the CEMLI Playbook and Master Sheet, ensuring transparency. Data cleaning and validation activities, such as spot-checking customer data (e.g., Registry ID, name, primary address) and comparing extracts to source data, reinforce quality standards. By adhering to these structured processes, the project delivers exceptional data quality, mitigates risks, and supports operational excellence and audit compliance.

ASSURANCE, AUDIT & CONTROL

Too often quality terminology is used interchangeably without understanding the differences and similarities. Begin with the distinctions between, quality assurance, quality audit and quality control, before moving forward to erudition of quality measurement tools.

Quality Assurance: *A proactive and preventive approach aimed at ensuring that quality standards are consistently met throughout the project lifecycle. Quality assurance focuses on process improvements, standardization, and compliance monitoring to prevent defects from occurring. This involves conducting regular reviews, implementing best practices, and fostering a culture of continuous improvement. For example, in software development, QA practices include code reviews, automated testing, and process audits to ensure products meet performance and reliability standards before deployment.*

Quality Audit *A systematic and objective examination of a project's quality-related processes, policies, and deliverables to verify compliance with established standards and identify areas for improvement. Quality audits assess whether best practices, regulatory requirements, and internal quality protocols are being followed. During an audit, independent reviewers evaluate documentation, workflows, and deliverables to identify gaps, inefficiencies, or noncompliance issues. The findings help organizations implement corrective actions, enhance quality practices, and improve overall project performance.*

Quality Control *A **reactive process** that involves inspecting, testing, and monitoring project deliverables to detect and correct defects, ensuring they comply with quality standards. Quality control activities include sampling, validation, and verification to confirm that outputs meet specified criteria. For example, in manufacturing, QC may involve testing random product samples for defects, while in software development, it could include bug testing and code validation. By identifying and addressing deviations from quality requirements, quality control helps maintain consistency and deliver defect-free products or services.*

QUALITY MEASUREMENT TOOLS

The following section reviews additional tools with associated use cases one could apply to their own specific projects. Many are effective in day-to-day operations.

Fishbone Diagram: *Also known as a **Cause-and-Effect Diagram** or an **Ishikawa Diagram**, the fishbone diagram is a visual tool used for root cause analysis. It helps teams systematically identify and categorize the potential causes of a quality issue by mapping them into major contributing factors. The diagram resembles the shape of a fishbone, with the problem statement at the head and the main categories of causes branching off like bones.*

Typical categories include:

- **People:** Human-related factors such as employee skills or training.
- **Processes:** Procedural inefficiencies or workflow issues.
- **Equipment:** Malfunctioning tools or outdated technology.
- **Environment:** External conditions or workplace factors.
- **Materials:** Quality or availability of raw materials.
- **Management:** Oversight, policies, or decision-making issues.

Sample Fishbone Diagram:

Illustrating the root causes of slow cloud service performance for a cloud provider.

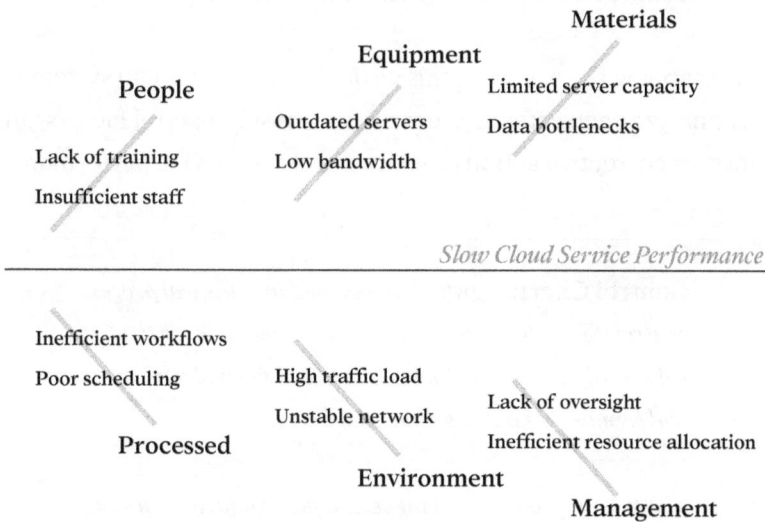

Materials

Equipment

People

Limited server capacity

Outdated servers   Data bottlenecks

Lack of training

Low bandwidth

Insufficient staff

Slow Cloud Service Performance

Inefficient workflows

Poor scheduling   High traffic load

Lack of oversight

Unstable network

Processed

Inefficient resource allocation

Environment

Management

Explanation of the Diagram:

The fishbone diagram illustrates the root causes of slow cloud service performance by categorizing potential factors into six key areas:

- **People:** Issues related to employee skills, such as lack of training and insufficient staffing, which can slow response times.
- **Processes:** Inefficient workflows and poor scheduling that create delays and bottlenecks.
- **Equipment:** Outdated servers and limited bandwidth, contributing to sluggish performance.
- **Environment:** High traffic loads and unstable networks that overwhelm resources.
- **Materials:** Limited server capacity and data bottlenecks, reducing processing efficiency.
- **Management:** Lack of oversight and inefficient resource allocation, which hinders optimization efforts.

By mapping the causes in this visual format, teams can systematically analyze each category, identify the most impactful factors, and prioritize corrective actions to improve cloud service performance.

Control Chart: *A graphical tool used in statistical process control (SPC) that tracks process performance over time. It helps project teams distinguish between normal variations and signals that indicate potential issues.*

5 Whys: *A problem-solving technique that involves asking "Why?" repeatedly (typically five times) to peel away the layers of symptoms and identify the root cause of an issue. This approach is widely used in lean management and Six Sigma methodologies to improve process efficiency and eliminate defects.*

Flowchart: *A* **flowchart** *is a visual representation of a process that outlines the sequence of steps, decision points, and interactions between tasks. It uses standard symbols such as ovals for start and end points, rectangles for processes or actions, diamonds for decision-making steps, and arrows to indicate the flow direction. Flowcharts are valuable tools for analyzing, documenting, and improving workflows, making them essential for quality management, process optimization, and troubleshooting.*

Check Sheet: *A structured, pre-formatted tool used for systematically collecting, organizing, and categorizing data related to quality observations. It is commonly referred to as a tally sheet or checklist due to its straightforward format, which typically includes columns for recording occurrences, dates, and categories of defects or events. By capturing real-time data, check sheets help identify patterns, trends, and recurring issues, making them valuable for root cause analysis and continuous improvement efforts.*

Check sheets are particularly effective in visualizing frequency distributions and tracking defect occurrences over time. They can be customized to monitor various parameters, such as error rates, process deviations, or product failures, providing teams with tangible insights into quality performance. By using check sheets, organizations can make data-driven decisions, streamline corrective actions, and enhance overall process reliability.

In an IT help desk, the quality control team uses a check sheet to monitor common defects from the issue log. This sheet includes predefined defect categories, such as login issues, application or defect tracking, failure points along with an aggregate summary representing the frequency of each defect. By reviewing the completed check sheet, the team identifies that scratches account for 60% of all defects, prompting them to focus on surface handling processes to reduce this recurring issue.

LEVERAGING STATISTICAL TOOLS FOR QUALITY MANAGEMENT IN CLOUD INFRASTRUCTURE (IAAS)

The old adage "you'll never use that again after high school" is an urban myth in my experience, most people already know of concepts in the following section, but we rarely use them in practice. In the realm of cloud infrastructure as a service (IaaS), ensuring quality, reliability, and performance consistency is vital for delivering seamless and efficient operations. Cloud providers manage vast datasets, monitor usage metrics, and track performance benchmarks to optimize service delivery. To achieve this, they rely heavily on statistical tools such as statistical sampling, normal distribution, standard deviation, and the mean. These techniques help cloud providers analyze resource usage patterns, detect anomalies, and improve service reliability.

For example, statistical sampling enables providers to assess infrastructure performance by testing subsets of virtual machines (VMs) rather than evaluating every instance. Normal distribution helps model response time variances across different regions, ensuring latency consistency. Standard deviation measures the variability in CPU or memory usage, while the mean reveals average utilization, aiding in capacity planning. By integrating these statistical tools, cloud providers can proactively manage infrastructure quality, optimize resource allocation, and enhance customer satisfaction.

Statistical Sampling: *A data collection technique used to select a representative subset from a larger population for inspection or analysis. By examining only a portion of the population, organizations can make inferences about the entire group without the need for exhaustive testing. This method is widely applied in quality control, market research, and performance assessments. Statistical sampling enhances efficiency by reducing the time, cost, and resources required for evaluation while still providing statistically valid insights.*

For example, a cloud service provider may offer IaaS solutions with thousands of virtual machines (VMs) running across multiple data centers. Statistical sampling in cloud infrastructure involves selecting a representative subset of VMs, servers, or storage units to assess performance, security, or reliability, rather than inspecting the entire environment. This streamlines the auditing process, making it more efficient without compromising accuracy. Instead of testing every VM for performance and security compliance, the provider uses random sampling to inspect 5% of the VMs in each region.

- If network latency and disk I/O rates in the sample meet performance thresholds, the entire infrastructure is assumed to meet the standards.
- If significant deviations are detected, further sampling or a full inspection is conducted. This approach ensures efficient quality control without excessive resource consumption.

Normal Distribution: *A bell-shaped probability curve representing how data points are distributed around the mean (average). In this symmetrical model, most values cluster around the mean, with fewer occurrences at the extremes. The curve's shape reflects the standard deviation, which measures data spread. The normal distribution helps analyze process performance, defect rates, and customer satisfaction scores.*

In cloud IaaS environments, normal distribution helps model performance metrics, such as API response times, uptime rates, or data transfer speeds. It allows providers to identify deviations from typical performance levels. A cloud provider tracks the response time of its API service across multiple regions. The response time follows a normal distribution with:

- Mean latency of 120 ms.
- Standard deviation of 10 ms.

According to the empirical rule:

- 68% of the API requests complete within 110–130 ms (±1 standard deviation).
- 95% complete within 100–140 ms (±2 standard deviations).
- 99.7% complete within 90–150 ms (±3 standard deviations).

When latency exceeds 150 ms, it indicates anomalous performance, triggering automated scaling or investigation into potential bottlenecks.

Standard Deviation: *A statistical measure of variability that indicates how much individual data points deviate from the mean. A lower standard deviation reflects consistent, tightly clustered data, while a higher standard deviation indicates greater variability. In quality management, standard deviation is used to assess process stability, measure consistency, and identify outliers.*

- Key insights from standard deviation:
- Low standard deviation: Data points are close to the mean, indicating consistency.
- High standard deviation: Data points are widely spread, indicating variability.

For example, standard deviation measures variability in cloud resource usage, such as CPU, memory, or bandwidth consumption. It helps identify performance inconsistencies and optimize load balancing strategies. A cloud provider monitors CPU utilization across a cluster of virtual machines (VMs):

- The average CPU utilization is 65%.
- Standard deviation is 5%.

If most VMs have utilization between 60% and 70% (±1 standard deviation), the environment is considered stable. However, if some VMs frequently exceed ±2 standard deviations (e.g., reaching 75%–80% CPU utilization), it signals resource contention or performance inconsistencies. The provider uses this insight to adjust autoscaling policies, allocating additional VMs to reduce the load on overburdened instances.

Mean: *Also known as the arithmetic average, is a fundamental statistical measure that represents the central value of a dataset. It is calculated by summing all data points and dividing by the total number of values. In quality management, the mean helps evaluate process performance, customer satisfaction, and product quality by identifying the average result of a series of measurements.*

The mean is a critical metric in cloud IaaS for capacity planning, performance analysis, and resource optimization. It represents the average consumption or performance level across the infrastructure. A cloud storage provider tracks the average daily data transfer rate across its regions.

- On a given day, the service handles 5,000 TB of data across 100 regions.
- The mean data transfer rate is:
  Mean=5000100=50 TB per region\text{Mean}
  = \frac{5000}{100} = 50 \text{ TB per region}
  Mean=1005000=50 TB per region

By calculating the mean, the provider identifies regions exceeding or falling below average usage. If Region A transfers 80 TB (60% above the mean), it indicates higher demand, potentially requiring more bandwidth or server capacity. Conversely, Region B transferring 30 TB signals underutilization, prompting potential resource redistribution.

Histogram: *A bar graph that visually represents frequency distributions of data. It is useful in identifying variations and trends in quality performance.*

Pareto Analysis: *A data-driven decision-making technique used to identify the most significant factors contributing to quality issues, based on the 80/20 rule. This principle suggests that 80% of problems typically stem from 20% of the causes. By applying Pareto analysis, organizations can focus their improvement efforts on the few critical factors that will yield the greatest impact. For example, in customer service, analyzing complaint data may reveal that a small number of recurring issues account for the majority of dissatisfaction. By addressing these key drivers, businesses can optimize resource allocation and achieve meaningful quality improvements.*

Pareto Chart: *A visual representation of Pareto analysis that combines a bar graph and a line graph to prioritize problem areas based on their frequency or impact. The bars represent individual problem categories, arranged in descending order of significance, while the cumulative line graph shows the cumulative impact of these issues. The point where the line flattens indicates the vital few causes responsible for most of the problems. Pareto charts are commonly used in quality control, project management, and process improvement to identify and focus on the most influential factors, enhancing decision-making efficiency.*

Here's a Pareto chart illustrating customer service issues for a cloud services provider. The chart shows how 80% of customer complaints stem from just two primary causes: slow response time and frequent service outages.

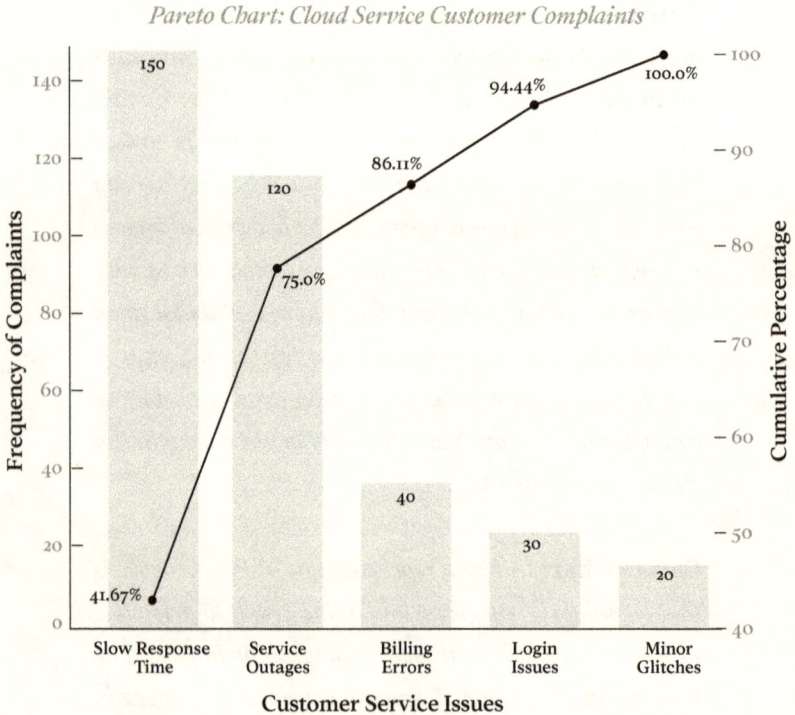

Pareto Chart: Cloud Service Customer Complaints

The Pareto chart displays customer service complaints for a cloud service provider. The bars represent the frequency of complaints, while the red line shows the cumulative percentage. From the chart, we can see that:

- Slow response time and service outages account for 80% of the total complaints, making them the primary areas of concern.

- Addressing these two issues first will yield the greatest improvement in customer satisfaction.
- The remaining issues, while still present, have a lower impact and can be addressed later.

By visualizing the data in this way, the organization can prioritize its quality improvement efforts effectively.

QUALITY MATURITY GRID FOR SOFTWARE DEVELOPMENT LIFECYCLE (SDLC)

Inspired by Philip Crosby's Quality Maturity Grid, this framework assesses an organization's quality management practices across the Software Development Lifecycle (SDLC).[132] The grid evaluates five maturity levels (Uncertainty, Awakening, Enlightenment, Wisdom, and Certainty) across six categories tailored to software development.

Maturity Model: *A structured framework that guides organizations in assessing and improving their processes over time, moving from initial levels of capability to optimized performance.*

Category Descriptions

I. Management Understanding and Attitude: Reflects leadership's perspective on the importance of quality in software development and its integration into organizational strategy.

2. Organizational Quality Focus: Measures the extent to which quality is a shared responsibility across teams versus being siloed in specific departments.

3. Problem Handling: Assesses how effectively the organization identifies, resolves, and prevents recurring issues.

4. Cost of Quality Awareness: Evaluates whether the organization tracks and understands quality costs, including prevention, appraisal, and failure costs.

5. Quality Improvement Actions: Tracks the implementation and effectiveness of initiatives aimed at enhancing quality, such as process improvements, training, and new tools.

6. Software Testing and Validation Practices: Focuses on the maturity and comprehensiveness of testing practices, from manual testing to advanced automation.[133]

Using the SDLC Grid

Organizations can use this SDLC Quality Maturity Grid to:

1. Evaluate Current Maturity: Assess where the organization stands in each category.

2. Set Improvement Goals: Identify target maturity levels and prioritize actions to achieve them.

3. Track Progress: Regularly review advancements in quality practices to ensure continuous improvement.

By progressing through the stages and aligning with the principles of quality philosophy, software organizations can minimize defects, improve efficiency, and deliver products that meet or exceed customer expectations.[134]

Maturity Levels	Management Understanding and Attitude	Organizational Quality Focus	Problem Handling
Stage 1: Uncertainty	Management views quality as an unnecessary expense and prioritizes speed over correctness.	Little to no focus on quality; quality is seen as the responsibility of QA only.	Problems are addressed reactively, often with blame assigned to individuals.
Stage 2: Awakening	Management begins to recognize the costs associated with defects but lacks a cohesive strategy.	Quality initiatives are sporadic and depend on individual teams or projects.	Problems are documented but addressed inconsistently; root cause analysis is rare.
Stage 3: Enlightenment	Management actively supports quality as a priority and allocates resources to improvement efforts.	Quality is a shared responsibility among all stakeholders, including developers and product managers.	Problems are systematically analyzed for root causes; solutions focus on preventing recurrence.
Stage 4: Wisdom	Management fully integrates quality into strategic goals and measures success through quality outcomes.	Organization-wide quality culture is established; all teams proactively contribute to quality assurance.	Problems are rare and resolved efficiently through collaborative efforts; blame culture is eliminated.
Stage 5: Certainty	Management views quality as essential and non-negotiable; it is an intrinsic part of organizational identity.	Quality is embedded in every aspect of the SDLC, from requirements gathering to deployment.	Problems are anticipated and mitigated proactively; quality processes function seamlessly.
Stage 1: Uncertainty	Management views quality as an unnecessary expense and prioritizes speed over correctness.	Little to no focus on quality; quality is seen as the responsibility of QA only.	Problems are addressed reactively, often with blame assigned to individuals.

152

Maturity Levels	Cost of Quality Awareness	Quality Improvement Actions	Software Testing and Validation Practices
Stage 1: Uncertainty	Quality costs are not measured or understood.	No formal improvement initiatives exist; errors are tolerated and normalized.	Manual and inconsistent testing; no standard test plans or automation tools.
Stage 2: Awakening	Quality costs are calculated sporadically and limited to direct failure costs (e.g., bug fixes, rework).	Some ad-hoc process improvements are attempted, but they lack organization-wide support.	Basic testing procedures are defined; limited use of automated tools, but coverage is low and unstructured.
Stage 3: Enlightenment	Quality costs are regularly tracked, including prevention and appraisal costs.	Formal quality improvement programs (e.g., CI/CD pipelines, code reviews) are implemented across teams.	Automated testing is adopted, with structured test plans for unit, integration, and regression testing.
Stage 4: Wisdom	Quality costs are monitored in detail and influence budget and planning decisions.	Continuous improvement practices (e.g., retrospectives, DevOps practices) are ingrained in all processes.	Comprehensive test automation and validation processes ensure high coverage; performance and security testing are standard.
Stage 5: Certainty	Cost of quality is a standard KPI and informs decision-making at all levels of the organization.	Advanced quality initiatives include predictive analytics, AI-driven testing, and real-time quality monitoring.	Fully automated end-to-end testing integrated into the SDLC, with real-time feedback loops and self-healing systems.
Stage 1: Uncertainty	Quality costs are not measured or understood.	No formal improvement initiatives exist; errors are tolerated and normalized.	Manual and inconsistent testing; no standard test plans or automation tools.

ISO 9000: *A globally recognized set of quality management standards developed by the International Organization for Standardization (ISO) to help organizations ensure consistent quality in their processes and products.*

CHAPTER 14

Testing: Build it and They Will Come

I N TODAY'S FAST-PACED world, we often find ourselves caught up in a cycle of endless talking and planning. Enter the salesperson or the IT manager, professionals we turn to with the expectation that they'll deliver a tailored solution. We articulate our needs, entrusting them to build something functional or provide a service that resolves our challenges. Yet, all too often, what follows is a prolonged ordeal: months of back-and-forth, millions of dollars spent, and an endless barrage of questions that consume our time and resources. At the end of this exhaustive process, we're left with little more than a polished piece of paper, a proposal, a requirements document, and a hefty bill, while the tangible solution remains elusive. This disconnect between expectation and delivery underscores a fundamental flaw in how we approach problem-solving: we prioritize talking over doing, and in doing so, we lose sight of what truly matters. It's time to shift our focus from words to actions, as words without deeds are dead.

These efforts, while well-intentioned, often fail to move the needle. Instead of showcasing a system through a glossy deck, imagine the impact of putting that system directly into the hands of the people who will use it. It's not enough to merely display functionality; users must interact with it, touch it, and explore its contours themselves. Robert Greene, in his seminal work Mastery, introduces the concept of the "tactical framework," which posits that human beings learn most effectively through hands-on engagement.[135] This isn't just a preference, it's an intuitive, primal aspect of how we process and internalize knowledge. Neuroscience supports this: tactile experiences activate the brain's sensory and motor cortices, forging stronger neural connections than passive observation ever could. For decision-makers evaluating a solution, this hands-on interaction is a critical step toward genuine understanding and confidence in their choices.

Consider Missouri, famously dubbed the "Show Me State." Its motto reflects a cultural skepticism toward empty promises, a demand for proof over persuasion. No amount of eloquent rhetoric or data-laden charts can rival the power of personal experience. When users engage directly with a system, they don't just see its potential, they feel it. This visceral connection reinforces their belief that the solution will work for them, aligning with their specific needs and workflows. Equally important, this exposure lays bare the system's imperfections. Far from being a drawback, revealing flaws is a value-add. When gaps or shortcomings surface, they illuminate areas ripe for improvement. Users, be they customers, employees, or stakeholders, can then assess the system through the lens of their own priorities, determining what's acceptable, what requires refinement, and what must be discarded entirely. This collaborative process fosters a sense of ownership and bridges divides between groups, transforming potential rancor into a unified pursuit of a common goal.

Contrast this with the traditional approach: months spent on exhaustive documentation, intricate design phases, and the painstaking transcription of requirements onto paper. This model, rooted in the waterfall methodology of project management, assumes that every detail can be anticipated and resolved upfront. But reality seldom cooperates. Requirements shift, priorities evolve, and the pristine documents that once seemed so vital quickly become obsolete, relegated to an archive where they gather dust. The true deliverable, the working product, remains the ultimate arbiter of success. Spending excessive time theorizing and planning, rather than building and testing, is a recipe for stagnation. It's a lesson echoed in the Agile Manifesto, which values "working software over comprehensive documentation."[136] By producing something tangible early and often, we enable real decisions based on real feedback, not hypothetical scenarios. This shift in mindset removes doubt and uncertainty, prompting a reflective question: "Knowing what I know now, would I go back and make the same choices again?" Too often, the answer is a resounding no, particularly when leadership clings to the illusion that requirements are static, ignoring the dynamic nature of human needs and market demands.

Robert Cialdini's Influence offers further insight into why this matters.[137] He describes how commitment and consistency shape human behavior: once we take a stand or make a choice, we face internal and external pressures to align our actions with that decision, even when evidence during later testing cycles suggests a pivot is warranted.[138] In the context of solution development, locking into rigid upfront requirements can trap us in a cycle of justification rather than adaptation. The antidote? Move swiftly to testing. Start with a "straw man", a rough, baseline prototype derived from initial conversations and interviews. This isn't about perfection; it's about progress. We take tests in school not to achieve flawlessness but to gauge where we stand and identify where we need to grow. Similarly, in development, testing provides a snapshot in time, a demarcation line that reveals what works, what doesn't, and where to pivot next.

Prototyping: *A development technique that involves creating a preliminary working model or simulation of a system, product, or feature to gather early user feedback, refine requirements, and improve design before full-scale implementation. Prototypes can be low-fidelity (such as wireframes or sketches) or high-fidelity (such as interactive software simulations). This method is especially useful in iterative development methodologies like Agile, where frequent testing and refinements are necessary to align with user needs and business goals.*

History's greatest innovators understood this implicitly. Leonardo da Vinci didn't merely theorize about flight or anatomy; he built physical models, dissected cadavers, and sketched his observations, letting his hands guide his genius. Benjamin Franklin flew a kite into a storm to unravel the mysteries of electricity, risking his life for empirical proof. Michelangelo sculpted marble not just to create art but to learn the stone's texture and temperament through his fingertips. Coco Chanel, too, eschewed static sketches, draping fabrics directly onto live models to see how they moved and fell. These tactile experiments weren't ancillary to their success; they were the bedrock of it.[139]

In software development, this translates to starting small and building fast. Whether crafting a mobile app from scratch, integrating complex systems with data mappings, or configuring enterprise software, begin with a "hello world" handshake, a minimal viable product that establishes core functionality. Deliver it quickly, at minimal cost, and get it into the team's hands immediately for testing. Don't let the fear of imperfection paralyze you. The incessant "what ifs", What if it's wrong? What if it's not what they want?, are the very questions testing seeks to answer.

Testing isn't about delivering a finished product; it's about establishing a starting point. It's a line in the sand that says, "This is where we are today." From there, we adapt, iterate, and refine. That's the essence of why we test, not to confirm preconceived notions, but to uncover truths and chart the path forward. In a world obsessed with over-planning and over-talking, the imperative is clear: stop debating, stop documenting, and start building. Create something real, something users can touch and critique. Build it, and they will come, not because of promises, but because of proof.

CRAWL - WALK - RUN - FLY
- TESTING STRATEGY

The "crawl, walk, run, fly" testing strategy is a progressive approach that builds user proficiency and system stability over time. In the initial "crawl" phase, novice users explore the system, learning its capabilities and limitations through basic testing cycles. This foundational stage helps identify early issues while allowing standout users, those who quickly grasp the system, to emerge as leaders. As testing progresses to the "walk" phase, the focus shifts from basic functionality to more challenging scenarios, leveraging accumulated knowledge to push the system harder. The "run" phase introduces full system integration, aligning diverse tracks, each at varying completion levels, through careful timing and cross-functional coordination, ensuring key activities sync up effectively. User Acceptance Testing (UAT) in this stage should mirror production as closely as possible, prioritizing progress over perfection. Finally, in the "fly" phase, the system goes live, with ownership handed to users and leaders who've grown with it. At each checkpoint, an acceptable level of risk is assessed for a go/no-go decision, recognizing that 100% perfection is unrealistic, steady improvement and confidence in the system are what matter most.

Testing Strategy: *A Testing Strategy is a high-level, systematic plan that outlines the overall approach and objectives for testing a software application or system. It defines the scope, objectives, testing methods, resources, tools, and timelines to ensure that the product meets quality standards. The strategy serves as a guiding framework, aligning the testing process with the project's goals and business requirements.*

Key Components of a Testing Strategy

I. **Testing Objectives:**
Clearly defines the goals and expected outcomes of the testing process, such as identifying defects, verifying functionality, validating performance, or ensuring security.
  - Outlines the acceptance criteria to determine when the product is ready for release.

Acceptance Criteria: *A set of predefined conditions or requirements that a software product, feature, or user story must meet to be accepted by stakeholders. They define the boundaries of functionality and serve as the basis for determining whether a feature works as intended. Acceptance criteria are essential in agile development, as they clarify* *the expectations for both developers and testers, ensuring alignment with business goals.*

2. **Scope of Testing:**
   Define the boundaries of what will and won't be tested. Reference the original statement of work to focus on what is required and avoid scope creep.
   - Specifies what features, modules, or systems will be tested.
   - Identifies in-scope and out-of-scope components to prevent ambiguity.
   - Includes details about supported platforms, devices, or browsers (for web apps).
     - **Features:** Unique characteristics of a product or service that enhance user experience and differentiate it from competitors. Features should align with customer needs and expectations.
     - **Functionality:** The capability of a product, system, or service to perform its intended functions as expected by the user.

3. **Testing Levels and Types:**
   Crawl, walk run iterative process progression. A comprehensive testing strategy ensures adequate coverage by including multiple testing types, reducing the likelihood of undetected defects.
   - Describes the different **levels of testing**, including: [140]
     - **Unit Testing**: Verifying individual components.
     - **Integration Testing**: Ensuring modules interact correctly.

- **System Testing**: Validating the complete system's functionality.
- **User Acceptance Testing (UAT)**: Ensuring the system meets business requirements.

Unit Test: *Unit testing is a fundamental practice in software quality assurance where individual components or modules of a program are independently tested to confirm they perform as expected. Typically performed by developers, unit tests verify the smallest testable parts of an application, such as functions, methods, or classes. This process helps catch bugs early in the development cycle, reduces the likelihood of defects in later phases, and ensures code reliability. Automated testing frameworks, such as JUnit, NUnit, or pytest, are commonly used to streamline unit testing, making it an essential part of continuous integration and delivery (CI/CD) pipelines.*

Integration Testing: *Integration testing is a phase in software testing where individual components or modules are combined and tested as a group to verify that they function together as intended. It focuses on validating the data flow, communication, and interaction between different parts of the system. This testing phase identifies issues related to interface mismatches, inconsistent data handling, and incorrect module interactions. Integration testing can be performed using various approaches, including top-down, bottom-up, and sandwich (hybrid) methods. It is essential for ensuring seamless collaboration between independently developed units, particularly in complex systems with multiple dependencies.* **See Use case at end of the section.**

System Testing: *Part of the software development life cycle (SDLC) where the entire application or system is tested as a whole. This phase evaluates whether the integrated system meets specified requirements and functions as expected. It includes testing the software's performance, reliability, and security under realistic conditions. System testing often involves black-box testing techniques, where the internal code structure is not considered, focusing instead on verifying external behaviors and outputs. The goal is to identify defects, ensure compliance with business requirements, and validate that the system behaves as intended in a production-like environment.*

User Acceptance Testing (UAT): *User Acceptance Testing (UAT) is the final phase of the testing process, where real-world end users validate whether the software meets their business needs and functional requirements. This phase is critical for confirming that the system is ready for production deployment. UAT scenarios often reflect real-life use cases and business processes to ensure the software performs as expected in practical conditions. UAT identifies any remaining issues, inconsistencies, or unmet expectations that developers may have overlooked. Successful completion of UAT signifies that the client or stakeholders formally accept the system, making it a key milestone before the software goes live.*

- *Includes different* **testing categories,** *such as.*[141]
- **Functional Testing:** *Verifying core functionalities.*
- **Non-Functional Testing:** *Performance, security, usability, and scalability.*

- **Regression Testing**: *Ensuring new changes do not break existing features.*
- **Disaster Recovery**: *Validate that critical data can be restored.*

Conference Room Pilot (CRP): *A Conference Room Pilot (CRP) is a hands-on, interactive testing session conducted in a controlled environment, typically in a conference room or designated testing area. It allows stakeholders, including business users and project team members, to review and validate the functionality of a new system, application, or business process. CRPs are commonly used during large-scale enterprise system implementations, such as ERP (Enterprise Resource Planning) deployments. The goal is to simulate real-world scenarios, identify gaps, and ensure that the system aligns with business requirements before full-scale implementation. CRPs provide valuable feedback that helps refine the system and improve user satisfaction.*

Role based Testing: *A software testing technique that focuses on personas, verifying whether users with different functions and permissions can access and interact with the system according to their assigned privileges. It ensures that the authorization and access control mechanisms are functioning correctly, and that each role can only perform the actions intended for it.*

Performance Testing : *A type of software testing that evaluates a system's speed, scalability, and stability under expected and peak workloads. It helps determine how well* *an application responds to various levels of user demand and identifies performance bottlenecks before deployment.*

Failover Testing: *A resilience testing technique that ensures a system can automatically switch to a backup or redundant system when the primary system fails. It validates high availability and fault tolerance in case of unexpected failures.*

Regression Testing: *Regression Testing is a type of software testing performed to ensure that new code changes (such as enhancements, bug fixes, or patches) have not negatively impacted existing functionality. It involves re-executing previously passed test cases to verify that the system still behaves as expected after modifications.*

Disaster Recovery: *Assess an organization's ability to restore IT systems and data after a catastrophic event, such as server failures, cyberattacks, or natural disasters. It ensures business continuity and minimal downtime.*

---

1. **Testing Methodology:**
   Describes how we will test.
   - Specifies whether the testing will follow a manual, automated, or hybrid approach.
   - Defines the testing model, such as:
     - **Waterfall**: Sequential and phase-wise testing.
     - **Agile**: Iterative testing with continuous feedback.
     - **DevOps/CI-CD**: Continuous testing integrated into the delivery pipeline.
2. **Test Environment:**
   Follow the Cloud based used case for details. Proper configuration of the test environment ensures

accurate and reliable test results, reducing the risk of defects in production.

- Describes the hardware, software, network configurations, and test data requirements.
- Specifies the use of staging or pre-production environments that replicate the production setup.

3. **Tools and Technologies:**
Identify the automation frameworks, test management tools, and defect tracking systems used during testing. What we will use to execute.

- Lists the test management, automation, and defect tracking tools (e.g., Selenium, JIRA, Postman, TestRail) used during the testing process.
- Includes any CI/CD integration tools (e.g., Jenkins, GitLab) for automated testing pipelines.

4. **Defect Management and Reporting:**
RAID Log used for tracking defects.

- Outlines how defects will be **reported, tracked, and managed**, including categorizing them by severity and priority.

Software Defect: *A software defect, also known as a bug, is any flaw, error, or inconsistency in a software application that prevents it from functioning as intended. Defects may arise from coding mistakes, incorrect logic, or design flaws and can lead to unexpected behavior or system crashes. Identifying and resolving defects is a core part of the testing and debugging process. Defects are typically categorized by severity (e.g., critical, major, minor) and priority, helping development teams prioritize fixes. Proper defect tracking* *and management are essential for ensuring software quality and stability before deployment.*

---

5. **Risk and Mitigation Plan:**
   See chapter on Risk.
   - Identifies potential risks (e.g., lack of test data, tight deadlines, resource constraints) and outlines mitigation strategies.
   - Includes contingency plans for handling unexpected issues.

6. **Test Deliverables:**
   Specifies the work products and artifacts produced, such as:
   - Test Plans
   - Test Cases
   - Test Execution Reports
   - Defect Logs
   - Final Test Summary Report

7. **Entrance and Exit Criteria:**
   Expectation metrics to start and close the testing cycle.

   Entrance criteria define the prerequisites that must be met before testing begins. These may include approved test plans, availability of test environments, complete test data, and a stable build ready for testing. Ensuring these conditions are met helps prevent incomplete or ineffective testing.

   Exit criteria, on the other hand, specify the conditions that must be satisfied to conclude testing. This may include meeting test coverage thresholds, passing critical test cases, resolving major defects, and obtaining stakeholder approvals. It ensures that testing is thorough, consistent, and meets quality expectations before release.

- Defines the conditions that must be met before testing is considered complete.
- Includes metrics like zero critical defects, test coverage percentage, and successful UAT sign-off.
- Establishes the formal approval process for transitioning to production.

NAVIGATING CLOUD-BASED IT PROJECTS

The advent of cloud computing has transformed how IT projects are developed, delivered, and maintained, introducing both opportunities and complexities that demand robust, continuous strategies. Here we explore the principles shaping cloud-based project development, the impact of cloud-specific policies and practices, and a tailored testing strategy to ensure quality and resilience in multicloud environments. From service contracts to patching cycles, cloud entitlements to support services, these elements redefine traditional project management, requiring a proactive, adaptive approach to testing that balances automation, human oversight, and risk mitigation.

PRINCIPLES, CHALLENGES, AND A CONTINUOUS TESTING

At the core of cloud project development lies a set of principles that prioritize flexibility, scalability, and service integration, all amplified by the cloud's dynamic nature. Cloud service policies and contracts dictate the terms under which services are provided, often embedding cloud products-specific hosting and delivery policies that outline how applications are deployed, whether on public, private, or hybrid platforms, and the responsibilities of providers like AWS, Azure, or Oracle Cloud. For instance, a contract might specify that a SaaS application is hosted on a vendor's servers with guaranteed uptime, shifting infrastructure management away from the client. Similarly, cloud product testing terms and conditions establish testing boundaries, such as limitations on penetration testing due to shared infrastructure risks, necessitating strategic planning to validate functionality without breaching agreements.

Cloud service entitlements further complicate this landscape, offering product-specific varying entitlements, rights to resources like storage, compute power, or additional features, that differ across vendors or tiers. A payroll application might include entitlements for parallel testing environments, while a CRM tool might restrict cloning to premium plans, impacting testing scope. Meanwhile, cloud updates and patching cycles introduce product-specific maintenance and update cycle policies, where vendors roll out fixes or enhancements, sometimes weekly, as with Salesforce, or quarterly, as with Oracle ERP, requiring projects to align development with these rhythms or risk compatibility issues. Cloud environment management becomes critical in multicloud setups, where juggling AWS for analytics and Azure for databases demands cohesive environment management for multicloud implementation projects. Finally, cloud support services play a pivotal role, requiring teams to work effectively with support across delivery teams, coordinating with vendor help desks and internal IT to resolve incidents swiftly.

These cloud-driven factors shift project strategies from static, one-time plans to continuous, iterative frameworks. Unlike traditional on-premises projects with fixed hardware, cloud projects must adapt to evolving policies, entitlements, and updates, embedding testing as an ongoing process to ensure stability and performance across this fluid ecosystem.

TESTING MULTICLOUD IT PROJECTS: STEP BY STEP

To address these challenges, a comprehensive testing strategy for multicloud IT projects must account for service contracts, entitlements, patching cycles, environment management, and support dynamics. This strategy leverages role-based, risk-based, and regression testing, judiciously incorporating automation while emphasizing human collaboration, and is outlined below.

1. Influences of Service Contracts and Testing Restrictions

Testing begins with understanding service contract and testing restrictions, identifying where limitations apply to critical areas:

- **Disaster Recovery Testing:** Contracts may restrict live failover simulations to avoid disrupting shared tenants, requiring synthetic tests (e.g., simulating a data center outage in a sandbox).
- **Performance Testing:** Caps on load testing, say, 10,000 virtual users, might necessitate phased assessments or vendor-approved stress tests.
- **Failover Testing:** Restrictions on switching live traffic could mean relying on pre-configured backups and validating switchover in controlled environments.

- **Security Testing:** Policies often ban unapproved penetration tests, so teams coordinate with vendors for whitelisting or use mock environments to simulate threats.

For an IT help desk system spanning Azure and Google Cloud, the strategy might involve testing disaster recovery by simulating Azure outages in a mirrored Google Cloud setup, respecting contract limits while ensuring recovery meets a 4-hour RTO (Recovery Time Objective).[142]

2. Influences of Cloud Service Entitlements

Entitlements shape testing scope and timing:

- **Lead Times for Service Requests:** Requesting additional compute power might take 48 hours, delaying performance tests unless pre-planned.
- **Concurrent Maintenance:** Patching or refreshes (e.g., cloning a production database) might clash with testing, requiring scheduling to reduce downtime— perhaps aligning clones with off-peak hours.
- **Migrating Configurations:** Moving setups across environments (dev to test) needs validation to avoid drift, adding test cycles.
- **Additional Testing Environments:** Needs vary, e.g., a payroll parallel environment for dual runs or an exclusive security/governance environment for compliance, each with lead times to enable services like VPNs, SSO, or IP whitelisting.

For the help desk, securing an extra Azure environment for security testing might require a week's lead time, prompting early requests and a cloned setup to mirror production configs, minimizing downtime during SSO integration tests.[143]

3. Influences of Cloud Patching Cycles and Environment Management

Patching cycles demand synchronized testing:

- **Mandated Regression Testing:** Continuous updates (e.g., monthly AWS patches) may require additional regression testing to ensure existing features hold, inflating effort if misaligned with project timelines.
- **Patching Misalignments:** Differing cycles, Azure's biweekly vs. Oracle's quarterly, could disrupt multi-cloud harmony, necessitating extra validation.
- **Conflicts with Patching Calendars:** Blackout periods (e.g., holiday freezes) clash with test schedules, requiring coordination to shift cycles or buffer with pre-patch snapshots.

Managing this, the help desk team might run regression tests post-AWS patches, aligning with a biweekly calendar, while scheduling major Oracle updates outside a December blackout, using snapshots to test pre- and post-patch states.[144]

4. Role-Based, Risk-Based, and Regression Testing

- **Role-Based Testing:** Assign testers by expertise, e.g., security specialists for penetration, support staff for help desk workflows, ensuring coverage matches skills.

- **Risk-Based Testing:** Prioritize high-risk areas (e.g., failover in disaster recovery) over low-risk (e.g., UI tweaks), optimizing effort.
- **Regression Testing:** Automate repetitive checks (e.g., ticket creation post-patches) but review manually for nuanced impacts, balancing speed and depth.

For the help desk, a risk-based approach might focus testing on ticket escalation (high-impact) over font changes (low-impact), with regression tests automated for core functions after each patch.[145]

5. Automated Testing Tools and Human Oversight

Automated testing tools, in my experience, have underperformed, requiring significant human effort to configure and interpret, as organizations thrive on people, not just scripts. The rise of artificial intelligence (AI) promises improvement, potentially enhancing *systematic and programmatic testing functions* like load simulation or defect detection. Yet, the term "artificial" hints at limits, AI excels at scale but lacks the intuition of human collaboration, vital for nuanced issues like user experience. This isn't to dismiss AI's power; tools like Selenium or JMeter can automate regression or performance tests, but success hinges on people to design, validate, and adapt them. For the help desk, AI might auto-test response times, but support staff must assess if tickets resolve user pain points, blending tech with human insight.

SUMMARY

The cloud's influence on IT projects, through policies, entitlements, updates, and support, demands continuous testing strategies that evolve with the environment. By addressing contract restrictions, entitlement logistics, patching cycles, and environment management, this strategy ensures quality in multicloud projects like an IT help desk. Role-based, risk-based, and regression testing, supported by selective automation and human expertise, navigate these complexities, proving that while the cloud reshapes delivery, disciplined testing remains the backbone of success. As AI advances, its integration will refine this balance, but people, collaborating across teams, will always drive the heart of effective project outcomes.

GROUP TESTING EFFECTIVENESS VERSES INDIVIDUAL TESTING: INSIGHTS FROM CASE STUDIES

Testing, whether in educational, industry, clinical, or organizational settings, traditionally emphasize individual performance to gauge personal competence or outcomes. However, emerging research suggests that group testing, where individuals collaborate to solve problems or demonstrate knowledge, can offer distinct advantages over solitary efforts.[146] Case studies from diverse domains, such as healthcare implementation and energy infrastructure, provide evidence of group testing's effectiveness, revealing improved outcomes, enhanced learning, and practical applicability.[147] This section examines key findings from such studies, summarizes their extracts, and analyzes why group testing proved successful, drawing on collaborative dynamics, shared accountability, and real-world relevance.

When individuals are tasked with executing test scripts on their own, they approach the process through the lens of their unique perspectives, goals, and needs. To channel this individuality, we employ role-based testing, tailoring test cases to job-specific functions. However, testing solo often reveals a disconnect: without a clear grasp of the broader purpose, why certain functions matter, individuals may struggle. Tasks outside their departmental scope can feel irrelevant, leading to skipped steps, failed tests, or the need for extra guidance. Each person's lens varies: some rush through, passing everything to simply finish; others, distracted by phones or emails, lack focus; and a few, driven by personal motivation, aim for precision. This disparity in intrinsic drive, whether fueled by desire for accuracy or hampered by disinterest, yields inconsistent results. The highly motivated produce thorough outcomes, while others deliver incomplete or superficial efforts, leaving us with a scattered picture of performance.

In contrast, group testing transforms this dynamic, weaving individual strengths into a cohesive force, much like strands forming a sturdy rope. Initially, grouping people sparks discomfort, most prefer working alone at their own pace, on their terms. Yet, combining diverse personalities, the procrastinator, the mission-driven leader, the partially focused, creates a richer outcome. In a group, multiple perspectives collide and complement: the leader steers with intent, minimizing distractions like external emails or calls, while others fill gaps where focus wanes. The partially engaged shine in areas they care about, and the collective effort compensates for individual shortcomings. Unlike solo testing, where results hinge on one person's motivation, group settings leverage this diversity to elevate quality. Our testing strategy has evolved through this shift, less about passing or catching every flaw, and more about learning. Groups reveal critical improvement areas, clarify priorities, and chart a path for the next cycle, delivering not just a stronger product but a smarter process.

CASE STUDY: SCHLUMBERGER'S ERP SUCCESS WITH A GROUP TESTING STRATEGY

Software implementation projects, particularly for complex systems like Enterprise Resource Planning (ERP), are notorious for their high failure rates due to inadequate planning, testing, and execution. However, Schlumberger's successful ERP implementation, in partnership with Scrum Inc., offers a compelling case study that demonstrates how a well-executed testing strategy, emphasizing group collaboration and quality principles, can lead to transformative outcomes. This case study examines Schlumberger's ERP journey, focusing on its testing approach, and integrates lessons from group testing effectiveness, Philip B. Crosby's quality philosophy, and an IT help desk context to illustrate why the implementation succeeded.[148]

CASE STUDY: SCHLUMBERGER'S ERP IMPLEMENTATION

Schlumberger, the world's largest oil and gas services provider, operates in over 120 countries and employs approximately 100,000 people. In 2019, the company embarked on a large-scale ERP implementation to unify its global operations, a project critical to its future competitiveness. Initially, the implementation faced significant challenges: the project team ballooned from 600 to 1,300 employees and contractors, and data readiness lagged at below the target of 70%. Partnering with Scrum Inc., Schlumberger adopted an agile Scrum methodology to turn the project around. By April 1, 2019, the ERP system launched successfully in North America, the company's largest market, achieving a 25% productivity increase and a 25% cost reduction, with one team delivering data at 93% readiness, a week ahead of schedule.[149]

TESTING STRATEGY: INTEGRATING GROUP TESTING AND QUALITY PRINCIPLES

Schlumberger's success hinged on a robust testing strategy that leveraged group dynamics, prioritized quality from the outset, and aligned with operational realities like an IT help desk workflow. The strategy unfolded in three key phases:

GROUP-BASED TESTING FOR COLLABORATION AND ACCURACY

Drawing on the principles of group testing, Schlumberger organized cross-functional teams to conduct testing collaboratively. Unlike individual testing, where a single tester might miss critical defects due to limited perspective, group testing involved developers, data analysts, and end-users working together to validate data migration, system integration, and functionality. For instance, a team of 10 might include data specialists ensuring 93% readiness, developers verifying code, and business users simulating real-world scenarios like invoice processing. This mirrors findings from studies like Booth et al. (2015), which showed group clinics in healthcare improving outcomes through shared learning, here, group testing enhanced defect detection and solution brainstorming, reducing errors by leveraging diverse expertise.

QUALITY ASSURANCE: MAKING QUALITY CERTAIN

Inspired by Philip B. Crosby's philosophy from Quality is Free, Schlumberger embedded the principle of "making quality certain" into its testing process.[150] Crosby's mantra, "quality is free; it is nonconformance that wastes assets", guided the team to "make it right the first time." Instead of rushing to meet deadlines, as seen in failed implementations like Hershey's 1999 ERP debacle (where inadequate testing led to $100 million in lost orders), Schlumberger prioritized thorough unit, integration, and user acceptance testing. For example, unit tests validated individual modules (e.g., payroll processing), while group-led integration tests ensured seamless data flow across the ERP's global modules. This prevention-focused approach minimized "unquality", the costly rework that Crosby warned against, saving Schlumberger an estimated 25% in costs by catching defects early.[151]

IT HELP DESK INTEGRATION: REAL-WORLD VALIDATION

To ensure the ERP system supported operational needs, Schlumberger incorporated an IT help desk workflow into its testing phase, reflecting a simplified process: Diagnose Issue → Resolve Issue → Follow-Up. End-users, acting as help desk agents, simulated ticket scenarios—e.g., a user in North America unable to access inventory data, while testers diagnosed issues (e.g., a data sync failure), resolved them (e.g., adjusting API configurations), and followed up to confirm resolution. This group-based simulation, involving help desk staff, developers, and business users, ensured the ERP could handle real-world support demands, enhancing system reliability and user satisfaction.

WHY THE APPROACH WORKED

Schlumberger's testing strategy succeeded for several reasons, rooted in the synergy of group dynamics, quality focus, and practical alignment:

COLLABORATIVE DYNAMICS ENHANCED OUTCOMES

Group testing fostered collaboration, as seen in educational studies where case study-based group discussions improved performance by nearly two letter grades (Journal of Microbiology & Biology Education, 2015). At Schlumberger, diverse teams brought varied perspectives, data analysts spotted migration gaps, developers fixed code, and users flagged usability issues, leading to the 93% data readiness that exceeded the 70% target. This collective problem-solving reduced blind spots, a common pitfall in individual testing, and accelerated issue resolution.

SHARED ACCOUNTABILITY DROVE COMMITMENT

Group testing created shared accountability, mirroring healthcare team studies where teamwork improved clinical outcomes (PMC, 2023). Team members felt responsible for the project's success, pushing them to deliver ahead of schedule. For instance, the team that achieved 93% readiness likely motivated each other to exceed expectations, knowing their collective effort impacted Schlumberger's global operations.

QUALITY-FIRST MINDSET PREVENTED COSTLY ERRORS

Crosby's emphasis on prevention over correction ensured Schlumberger avoided the "unquality" that derails projects. By integrating thorough testing across phases, unit, integration, and user acceptance, the company caught defects early, aligning with Crosby's idea that "there is no such thing as a quality problem," only preventable failures. This approach saved 25% in costs, proving quality is indeed free when done right.

REAL-WORLD RELEVANCE VIA IT HELP DESK SIMULATION

The IT help desk communication workflow ensured testing mirrored operational realities, much like the biology case studies prepared students for collaborative workplaces. By simulating help desk scenarios, Schlumberger validated the ERP's usability and support readiness, ensuring it could handle real user issues post-launch, which contributed to the smooth North American rollout.

CRITICAL REFLECTION

Schlumberger's ERP implementation, launched successfully on April 1, 2019, demonstrates how a group testing strategy, underpinned by Crosby's quality principles and practical IT help desk simulations, can transform a struggling project into a success. By achieving 93% data readiness, a 25% productivity increase, and a 25% cost reduction, Schlumberger proved that collaborative testing, a prevention-first mindset, and real-world validation are key to overcoming implementation challenges. This case study offers a blueprint for organizations aiming to implement software effectively, showing that when teams work together to ensure quality from the start, the results can exceed expectations.

Schlumberger's success highlights the power of group testing and quality focus, but it's not without caveats. The case study lacks detail on specific testing tools or AI integration, which could have further optimized efficiency, using automated testing's potential with AI advancements. Additionally, the 25% productivity gain, while impressive, might vary in smaller firms with fewer resources to support large group testing teams. Still, the principles, collaboration, prevention, and practical testing, offer universal lessons for software implementations.

RISK BASED TESTING

Risk Based Testing (RBT): *A strategic testing approach where test cases are prioritized based on the likelihood of defects occurring and the impact of those defects on the system. It ensures that testing efforts focus on the most critical areas, optimizing resource utilization and enhancing defect detection efficiency.*

Test Priorities:

- **P1 –Critical Risk:** Must be tested
  Nature: These are the riskiest and business-critical areas. Defects in this quadrant would cause major failures and are likely to occur.

Action: Test these areas extensively with detailed and exhaustive test cases. Apply multiple testing types (functional, performance, security) to ensure thorough coverage. Prioritize early and frequent testing.

I. **P2 –High Risk:** Should be tested
    Nature: These are high-impact but less probable risks. While they are unlikely to occur, their consequences would be severe.
    Action: Perform targeted and in-depth testing to reduce the chances of missed defects. Implement negative and edge case testing. Include these in regression suites to prevent future defects.

- **P3 –Medium Risk**: May be tested if schedule permits
    Nature: These are frequent but low-severity issues that do not significantly affect the system's functionality.
    Action: Perform basic functional testing but avoid extensive coverage. Automate repetitive test cases to save time. Prioritize fixing only if they affect the user experience significantly.
- **P4 –Low Risk:** Don't test
    Nature: These are low-risk and rare issues that have minimal impact on the system or user experience.
    Action: Minimal or no testing required. These issues are often deferred or addressed in future releases. May be flagged as low-priority defects.

EXAMPLE: TESTING PRIORITY QUADRANT (BUSINESS EVENTS-DRIVEN): HCM EXAMPLE

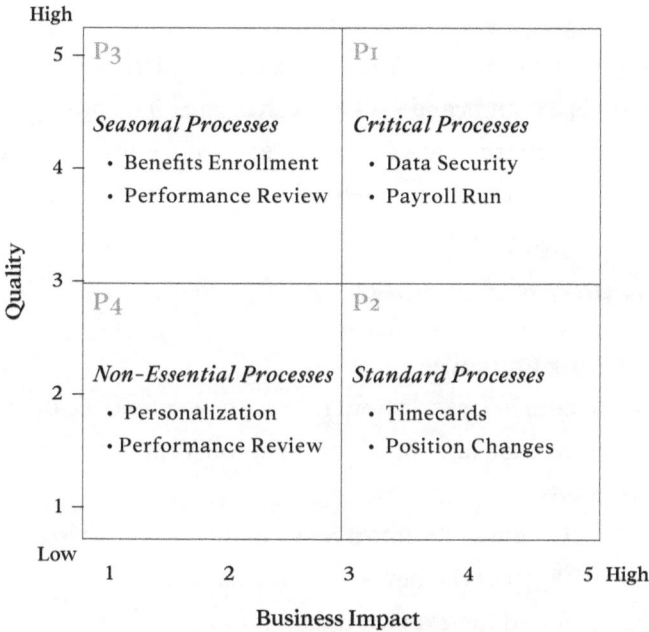

SYSTEM INTEGRATION TESTING EXAMPLE

System Integration Test Plan: SaaS to Payroll Vendor

This integration test plan ensures thorough validation of data extraction and loading from SaaS to Payroll Vendor. By involving business users and employing robust testing techniques, the plan aims to achieve accurate and reliable data integration.

Objective:

To validate the successful extraction of data from SaaS and its subsequent loading into Payroll Vendor using specific test scenarios such as hiring an employee and termination. The business will log into the test environment to review the data, and the tech team will validate record counts and success/error rates. The business team will then compare the data in the test environment to the changes and events that occurred in the SaaS source environment.

Test Scenarios: Examples

I. **Hiring Employee**
   - **Scenario Description:** Extract new employee data from SaaS and load it into Payroll Vendor.
   - **Steps:**
     1. Create or update a new employee record in SaaS.
     2. Extract the new employee data.
     3. Load the extracted data into Payroll Vendor.
     4. Log into the Payroll Vendor test environment and verify the new employee record.
     5. Validate record counts and success/error rates.
     6. Compare the Payroll Vendor test environment data with the SaaS source data.

2. **Terminating Employee**
   - **Scenario Description:** Extract employee termination data from SaaS and update the status in Payroll Vendor.
   - **Steps:**
     1. Terminate an employee record in SaaS.
     2. Extract the termination data.
     3. Update the employee status in Payroll Vendor using the extracted data.

4. Log into the Payroll Vendor test environment and verify the terminated employee record.
5. Validate record counts and success/error rates.
6. Compare the Payroll Vendor test environment data with the SaaS source data.

Testing Techniques and Guidance:

1. **Data Mapping and Transformation:**
   - Ensure that data fields in SaaS map correctly to corresponding fields in Payroll Vendor.
   - Document any transformations applied during data extraction and loading.

2. **Validation and Verification:**
   - **Record Counts:** Ensure the number of records extracted from SaaS matches the number loaded into Payroll Vendor.
   - **Field-Level Validation:** Verify that all fields are correctly populated in Payroll Vendor.
   - **Success/Error Rates:** Track and document the number of successful and failed records during the loading process.

3. **Automated Testing Tools:**
   - Use ETL (Extract, Transform, Load) testing tools to automate the data extraction and loading processes.
   - Implement scripts to automate validation steps, including record count checks and field-level comparisons.

4. **Error Handling and Logging:**
   - Implement robust error handling mechanisms to capture and log errors during data extraction and loading.
   - Review error logs to identify and resolve issues promptly.

5. **Business User Involvement:**
   - Engage business users in the review process to ensure data accuracy and business rule compliance.
   - Provide business users with access to the test environment for hands-on verification.
6. **Comparative Analysis:**
   - Perform a comparative analysis between the source data in SaaS and the loaded data in Payroll Vendor.
   - Use SQL queries or reporting tools to compare key data points and ensure consistency.

Test Execution:

Hiring Employee Scenario:

1. **SaaS:**
   - Create a new employee record.
   - Extract the employee data using an ETL tool.
2. **Payroll Vendor:**
   - Load the extracted data into Payroll Vendor.
   - Log into the Payroll Vendor test environment and verify the new employee record.
   - Validate record counts and success/error rates.
3. **Comparison:**
   - Compare the new employee record in Payroll Vendor with the SaaS source data.
   - Ensure all fields are correctly populated and consistent.

Terminating Employee Scenario:

1. **SaaS:**
   - Terminate an existing employee record.
   - Extract the termination data using an ETL tool.
2. **Payroll Vendor:**
   - Update the employee status in Payroll Vendor with the extracted data.
   - Log into the Payroll Vendor test environment and verify the terminated employee record.
   - Validate record counts and success/error rates.
3. **Comparison:**
   - Compare the terminated employee record in Payroll Vendor with the SaaS source data.
   - Ensure the status and other relevant fields are updated correctly.

Reporting and Documentation:

- Document all test cases, including expected results and actual outcomes.
- Capture screenshots of the test environment for visual verification.
- Maintain a log of issues encountered and resolutions implemented.

The Cheerful Crowd That Cheers Them On

NOW THAT YOU have completed this book, you should be able to:

- Initiate a project leadership incubator for creativity and innovation.
- Spark curiosity to develop a clear and compelling vision for the future.
- Shape skilled communicators who can inspire and motivate others.
- Provide a structured framework for effective project leadership and decision making.
- Encourage critical thinking and empathetic listening.
- Understanding accountability in each project knowledge area.

We are project managers from every corner of the globe, representing diverse industries, political views, economic backgrounds, and social contexts. We are a group that, under normal circumstances, would not converge. Yet, we share an extraordinary bond, a fellowship rooted in mutual understanding and camaraderie that defies description. Picture the passengers of a great ocean liner, moments after being rescued from a shipwreck. The joy, unity, and democratic spirit that sweep from steerage to the captain's table mirror the connection we feel. But unlike those passengers, whose elation fades as they resume their separate lives, our sense of shared triumph over project management challenges only grows stronger.

This enduring connection is not merely the result of shared struggles. It is forged by the discovery of a powerful, common solution, a proven approach to project management that unites us in purpose and action. This solution is the cornerstone of our victory, transforming projects once deemed hopeless, like the fabled Project Phoenix, into successes. We have found a way out, an approach we can all agree upon and apply with harmony and precision.

COMMITMENT TO EXCELLENCE

At Asha One we understand that change is not always easy. Since 1999, we've been helping companies of all sizes respond to industry transitions to stay competitive. Our years of experience have taught us always to make your business success our priority. Looking to develop your business but not sure where to turn? Need help planning or executing your next project? Let us guide you. Any organization can move forward with small incremental changes, but building for the future in today's rapidly evolving environment means taking bold chances and making insightful decisions.

ENDNOTES

1 McKinsey & Company, & Oxford University (2012). *Delivering largescale IT projects on time, on budget, and on value.* McKinsey & Company.

2 Standish Group. (2015). *CHAOS Report 2015.* The Standish Group International, Inc

3 Hegseth, P. (2025, March 20). *Continuing Elimination of Wasteful Spending at the Department of Defense [Memorandum].*

4 U.S. Government Accountability Office. (2023). *Defense Business Systems: DoD Needs to Improve Performance Reporting and Acquisition Oversight for Systems Supporting Business Operations.* GAO-23-105336. Retrieved from https://www.gao.gov/products/gao-23-105336

5 Hegseth, P. (2025, March 20). *Continuing Elimination of Wasteful Spending at the Department of Defense [Memorandum].*

6 U.S. Government Accountability Office. (2023). *Defense Business Systems: DoD Needs to Improve Performance Reporting and Acquisition Oversight for Systems Supporting Business Operations.* GAO-23-105336. Retrieved from https://www.gao.gov/products/gao-23-105336

7 Hegseth, P. (2025, March 20). *Continuing Elimination of Wasteful Spending at the Department of Defense [Memorandum].*

8 U.S. Government Accountability Office. (2023). *Defense Business Systems: DoD Needs to Improve Performance Reporting and Acquisition Oversight for Systems Supporting Business Operations.* GAO-23-105336. Retrieved from https://www.gao.gov/products/gao-23-105336

9 Hegseth, P. (2025, March 20). *Continuing Elimination of Wasteful Spending at the Department of Defense [Memorandum].*

10 U.S. Government Accountability Office. (2023). *Defense Business Systems: DoD Needs to Improve Performance Reporting and Acquisition Oversight for Systems Supporting Business Operations. GAO-23-105336.* Retrieved from https://www.gao.gov/products/gao-23-105336

11 Standish Group. (2015). *CHAOS Report 2015.* The Standish Group International, Inc

12 Project Management Institute. (n.d.). *Pulse of the Profession: The impact of project management frameworks on organizational success.* https://www.pmi.org

13 Covey, S. R. (1991). *The seven habits of highly effective people.* Provo, UT: Covey Leadership Center.

14 Goleman, D. (2019). *The emotional intelligent leader.*

15 Raj, P., & Sinha, P. (2015). *Project management in era of agile and DevOps methodologies.* In International Conference on Applied Sciences (Vol. 9, No. 1, pp. 1024–1033).

16 Kim, G., Behr, K., & Spafford, K. (2014). *The phoenix project: A novel about IT, DevOps, and helping your business win.* IT Revolution.

17 Ibid.

18 Highsmith, J. (2009). *Agile Project Management: Creating Innovative Products.* Addison-Wesley.

19 Ibid.

20 Project Management Institute. (2021). *A Guide to the Project Management Body of Knowledge (PMBOK® Guide) – Seventh Edition.* Project Management Institute.

21 Project Management Institute. (n.d.). *Pulse of the Profession: The impact of project management frameworks on organizational success.* https://www.pmi.org

22 Project Management Institute. (2021). *A Guide to the Project Management Body of Knowledge (PMBOK® Guide) – Seventh Edition.* Project Management Institute.

23 Deming, W. E. (2000). *The new economics for industry, government, education.* MIT Press.

24 Ibid.

25 Ibid.

26 Bolman, L. G., & Deal, T. E. (most recent edition 2017). *Reframing Organizations: Artistry, Choice, and Leadership (6th ed.).* Jossey-Bass. Booth, J. M., et al. (2015). *Group testing insights.* Journal of Microbiology & Biology Education. Adapted from prior responses and PMC (2023).

27 Mintzberg, H., & Van der Heyden, L. (1999). *Organigraphs: Drawing how companies really work.* Harvard Business Review, 77, 87–95.

28 Duhigg, C. (2012). *The Power of Habit: Why We Do What We Do in Life and Business.* Random House.

29 Ibid.

30 Prosci. (2006). *ADKAR: A model for change in business, government and our community.* Prosci Learning Center.

31 Ibid.

32 Kerzner, H. (2017). *Project management: A systems approach to planning, scheduling, and controlling (12th ed.).* John Wiley & Sons.

33 Project Management Institute. (2021). *A Guide to the Project Management Body of Knowledge (PMBOK® Guide) – Seventh Edition.* Project Management Institute.

34 Oracle University. (n.d.). *Oracle Cloud Project Management Practitioner.* Oracle Partner Revenue Enablement Services. Retrieved from learn.oracle.com

35 Ibid.

36 Brue, G. (2002). *Six Sigma for managers.* McGraw-Hill.

37 Williams, L. (2017). *Microsoft's journey to Agile: Transforming enterprise software development.* Microsoft Adoption.

38 Highsmith, J. (2009). *Agile Project Management: Creating Innovative Products.* Addison-Wesley.

39 Ibid.

40 Taylor, F. W. (1911). *The principles of scientific management.* Harper & Brothers.

41 Ibid.

42 Leffingwell, D. (2007). *Mastering the iteration: An agile white paper.* Rally Software Development Corporation.

43 Ibid.

44 Dalio, R. (2017). *Principles: Life and work.* Simon & Schuster.

45 Ibid.

46 Ibid.

47 Kerzner, H. (2017). *Project management: A systems approach to planning, scheduling, and controlling (12th ed.).* John Wiley & Sons.

48 Ibid.

49 Ibid.

50 Project Management Institute. (2021). *A Guide to the Project Management Body of Knowledge (PMBOK® Guide) – Seventh Edition.* Project Management Institute.

51 Kerzner, H. (2017). *Project management: A systems approach to planning, scheduling, and controlling (12th ed.).* John Wiley & Sons.

52 Choo, C. W. (2002). *Information management for the intelligent organization: The art of scanning the environment.* Information Today, Inc.

53 Ibid.

54 Vij, N. (2021, June 26). *Ethnographic Faculty of Health and Medical Sciences research process for successful UI/UX research.* Net Solutions. Retrieved from https://www.netsolutions.com/insights/how-to-do-ethnographic-research/

55 Jakob, N. (2005). *Ten usability heuristics.* Retrieved from http://www.useit.com/papers/heuristic/heuristic_list.html

56 Ibid.

57 Reason, J. (1990). *Human Error.* Cambridge University Press.

58 Schulz, K. F., Chalmers, I., Hayes, R. J., & Altman, D. G. (1995).

59 Project Management Institute. (2021). *A Guide to the Project Management Body of Knowledge (PMBOK® Guide) – Seventh Edition.* Project Management Institute.

60 Fayol, H. (1949). *General and industrial management (C. Storrs, Trans.).* London: Pitman. (Original work published 1916)

61 Kerzner, H. (2017). *Project management: A systems approach to planning, scheduling, and controlling (12th ed.).* John Wiley & Sons.

62 Goldratt, E. M. (1997). *Critical chain.* Great Barrington, MA: North River Press.

63 Ibid.

64 Ibid.

65 Ibid.

66 Taleb, N. N. (2007). *The black swan: The impact of the highly improbable.* Random House.

67 Covey, S. R. (1991). *The seven habits of highly effective people.* Provo, UT: Covey Leadership Center.

68 Ibid.

69 Tuckman, B. W. (1965). *Developmental sequence in small groups.* Psychological Bulletin, 63(6), 384–399. https://doi.org/10.1037/h0022100

70 Ibid.

71 Brown, J. S., & Duguid, P. (2000). *The social life of information.* Boston, MA: Harvard Business School Press.

72 Ibid.

73 Ibid.

74 Ibid.

75 Ibid.

76 Goleman, D. (2019). *The emotional intelligent leader*.

77 Ibid.

78 Ibid.

79 Ibid.

80 Ibid.

81 Ibid.

82 Ibid.

83 Myers & Briggs Foundation. (2021). *MBTI basics.* https://www. myersbriggs.org/my-mbti-personality-type/mbti-basics/

84 Ibid.

85 Ibid.

86 Ibid.

87 Follett, M. P. (1924). *Power. In Creative experience* (pp. 178–193). New York, NY: Longmans, Green and Co.

88 Ibid.

89 Ibid.

90 Ibid.

91 Ibid.

92 Ibid.

93 Ibid.

94   Ibid.

95   Taylor, F. W. (1911). *The principles of scientific management.* Harper & Brothers.

96   Follett, M. P. (1924). *Power. In Creative experience* (pp. 178–193). New York, NY: Longmans, Green and Co.

97   Ibid.

98   Gross, J. J. (1998). *The emerging field of emotion regulation: An integrative review.* Review of General Psychology, 2(3), 271–299. https://doi.org/10.1037/1089-2680.2.3.271

99   Ibid.

100   Byrne, R. (2006). *The Secret.* Atria Books.

101   Follett, M. P. (1924). *The circular response. In Creative experience* (pp. 54–70). New York, NY: Longmans, Green and Co.

102   Ibid.

103   Ibid.

104   Goldratt, E. M. (1997). *Critical chain.* Great Barrington, MA: North River Press.

105   Kahneman, D. (2011). *Thinking, fast and slow.* Macmillan.

106   Ibid.

107   Ibid.

108   Covey, S. R. (1991). *The seven habits of highly effective people.* Provo, UT: Covey Leadership Center.

109   Kotler, P., & Keller, K. L. (2022). *Marketing management* (16th ed.). Pearson.

110   Ibid.

111   Cooper, J. O., Heron, T. E., & Heward, W. L. (2020). *Applied behavior analysis* (3rd ed.). Pearson.

112   Cialdini, R. B. (1993). *The psychology of persuasion.* New York.

113   Ibid.

[114] Ibid.

[115] Kahneman, D. (2011). *Thinking, fast and slow.* Macmillan.

[116] Ibid.

[117] Suchard, L. (2012). *Mind reader.* Harper Collins Publishers.

[118] Kahneman, D. (2011). *Thinking, fast and slow.* Macmillan.

[119] Alenezi, A. M., & Ahmad, M. H. (2014). *Measuring the function points for migration project: A case study. International Journal of Software Engineering and Its Applications,* 8(10), 171–182.

[120] Kahneman, D. (2011). *Thinking, fast and slow.* Macmillan.

[121] Slovic, P. (2016). *Perception of risk. In The perception of risk* (pp. 220–231). Routledge.

[122] Kahneman, D. (2011). *Thinking, fast and slow.* Macmillan.

[123] Taleb, N. N. (2007). *The black swan: The impact of the highly improbable.* Random House.

[124] Crosby, P. B. (1979). *Quality is free: The art of making quality certain.* McGraw-Hill.

[125] Deming, W. E. (2000). *The new economics for industry, government, education.* MIT Press.

[126] Ibid.

[127] Crosby, P. B. (1979). *Quality is free: The art of making quality certain.* McGraw-Hill.

[128] Ibid.

[129] Fayol, H. (1949). *General and industrial management* (C. Storrs, Trans.). London: Pitman. (Original work published 1916)

[130] Crosby, P. B. (1979). *Quality is free: The art of making quality certain.* McGraw-Hill.

[131] Ibid.

[132] Ibid.

[133] Ibid.

[134] Ibid.

[135] Greene, R. (2013). *Mastery.* Penguin.

[136] Highsmith, J. (2009). *Agile Project Management: Creating Innovative Products.* Addison-Wesley.

[137] Cialdini, R. B. (1993). *The psychology of persuasion.* New York.

[138] Highsmith, J. (2009). *Agile Project Management: Creating Innovative Products.* Addison-Wesley.

[139] Oracle University. (n.d.). *Oracle Cloud Project Management Practitioner. Oracle Partner Revenue Enablement Services.* Retrieved from learn.oracle.com

[140] Greene, R. (2013). *Mastery.* Penguin

[141] Oracle University. (n.d.). *Oracle Cloud Project Management Practitioner. Oracle Partner Revenue Enablement Services.* Retrieved from learn.oracle.com

[142] Ibid.

[143] Ibid.

[144] Ibid.

[145] Ibid.

[146] McGuier, E. A., Kolko, D. J., Aarons, G. A., Schachter, A., Klem, M. L., Diabes, M. A., Weingart, L. R., Salas, E., & Wolk, C. B. (2024). *Teamwork and implementation of innovations in healthcare and human service settings: A systematic review [Systematic review].* Implementation Science, 19, 49. https://doi.org/10.1186/s13012-024-01381-9

[147] Bolman, L. G., & Deal, T. E. (most recent edition 2017). *Reframing Organizations: Artistry, Choice, and Leadership (6th ed.).* Jossey-Bass. Booth, J. M., et al. (2015). Group testing insights. Journal of Microbiology & Biology Education. Adapted from prior responses and PMC (2023).

[148] Schlumberger. (2019). *Case study on successful software implementation with a focus on testing.* Scrum Inc. (Web ID 13).

[149] Ibid.

[150] Ibid.

[151] Crosby, P. B. (1979). *Quality is free: The art of making quality certain.* McGraw-Hill.

[152] Crosby, P. B. (1979). *Quality is free: The art of making quality certain.* McGraw-Hill.

ASHA ONE CORP

WWW.ASHAONE.COM

Centre Island, New York, United States

(631)-210-6044

WWW.MAXIMUM-DELIVERY.COM

WWW.MAXIMUM.DELIVERY.COM

WWW.PROJECT-TOOLKIT.COM

www.ingramcontent.com/pod-product-compliance
Lightning Source LLC
Chambersburg PA
CBHW021917190326
41519CB00009B/814